Revelation Revealed

Verse by Verse

by
Dr. Jack Van Impe

Revised edition, 1992
Second printing, 1993

Jack Van Impe Ministries
P.O. Box 7004 • Troy, Michigan 48007
In Canada: Box 1717, Postal Station A
Windsor, Ontario N9A 6Y1

ISBN 0-934803-67-1

Dedicated

to

DR. DAVID D. ALLEN

who, upon my conversion to Christianity, opened my mind, eyes, and heart to prophetical truth as a professor at Detroit Bible College (now William Tyndale College)

and

MR. GREG HARRELL

whose expertise as a writer was tremendously helpful in editing this work

and

MRS. REBECCA (SHELTON) KILGUS

my niece, whose untiring efforts in preparing the final manuscript are deeply appreciated.

—Dr. Jack Van Impe

Contents

PREFACE

The Book of Revelation is the culmination of Bible prophecy—the point at which all the prophecies of the ages converge and find their ultimate fulfillment. Revelation discloses the future of the Jew, Gentile, and the Church of the Lord Jesus Christ. Within its pages are specific details concerning the Saviour's return, the establishment of His Millennial kingdom and, finally, the eternal state of both the saved and the lost.

The word *revelation* comes from the Greek *apokalupsis,* meaning "an uncovering or unveiling." For this reason, the Book of Revelation is also known as the Apocalypse. In either case, the definition reflects the fact that God has made known to mankind those eternal, supernatural truths and realities which man, on his own, could never realize or discover.

The Book of Revelation is the final work of the New Testament and the Revelation of Jesus Christ which details world history from the time of John (the Early Church Age) to eternity. It constitutes God's last special revelation to mankind this side of heaven. Simply stated, Bible prophecy and Revelation are history written in advance. They form God's description of future facts and events. Such prophecy is completely trustworthy because God is omniscient. He knows all things, whether they be actual or merely possible, and He knows them perfectly from all eternity. Acts 15:18 states: *Known unto God are all His works from the beginning of the world.* Thus, the

Almighty is able to fully and accurately describe the future in advance of its actual occurrence.

Current international events reflect exactly the conditions and happenings predicted throughout the Bible for the last days of this age. Yet, comparatively little prophetic teaching and preaching are currently taking place. This is probably due to the fact that this field of endeavor involves a great amount of research and study (see 2 Timothy 2:15). Millions more prefer not to have prophecy explained to them because they would rather live by the world's standards and dictates. As individuals who are seeking satisfaction and rewards in this life, they are obviously not anxiously anticipating Christ's return.

As we walk through the Book of Revelation together, remember that this special message has been given to reveal God's truth, not conceal it; and to clarify God's eternal purpose, not mystify it. I have not attempted to present an elaborate outline or engage in the use of heavy theological terminology. My goal is simplicity through a verse-by-verse analysis. I trust that, as a result, each reader will gain a clear understanding of the blessed truths the Book of Revelation contains.

This work was prepared to alert millions to the fact that Jesus is coming soon—perhaps today!

1

Verse 1: *The Revelation of Jesus Christ, which God gave unto him, to shew unto his servants things which must shortly come to pass; and he sent and signified it by his angel unto his servant John:*

We begin our study by immediately recognizing that the noun is *revelation,* singular, not *revelations,* plural. This term comes from the Greek word *Apokalupsis* and means "an unveiling or uncovering." It is often used in the epistles as a "manifestation" (Romans 8:19), a "coming" (1 Corinthians 1:7), a "revealing" (2 Thessalonians 1:7), and an "appearing" (1 Peter 1:7). The Book of Revelation, then, concerns the unveiling or appearing of our precious Saviour, the Lord Jesus Christ. It is not the unfolding of the story of St. John the Divine, or even of prophetical truth, but rather the message of the "appearing of Christ." This appearing takes place at the Rapture (chapter 4, verse 1), as well as at the hour of His return to earth when every eye shall see Him (chapter 1, verse 7).

Secondly, we see that this revelation was given to Jesus Christ, as is everything, for Jesus said, *All things are delivered unto me of my Father* (Matthew

11:27). They are presented unto Him *to shew unto his servants things which must shortly come to pass.* The term *shortly* in the original means "rapidity of action once there is a beginning." This certainly pictures the present hour when signs pointing to His return are beginning to appear with alarming frequency. These truths, then, are sent and signified by Christ's angel unto John, the writer of the book, under the inspiration of the Holy Spirit. Notice that the first four letters of the word *signified* spell SIGN. Why? The Book of Revelation is a study of signs. There is the sign of the Holy Spirit presented as seven spirits (verse 4) and the sign of the seven golden candlesticks and the seven stars (verse 20). Thus, through signs, we come to an understanding of this gloriously revealed portion of Scripture.

Verse 2: [John] *bare record of the word of God, and of the testimony of Jesus Christ, and of all things that he saw.*

This statement is self-explanatory.

Verse 3: *Blessed is he that readeth, and they that hear the words of this prophecy, and keep those things which are written therein: for the time is at hand.*

Verse three proves that the apocalypse is not some deep, mysterious, confusing book. God would not be an omniscient, all-knowing God if He promised a special blessing to those who read, hear, and keep what they read and hear, if they were unable to comprehend the truth. No, the Book of Revelation is understandable and fills the heart with joy once one sees its glorious message concerning the Saviour.

One reason that readers and hearers are to keep that which they have heard is because the time of Christ's return is at hand. The words *at hand* mean "imminent." *Near* and *imminent* are not synonymous. Imminent means "impending." Hence, the event could happen immediately or within ten minutes, ten months, or even ten years. "Imminence" is always the meaning of *at hand* when speaking about the return of the Lord. For example, Romans 13:12 says, *The night is far spent, the day is at hand* [imminent]. Philippians 4:5 declares, *Let your moderation be known unto all men. The Lord is at hand.* And 1 Peter 4:7 says, *But the end of all things is at hand: be ye therefore sober, and watch unto prayer.* Thus, the next event on God's calendar, the return of Christ for His Church, may happen momentarily. That is why we, as Christians, should keep our eyes fixed heavenward, *looking for that blessed hope, and the glorious appearing of the great God and our Saviour Jesus Christ* (Titus 2:13).

Verse 4: *John to the seven churches which are in Asia: Grace be unto you, and peace, from him which is, and which was, and which is to come; and from the seven spirits which are before his throne;*

John now focuses his attention on seven local churches located in a land area called Asia. This is not Asia as we know it today, but probably a portion of Turkey. Only seven churches are mentioned, although there were undoubtedly more in existence. Seven is God's number of perfection. The number also pictures seven different sets of conditions reflecting the history of God's people through the Church Age.

God's salutation, found in nineteen of the twenty-seven books of the New Testament, is presented here as well: *Grace be unto you, and peace.* It is not "peace and grace" but "grace and peace," because this is God's program for sinners. They cannot have peace until He has shown them His lovely grace. God must show His unmerited favor and love, called "grace," before one can experience peace. This grace is shown through the sacrifice of Calvary and is freely bestowed upon all who believe and receive Christ. *For by grace are ye saved through faith; and that not of yourselves: it is the gift of God: Not of works, lest any man should boast* (Ephesians 2:8,9).

For the grace of God that bringeth salvation hath appeared to all men (Titus 2:11). When grace has done its job, peace follows: *Therefore being justified by faith, we have peace with God through our Lord Jesus Christ* (Romans 5:1). This peace was made *through the blood of his cross* (Colossians 1:20). Thus, Romans 15:13 states: *Now the God of hope fill you with all joy and peace in believing, that ye may abound in hope, through the power of the Holy Ghost.*

Only Jesus can give this peace. An unsaved psychiatrist is unable to do the job. Psychiatrists need the same peace that they strive to give. Thus, we must turn our problems over to the Son of God.

We also find that the message of grace and peace is from the entire Trinity. First, the Father which is, which was, and which is to come; then from the seven Spirits which are before the throne (a designation of the blessed Holy Spirit in all of His holiness, for seven means perfection)...

Verse 5: *And from Jesus Christ, who is the faithful witness, and the first begotten of the dead, and the prince of the kings of the earth. Unto him that loved us, and washed us from our sins in his own blood,*

The question is often asked, "Why is Christ the first begotten from the dead, when Lazarus and others were raised first?" The answer is simple. Others were raised to life, but they died again. They were raised from physical death to physical life only to eventually die a second time. Jesus Christ was raised from the dead to immortality—never to die again! He is the first to have been resurrected with a new neverdying body. This is why Christ *should be the first that should rise from the dead* (Acts 26:23)...and why He *only hath immortality* (1 Timothy 6:16).

Five times Christ is called "the first begotten" or "the firstborn from the dead." Another five times He is called "the only begotten." The term "only begotten" refers to His incarnation, whereas "first begotten (or firstborn) refers to His resurrection. For instance, *he bringeth in the first begotten into the world* (Hebrews 1:6). [Christ] *is the image of the invisible God, the firstborn* [first begotten] *of every creature* (Colossians 1:15). *And he is the head of the body, the church: who is the beginning, the firstborn* [first begotten] *from the dead; that in all things he might have the preeminence* (Colossians 1:18).

Romans 8:29 declares, *For whom he did foreknow, he also did predestinate to be conformed to the image of his Son, that he might be the firstborn* [yea,

13

the first begotten] *among many brethren*. Think these
verses through carefully so that no cultist can trip you
up on the terms "first begotten" and "firstborn," in his
attempts to make the eternal Christ have a beginning.
No, praise God, Christ is *from of old, from everlasting* (Micah 5:2). Yea, He is one with the *everlasting
Father* (Isaiah 9:6).

The Lord Jesus Christ is also called *the prince of
the kings of the earth*. This, of course, refers to the
future, when *the Prince of Peace* (Isaiah 9:6) returns
to earth as the *KING OF KINGS, AND LORD OF
LORDS* (Revelation 19:16). This glorious event will
be the fulfillment of Psalm 2:6, which states: [I have]
set my king upon my holy hill of Zion. At that time *the
Lord Jesus shall have dominion also from sea to sea,
and from the river unto the ends of the earth* (Psalm
72:8).

Verse 6: *And* [He] *hath made us kings and
priests unto God and his Father; to him be glory and
dominion for ever and ever. Amen.*

Verses 5 and 6 contain three glorious statements
concerning Christ's work on our behalf: (1) He loved
us; (2) He washed us from our sins in His own blood;
and (3) He hath made us kings and priests unto God
and His Father. The order is beautiful. Let's examine
it in detail.

First, the Lord Jesus had to love us in order to
wash us and make us kings and priests. However, it is
even more thrilling when one sees that His love is in
the present tense, meaning that He continues loving
those He has washed. This is why John 13:1 triumphantly declares, [Jesus], *having loved his own which*

14

were in the world, he loved them unto the end. Can you understand such love? Oh, that *you may be able to comprehend with all saints what is the breadth, and length, and depth, and height; and to know the love of Christ, which passeth knowledge* (Ephesians 3:18,19). This love is forever. That is why Paul declared in Romans 8:37-39: *Nay, in all these things we are more than conquerors through him that loved us. For I am persuaded, that neither death, nor life, nor angels, nor principalities, nor powers, nor things present, nor things to come, Nor height, nor depth, nor any other creature, shall be able to separate us from the love of God, which is in Christ Jesus our Lord.*

The love which Jesus Christ has bestowed upon each born-again believer should manifest itself in daily living, for He said to His own, *A new commandment I give unto you, That ye love one another; as I have loved you, that ye also love one another. By this shall all men know that ye are my disciples, if ye have love one to another* (John 13:34,35). This love for you and me brought Christ from heaven's glory to the cruel cross of Golgotha's hill. Love made Him shed His blood for the remission of our sins.

Secondly, He washed us! Some do not like the teaching about the blood. They want to earn heaven by their own meritorious works. However, being whitewashed is not the same as being *washed white.* There is a vast difference! It is not *less* toil that solves the difficulty, it is *no* toil. Listen to God: *Not by works of righteousness which we have done, but ac-*

15

cording to his mercy he saved us, by the washing of regeneration (Titus 3:5).

When one trusts in the merits of Christ's shed blood, his sins are gone, *As far as the east is from the west, so far hath he removed our transgressions from us* (Psalm 103:12). Isaiah 38:17 declares, *Thou hast cast all my sins behind thy back.* God says, *I have blotted out, as a thick cloud, thy transgressions, and, as a cloud, thy sins* (Isaiah 44:22). Yes, He has cast all our sins *into the depths of the sea* (Micah 7:19). Oh, come to Jesus and He will lift all your load. Here's proof! *To him give all the prophets witness, that through his name whosoever believeth in him shall receive remission of sins* (Acts 10:43). It matters not how far astray the wayward son or daughter has gone, *the blood of Jesus Christ* [God's] *Son cleanseth us from all sin* (1 John 1:7).

Thirdly, because of His love and the washing of regeneration, Christ is able to make us *kings and priests unto God and his Father.* "Priest" is the title of every believer. It is also the reason one does not need a minister to help him get closer to God. If you have been born again, you are a priest in the eyes of the Almighty. You can bring your own petitions to God. One is not heard any more rapidly because he has been ordained by men, for all born-again believers are on the same level. All are members of *a royal priesthood, an holy nation, a peculiar people; that* [we] *should shew forth the praises of him who hath called* [us] *out of darkness into his marvellous light* (1 Peter 2:9). What a calling! Thank you, Jesus. John

16

adds, *To him be glory and dominion for ever and ever. Amen.*

Verse 7: *Behold, he cometh with clouds; and every eye shall see him, and they also which pierced him: and all kindreds of the earth shall wail because of him. Even so, Amen.*

This verse announces the Lord's return to earth. Notice that every eye sees Him. That is why this great event is described as the "revealing" or "revelation" of Christ and occurs when He comes as the *KING OF KINGS, AND LORD OF LORDS* (Revelation 19:11-16). Thus, our text is actually a preview of what will happen when He returns with His saints in chapter 19. Isn't it thrilling to know that when *the lightning cometh out of the east, and shineth even unto the west* (Matthew 24:27), every eye will witness the spectacle of the ages? Notice also that the Israelites—a special group—will observe this momentous event, for *they shall look upon* [Him] *whom they have pierced* (Zechariah 12:10).

Furthermore, when He comes in power and great glory to smite the nations, *all kindreds of the earth shall wail because of him.* This is because He comes for judgment and none will escape. As John envisions the hour when *the Lord cometh with ten thousands of his saints* (Jude 14), he victoriously cries, "Amen! Amen!" The Greek for *even so* is "Amen," and "Amen" is the Hebrew for *even so.* John is literally shouting the praise or praises of God in two languages as he says, "Amen and Amen, He is coming!"

Verse 8: *I am Alpha and Omega, the beginning*

and the ending, saith the Lord, which is, and which was, and which is to come, the Almighty.

This text speaks of the eternal Christ. Alpha and Omega are the beginning and ending letter of the Greek alphabet. Christ is saying, "I am the beginning and ending of all things." He uses the title "I am," which is a verb indicating being, but not becoming. He always was. He was before all things and created all things. *All things were made by him; and without him was not any thing made that was made* (John 1:3). *For by him were all things created, that are in heaven, and that are in earth, visible and invisible, whether they be thrones, or dominions, or principalities, or powers: all things were created by him, and for him: And he is before all things, and by him all things consist* (Colossians 1:16,17). He also controls all things by *upholding all things by the word of his power* (Hebrews 1:3), and He will consummate all things as well (see Ephesians 1:10). Yes, Jesus Christ is *Alpha and Omega, the beginning and the ending.*

The terminology, *I am...the Lord which is, and which was, and which is to come,* expresses Christ's oneness with the Father (see verse 4). In fact, He adds the term, the Almighty, a name used for the Father in connection with His person. This term is used forty-eight times in the Old Testament. This verse clearly refutes the doctrine of anti-trinitarianism, which is anti-God, anti-Christ, and anti-Holy Spirit.

Verse 9: *I John, who also am your brother, and companion in tribulation, and in the kingdom and patience of Jesus Christ, was in the isle that is called*

Patmos, for the word of God, and for the testimony of Jesus Christ.

John realizes that he is an old man and highly revered, yet he wants no praise from men for his sufferings. He immediately identifies himself as a brother in Christ and a companion in heartache and suffering. He tells of the tribulation he endured during his incarceration at Patmos, but he rejoices that the other blood-bought sons of God will miss the Tribulation. How true!

The Saviour stated: *In the world ye shall have tribulation* (John 16:33). However, this does not include the Tribulation hour out of which the saints are kept (see Revelation 3:10). John's persecution came because of his devotion to Christ. This is always true when one takes a stand for the Saviour. Jesus said in John 15:18-20, *If the world hate you, ye know that it hated me before it hated you. If ye were of the world, the world would love his own: but because ye are not of the world, but I have chosen you out of the world, therefore the world hateth you. Remember the word that I said unto you, The servant is not greater than his lord. If they have persecuted me, they will also persecute you.*

Verse 10: *I was in the Spirit on the Lord's day, and heard behind me a great voice, as of a trumpet,*

Beginning with this verse, we enter into the revelation experience with John and observe firsthand all that is presented to him through the remainder of the book.

Joseph A. Seiss says that John was carried forward through the centuries until he saw a vision of the

19

great and terrible day of the Lord—the Tribulation hour. A majority of scholars, however, believe that the phrase, *on the Lord's day,* refers to the first day of the week. Thus, on Resurrection day—Sunday, the first day of the week—John is visited by the One who had so loved him while on earth—Jesus himself. As He appears, John hears the trumpet-like voice of Christ...

Verse 11: *Saying, I am Alpha and Omega, the first and the last: and, What thou seest, write in a book, and send it unto the seven churches which are in Asia; unto Ephesus, and unto Smyrna, and unto Pergamos, and unto Thyatira, and unto Sardis, and unto Philadelphia, and unto Laodicea.*

Alpha and Omega are the titles we discussed in verse 8. Verse 11 pictures the eternal Christ giving instructions to His beloved servant concerning the seven churches mentioned in verse 4 and to be discussed in chapters 2 and 3. Then, John adds...

Verse 12: *And I turned to see the voice that spake with me. And being turned, I saw seven golden candlesticks.*

When the trumpet-like voice of Christ sounded in verse 11, John turned to see the voice that spoke to him. This is different! One does not normally "see" a voice. Yet John *turned to see the voice.* As he looks in that direction, he sees seven golden candlesticks or lampstands. Verse 20 clearly explains the meaning of verse 12 as follows: *The mystery of the seven stars which thou sawest in my right hand, and the seven golden candlesticks* [means this:] *The seven stars are the angels of the seven churches: and the seven candlesticks which thou sawest are the seven churches.*

The fact that the seven churches are pictured as seven lampstands is significant because believers *are the light of the world* (Matthew 5:14). Sad, as we shall see, is the fact that the history of the seven churches often diminished that light. Oh, pray that it shall not be so in your life. Jesus said, *Let your light so shine before men, that they may see your good works, and glorify your Father which is in heaven* (Matthew 5:16).

Now that we have observed verse 12 in light of verse 20, let's take a closer look at the glorious Saviour who appears in the midst of the lampstands or churches.

Verse 13: *And* [I saw] *in the midst of the seven candlesticks one like unto the Son of man, clothed with a garment down to the foot, and girt about the paps with a golden girdle.*

The Lord is clothed with the garments of the Old Testament high priest because He is risen and in heaven, performing His ministry of intercession. For this reason, *he is able also to save them to the uttermost that come unto God by him, seeing he ever liveth to make intercession for them* (Hebrews 7:25). Thus, sixty years after Christ's death and resurrection, John sees Him as the High Priest in the heavenlies. Paul also testified to this blessed fact by stating: *Seeing then that we have a great high priest, that is passed into the heavens, Jesus the Son of God, let us hold fast our profession* (Hebrews 4:14). Next our precious Lord is described in detail.

Verse 14: *His head and his hairs were white like wool, as white as snow; and his eyes were as a flame of fire;*

John's description speaks of antiquity and coincides with the vision Daniel had in chapter 7, verses 9 through 13. This *Ancient of days*, the eternal One, Jesus Christ, is also pictured in terms of whiteness because of His righteousness, for He *is holy, harmless, undefiled, separate from sinners, and made higher than the heavens* (Hebrews 7:26). The Greek also emphasizes the fact that His eyes "shot out fire." Christ is righteously angry concerning the sin of the churches depicted in Revelation, chapters 2 and 3.

Verse 15: *And his feet* [were] *like unto fine brass, as if they burned in a furnace; and his voice* [was] *as the sound of many waters.*

Christ's feet picture judgment and relate to the events that take place when He returns to the earth in chapters 19 and 20. *His voice as the sound of many waters* also depicts judgment.

Verse 16: *And he had in his right hand seven stars: and out of his mouth went a sharp twoedged sword: and his countenance was as the sun shineth in his strength.*

The seven stars of this verse are the angels or messengers of the seven churches (see verse 20), while the twoedged sword is the Word of God as described in Hebrews 4:12: *The word of God is quick, and powerful, and sharper than any twoedged sword, piercing even to the dividing asunder of the soul and spirit, and of the joints and marrow, and is a discerner of the thoughts and intents of the heart.*

22

Then the expression, *his countenance was as the sun shineth in his strength,* takes our minds back to the transfiguration scene in Matthew 17:2 and thus pictures the glory of Christ, who is to be the Judge during the Great Tribulation hour, Armageddon, and the Great White Throne assembly of Revelation 20:11-15. Because of it, John is stunned, astonished, and humbled at the experience and cries...

Verse 17: *And when I saw him, I fell at his feet as dead. And he laid his right hand upon me, saying unto me, Fear not; I am the first and the last:*

Verse 18: *I am he that liveth, and was dead; and, behold, I am alive for evermore, Amen; and have the keys of hell and of death.*

The sight of Christ glorified was breathtaking, and the one who laid his head upon Jesus at the Last Supper now falls prostrate at His feet. As John falls before his blessed Lord in fear, Jesus lovingly says, *Fear not.* He is saying the same to us today. In the midst of wars, rumors of wars, heartaches, and death, the blessed Lord says, *Let not your heart be troubled* (John 14:1). This message to John is from *the first and the last, the Alpha and Omega,* the eternal One, Jesus Christ. The One *that liveth* (resurrection), *and was dead* (crucifixion) and who cries, *behold, I am alive for evermore* (ascension), *Amen.* He also has the keys of hell and of death. Because of this tremendous fact, Christians are not to fear, for *through death* ... [Christ destroyed] *him that had the power of death, that is, the devil; And* [delivered] *them who through fear of death were all their lifetime subject to bondage* (Hebrews 2:14,15). Not only have we been delivered from the fear of death but from the fear of Hades as well.

Let me explain: *Hades* was the place where the souls and the spirits of all humans went until the cross. *Sheol* (Old Testament) and Hades (New Testament) were one and the same. In Sheol and Hades were two compartments, one for the wicked and the other for the righteous. In Luke 16:22,23, the rich man and Lazarus went to their respective places— one to suffering and the other to comfort. The thief on the cross went to the comfort side, or paradise, as promised by Christ when He said, *To day shalt thou be with me in paradise* (Luke 23:43). This is where Christ went upon His death (Acts 2:27,31). There He ministered to His people and *led captivity captive* (Ephesians 4:8-10), literally releasing them for their entrance into the third heaven of 2 Corinthians 12:2.

Presently the comfort side of Hades has been emptied by Him who has the keys of death and Hades (hell), but the torment side is still full. This will be emptied for the Judgment Day when...*death and* [Hades deliver] *up the dead which* [are] *in them: and they* [are] *judged...* (Revelation 20:13). (For a detailed study of this subject, order my full-length audio cassette entitled "Hell Without Hell.")

Verse 19: *Write the things which thou hast seen, and the things which are, and the things which shall be hereafter;*

This verse gives us the order of the Book of Revelation, which is written chronologically, or as the events happen. One immediately recognizes the three tenses—past, present, and future. *Write the*

24

things which thou hast seen—past, chapter 1; *the things which are*—present, chapters 2 and 3; *and the things which shall be hereafter*—future, chapters 4 through 22.

Verse 20: [God explains to John:] *The mystery of the seven stars which thou sawest in my right hand, and the seven golden candlesticks. The seven stars are the angels of the seven churches: and the seven candlesticks which thou sawest are the seven churches.*

Since we have discussed the closing verse of this chapter in connection with verse 12, let us move on to the study of the seven candlesticks, or the history of the seven churches.

2

Chapters 2 and 3 contain seven letters to the seven literal, local churches mentioned in chapter 1, verse 11. These letters have a number of applications. First, they are seven actual letters to seven actual churches situated in seven different cities. Second, they are letters to seven individuals within the seven churches. Third, they are messages applicable to all churches in all ages, for the seven churches picture seven periods, or stages, of church history. In each period, the Lord speaks to the churches in a judgmental way, portraying their failures, then He calls them to repentance and zealousness.

Ephesus

Verse 1: *Unto the angel of the church of Ephesus write; These things saith he that holdeth the seven stars in his right hand, who walketh in the midst of the seven golden candlesticks* [or the seven churches represented throughout history];

The first church addressed is the church of Ephesus, covering the time period from approximately 33 A.D. (the birth of the church at Pentecost) until 100 A.D. when John, who wrote the Book of Revelation, died. The letter is to the *angel* or, literally, the "messenger" of the church of Ephesus, and is from the One who holds *the seven stars in his right hand and who* [walks] *in the midst of the seven golden candlesticks.* This, of course, is the glorified Christ, as we learned in chapter 1, verse 20. How thrilling to note that the Lord both holds the churches (all believers) in His hand and walks in the midst of them, as well! This is the Christian's security. The Saviour's walk among us is to bring us closer to himself. Next, Christ speaks...

Verse 2: *I know thy works, and thy labour, and thy patience, and how thou canst not bear them which are evil: and thou hast tried them which say they are apostles, and are not, and hast found them liars:*

Notice that, in each of the seven letters, the Lord begins by commending the local assembly for whatever He can find in them that is good before scolding them for their sins. The Ephesus church began in all purity, as can be observed from a study of the Book of Acts. Then false prophets entered in. This is exactly the warning Paul had sounded during his last gathering in Ephesus: *For I know this, that after my departing shall grievous wolves enter in among you, not sparing the flock. Also of your own selves shall men arise, speaking perverse things, to draw away disciples after them. Therefore watch, and remember* (Acts 20:29-31). The leaders of the church judged these false prophets in earlier days, but became lax as they lost their first love.

Today many think it is wrong to judge heresy or wickedness. Not so! The same Christ who said,

Judge not, that ye be not judged (Matthew 7:1) also declared, *Judge righteous judgment* (John 7:24). A believer is never to judge a person as far as character and motives are concerned. However, he should definitely judge one when that individual's doctrine is heretical or his life is filled with wickedness. This is why John said, *Try the spirits whether they are of God: because many false prophets are gone out into the world* (1 John 4:1), and why Paul stated in 1 Timothy 5:19 and 20: *Against an elder receive not an accusation, but before two or three witnesses. Them that sin rebuke before all, that others also may fear.* The church at Ephesus had slipped from its original moorings and was on the way down. Is it any wonder that Mohammedanism swept through the land and destroyed the compromising church that once was mighty under Paul?

Verse 3: *And hast borne, and hast patience, and for my name's sake hast laboured, and hast not fainted.*

Part of the reason this church (who had *borne*, and had *patience*, and for His name's sake had *laboured*, and had *not fainted*) failed may have been that they were too busy serving and not taking time for sweet fellowship at the feet of Jesus. When one is so active that he has no time for the Bible and prayer, he is too busy. Many have fallen to the indictment of...

Verse 4: *Nevertheless I have somewhat against thee, because thou hast left thy first love.*

How true of multitudes today! When they were first saved they loved Jesus, loved to pray, loved to

29

read the Word, loved to attend the services at God's house and loved to witness. Ah, but they have lost that first love!

Verse 5: *Remember therefore from whence thou art fallen, and repent, and do the first works; or else I will come unto thee quickly, and will remove thy candlestick* (or your local church) *out of his place, except thou repent.*

It happened! After the conquest of Mohammedanism, the church of Ephesus became nonexistent. Do not let this happen to your church or to you! Before God finishes His pronouncement of commendations and condemnations upon the church of Ephesus, he adds...

Verse 6: *But this thou hast, that thou hatest the deeds of the Nicolaitans, which I also hate.*

Who were the Nicolaitans and what was it about them that so angered Almighty God? The term comes from two Greek words which mean "victory over the laity"—a religious dictatorship that allowed little or no freedom to its members. This is precisely what the Holy Spirit had in mind when He told the church elders not to be *lords over God's heritage, but...ensamples* [examples] *to the flock* (1 Peter 5:3). How this message needs to be emphasized in our day as religious leaders try to impose their man-made rules on each and every member! After presenting this series of commendations and warnings, the Spirit of God adds...

Verse 7: *He that hath an ear, let him hear what the Spirit saith unto the churches; To him that over-*

cometh will I give to eat of the tree of life, which is in the midst of the paradise of God.

How can one be an overcomer? By trusting in the merits of the shed blood of Jesus Christ: *Who is he that overcometh the world, but he that believeth that Jesus is the Son of God?* (1 John 5:5).

Verse 8: *And unto the angel of the church in Smyrna write; These things saith the first and the last, which was dead, and is alive;*

We saw in chapter 1, verse 11, that this first and the last, or *Alpha and Omega,* is the Lord Jesus Christ. He now begins His message to the church of Smyrna.

Verse 9: *I know thy works, and tribulation, and poverty (but thou art rich) and I know the blasphemy of them which say they are Jews, and are not, but are the synagogue of Satan.*

The Smyrna period of church history takes us from 100 A.D. to 312 A.D. These people probably suffered the greatest persecution in all Christianity. Their works, faithfully performed in the name of Jesus, brought great tribulation and accompanying poverty, materially. However, great riches were laid up for them in heaven. In addition, their relentless, dedicated efforts brought the Word of God to the entire Roman Empire. During the second and third centuries, the Smyrna church members were fed to the lions at Rome while multitudes cheered. Church history informs us that five million may have been martyred during this era. Every Christian ought to read *Foxe's Christian Martyrs of the World.* He will quickly discover the foolishness of complaining in this day of luxury and ease.

Believe it or not, the church flourished and grew during the Smyrna period! Perhaps a little persecution would do us some good today. We might learn to love other brothers in Christ who have a different religious label than ours. God forgive us for our sectarianism!

Much of Smyrna's heartache came through false professors of religion—those who said they were Jews as defined in Romans 2:29 (circumcised *of the heart* and *the spirit* rather than *the letter*) but who, in reality, were not! They did not really believe and were actually members of the synagogue of Satan! Beware of those who claim to be Christians but deny the deity of Christ. They, too, are of the synagogue of Satan: [For] *every Spirit that confesseth not that Jesus Christ is come in the flesh is not of God* (1 John 4:3). The same is true of those who mix law and grace. Paul said, *I marvel that ye are so soon removed from him that called you into the grace of Christ unto another gospel: Which is not another; but there be some that trouble you, and would pervert the gospel of Christ. But though we, or an angel from heaven, preach any other gospel unto you than that which we have preached unto you, let him be accursed. As we said before, so say I now again, If any man preach any other gospel unto you than that ye have received, let him be accursed* (Galatians 1:6-9).

Because of the false brethren propagating false doctrine and despising the true believers, persecution came from within and from without. In the face of such satanic opposition, Christ's message was...

Verse 10: *Fear none of those things which thou shalt suffer: behold, the devil shall cast some of you into prison, that ye may be tried; and ye shall have tribulation ten days: be thou faithful unto death, and I will give thee a crown of life.*

When the hour of trial arrived, the believers were not to fear. They were to keep their eyes on eternal rewards as mentioned in James 1:12: *Blessed is the man that endureth* [testing]*: for when he is tried, he shall receive the crown of life, which the Lord hath promised to them that love him.* Many Bible scholars believe that the ten days of persecution consisted of ten literal periods of suffering. I agree, since church history emphatically supports this assertion. Still, the church of Smyrna was guaranteed final victory through the Lord's promises, power, and provision...

Verse 11: *He that hath an ear, let him hear what the Spirit saith unto the churches; He that overcometh shall not be hurt of the second death.*

Pergamos

Verse 12: *And to the angel of the church in Pergamos write; These things saith he which hath the sharp sword with two edges;*

Again, chapter 1, verse 16, proves that the speaker is the Lord Jesus Christ.

Verse 13: *I know thy works, and where thou dwellest, even where Satan's seat is: and thou holdest fast my name, and hast not denied my faith, even*

*in those days wherein Antipas was my faithful martyr,
who was slain among you, where Satan dwelleth.*

The letters to the first three churches begin with
a commendation. To each Christ says, *I know thy
works.* God sees what we do for Him. How sad when
backsliding destroys the many good deeds performed
in His name! We see this strange twist at Pergamos.
Here the bad works outweigh the good ones.

This church period, extending from 312 A.D. to
606 A.D., was one of materialism, self-indulgence,
and worldliness. Wickedness spread like a brushfire.
The name *Pergamos* has in it the same root from
which we get our English words *bigamy* and *polyga-
my.* Pergamos signifies a mixed marriage of the
church and the world. This happened because the
Babylonian religion established its headquarters at
Pergamos and infiltrated Christianity. No wonder
this local church is charged with dwelling in the area
of Satan's seat or literally, "throne." They were
perched on the doorstep of the devil's headquarters!

Of necessity, the believer in Christ is in the world.
However, he must constantly guard against becoming
involved in its ungodliness. The church of Pergamos
became part and parcel of Satan's worldly establishment. They called themselves by Christ's name (Christians) and made verbal and written assent to the faith,
even though they saw the danger of martyrdom in the
example of Antipas. Nevertheless, they backslid.

Verse 14: *But I have a few things against thee,
because thou hast there them that hold the doctrine of
Balaam, who taught Balac to cast a stumblingblock*

before the children of Israel, to eat things sacrificed unto idols, and to commit fornication.

The first grievance against the church of Pergamos was the fact that they had embraced the pleasure of the world or become a worldly church. Secondly, they had given heed to false doctrine—the theology of Balaam. Remember Balaam? He had a smart donkey! How sad to be famous because of one's donkey. The animal was so smart it could outtalk Balaam. What was the doctrine of Balaam taught to Balac? First, *to eat things sacrificed to idols,* and second, *to commit fornication.* Balac had hired Balaam to curse Israel, and Balaam, the false prophet, was unable to get the anointing of Satan upon his spirit for the task. So he figured out a plan of destruction for the Jews. He said, "Let the choice of the women of Balac's kingdom display themselves before the eyes of God's people." As expected, the Jewish men became enamored with the beauty of the daughters of Balac's kingdom, committed fornication with them, married them, and were eventually drawn into idolatry. How wrong! Those who name the name of Jesus are not to become involved with the world in any manner, [for] *ye cannot drink the cup of the...Lord's table, and of the table of devils* (1 Corinthians 10:21).

Verse 15: *So hast thou also them that hold the doctrine of the Nicolaitans, which thing I hate.*

Not only were the people of the first church of Pergamos worldly, sinful, and idolatrous, but they also shared in the wicked practice of Nicolaitanism as did the church at Ephesus. This, again, is ecclesiastical Hitlerism. It is when the minister or leader says, "I am the head, and you have no choice in the matter," allowing laymen no voice in the affairs of the church. Concerning the doctrine of the Nicolaitans, the condemnatory statement, *which thing I hate,* is uttered by the Lord God himself. The solution?

Verse 16: *Repent; or else I will come unto thee quickly, and will fight against them with the sword of my mouth.*

This is serious business. The Christian is not to close his mind, heart, and ears to God's warning.

Verse 17: *He that hath an ear, let him hear what the Spirit saith unto the churches; To him that overcometh will I give to eat of the hidden manna, and will give him a white stone, and in the stone a new name written, which no man knoweth saving he that receiveth it.*

As previously noted, the overcomer is the true believer in Jesus (see 1 John 5:4). He is given the *hidden manna* (the Word of God) and is presented a *white stone.* During ancient court trials, the jurors would lay down white stones to signify a decision of acquittal. Praise the Lord, through the blood of Jesus, the white stones of acquittal have been presented and every Christian has a new name written down in glory!

Thyatira

Verse 18: *And unto the angel of the church in Thyatira write; These things saith the Son of God, who hath eyes like unto a flame of fire, and his feet are like fine brass;*

Once again we see that the speaker is the Son of God. The description of His eyes and feet were discussed in chapter 1, verses 14 and 15.

Verse 19: *I know thy works, and charity, and service, and faith, and thy patience, and thy works; and the last to be more than the first.*

To this point, all four churches have been complimented for their works. Thyatira, however, was loaded with meritorious service and unusual deeds. She was known for her good works, love, service, faith, patience, and last works. The term "last works" means that this church outdid herself. Her works became greater toward the end of her lifetime than they were at the beginning.

Historically, Thyatira covers the years 606 A.D. to 1520 A.D. However, many scholars believe that this church is found in the world until she is destroyed by the revived Roman Empire in chapters 17 and 18. Although Thyatira had many admirable qualities, she nevertheless had some deep-rooted problems as well.

Verse 20: *Notwithstanding I have a few things against thee, because thou sufferest that woman Jezebel, which calleth herself a prophetess, to teach and to seduce my servants to commit fornication, and to eat things sacrificed unto idols.*

Who was Jezebel? In the Old Testament she was perhaps the most wicked woman of her day. She became so hated that she was thrown from a window and the dogs ate her flesh. The sin of this self-appointed prophetess was to bring Baalism into Israel as a new religion. She is accused of seducing God's servants to commit fornication and to eat things sacrificed to idols. This constituted the breaking of two of God's commandments to His people Israel: (1) *Thou shalt not make unto thee any graven image, or any likeness of any thing that is in heaven above, or that is in the earth beneath, or that is in the water under the earth: Thou shalt not bow down thyself to them* and (2) *Thou shalt not commit adultery* (Exodus 20:4,5,14). God called upon Thyatira to turn from her wicked ways.

Verse 21: *I gave her space to repent of her fornication; and she repented not.*

The long-suffering and loving God gave Thyatira approximately 1,000 years to do what was right, but she resisted. How like many twentieth-century Christians, constantly rejecting the wooings of the blessed Holy Spirit. The result...

Verse 22: *Behold, I will cast her into a bed, and them that commit adultery with her into great tribulation, except they repent of their deeds.*

Judgment always comes: *Be sure your sin will find you out* (Numbers 32:23). The Lord promises to cast this church and her bed partners—those who have partaken of her abominable iniquity, including idolatry and unfaithfulness to the Bridegroom, Jesus Christ—into the Great Tribulation. At that point, the church which sits upon seven hills (chapter 17, verse 9) will be destroyed. The details concerning this event are discussed in chapters 17 and 18.

The obvious lesson here is that God hates sin. Sentimentalists say, "Oh, the blessed, loving Jesus would never condemn anyone." Really? We know that *God is love* (1 John 4:8) and *God sent not his Son into the world to condemn the world* (John 3:17). Nevertheless, when His love is repeatedly spurned and one deliberately follows a course of sin, God's holiness demands that the sinner be punished. Remember Christ himself is speaking the following verse:

Verse 23: *And I will kill her children with death; and all the churches shall know that I am he which searcheth the reins and hearts: and I will give unto every one of you according to your works.*

How sad that the church of Thyatira, so highly praised for good works in the opening passages, must be horribly judged because of having undone every good thing that had been originally performed in the name of the Saviour. Likewise, today it is possible for the Christian to lose every reward he has earned, so *look to yourselves, that* [you] *lose not those things which* [you] *have wrought* [or earned] (2 John 8). The only good news concerning Thyatira was that a remnant remained faithful in spite of the deterioration of this local church.

Verse 24: *But unto you I say, and unto the rest in Thyatira, as many as have not this doctrine, and which have not known the depths of Satan, as they speak; I will put upon you none other burden.*

The Lord Jesus informed John that those who did not succumb to Jezebel's theological follies or fall into the fornication and idolatry propagated by this false Babylonian religion, would not have any other burden. They had experienced enough heartache.

Verse 25: *But that which ye have already hold fast till I come.*

Here the faithful remnant was admonished to

continue in the truth of God's Word until Jesus returned.

Verse 26: *And he that overcometh, and keepeth my works unto the end, to him will I give power over the nations:*

Verse 27: *And he shall rule them with a rod of iron; and as the vessels of a potter shall they be broken to shivers: even as I received of my Father.*

Verse 28: *And I will give him the morning star.*

Christ has promised faithful believers three rewards upon His return to the earth: (1) rulership over the nations during the Millennium: *For they lived and reigned with Christ a thousand years* (chapter 20, verse 4); (2) sharing in this glorious time of perfect righteousness resulting from Christ's personal enforcement and order (see Psalm 2:8,9); and (3) the abiding presence of the blessed Saviour throughout time and eternity as Christ himself, *the bright and morning star,* is given (chapter 22, verses 14 and 16).

If your life is not what it once was for Christ, don't be a loser when rewards are distributed. Instead, about-face! Live for Him! Heed the warning of the next verse.

Verse 29: *He that hath an ear, let him hear what the Spirit saith unto the churches.*

3

Let's move on to the next church. The fifth letter, written to the local church in Sardis, is also from the Saviour, for Christ has the seven stars in His right hand in Chapter 1, verse 16. Again, the Saviour begins by commending Sardis for her works.

Verse 1: *And unto the angel of the church in Sardis write; these things saith he that hath the seven spirits of God, and the seven stars; I know thy works, that thou hast a name that thou livest, and art dead.*

Sardis began in 1520 A.D., and undoubtedly extends, historically, into the Tribulation. This period of time covers the Reformation (with its dead, lukewarm churches) and is presently part of the Laodicean period as well. The reason for the deadness is that, during the Reformation, entire countries became Protestant without being born again. Protestantism was made the state religion, and was freely embraced by millions who did not know what it meant to become new creations in Christ Jesus (see 2 Corinthians 5:17). Thus, Sardis became the mother of dead orthodoxy. Her theme song was not "Standing on the Promises"—her members were dead! God help us to have life! Hundreds of churches follow Sardis' lead today. This is the reason millions are leaving liberal churches for good, old-fashioned, gospel-preaching lighthouses. Immediately, God called for a fivefold revival package.

Verse 2: *Be watchful, and strengthen the things which remain, that are ready to die: for I have not found thy works perfect before God.*

Verse 3: *Remember therefore how thou hast received and heard, and hold fast, and repent. If therefore thou shalt not watch, I will come on thee as a thief, and thou shalt not know what hour I will come upon thee.*

Sardis was admonished to: (1) *Be watchful* or alert: *knowing the time, that now it is high time to awake out of sleep* (Romans 13:11); (2) *Strengthen the things which remain, that are ready to die:* Her people were to do everything possible to salvage the little good that still remained in their bastion of dead orthodoxy; (3) *Remember therefore how thou hast received and heard*: The Sardis Christians were commanded to recall the former days—the early days of their salvation when they were filled with purity and zeal; (4) *Hold fast:* They were to retain the simple truth of the gospel and discard the excess baggage of ecclesiastical pomp and ceremony; and (5) *Repent:* They were to change their minds. Christ's call was not for personal repentance but for the entire church, yea, the entire movement, to change. The Reformation churches needed to turn back to Christ, seeking His will and His Spirit's teachings rather than man-made ideas about theological truth.

One of the areas of truth the Reformation churches

failed to proclaim was the return of Christ. There-fore, the Lord said that this event would catch them unawares: *Thou shalt not know what hour I will come upon thee.* No wonder many of the present-day off-spring of the Reformation have ministers who say, "No one can understand the Book of Revelation. It is a deep, mysterious, symbolical, figurative book." Baloney! Preacher, layman, you are the one Christ had in mind. *Awake thou that sleepest...and Christ shall* [raise you from the dead] (spiritually speaking).

In the midst of this deadness, Sardis had a few who could still wiggle, spiritually.

Verse 4: *Thou hast a few names even in Sardis which have not defiled their garments; and they shall walk with me in white: for they are worthy.*

Though the Reformation churches, like the mother out of whom they came, did not practice holiness unto the Lord, there were individuals who did not defile their garments in compromise with the world, the flesh, and the devil. They came *out from among them, and* [touched] *not the unclean thing* (2 Corin-thians 6:17). As a result, they were promised the reward of being clothed in white garments, as stated in the latter part of verse 4 and in verse 5:

Verse 5: *He that overcometh, the same shall be clothed in white raiment; and I will not blot out his name out of the book of life, but I will confess his name before my Father, and before his angels.*

This white raiment is found upon the bride of Christ at the Marriage Supper of the Lamb: *Let us be glad and rejoice, and give honour to him: for the marriage of the Lamb is come, and his wife hath*

43

made herself ready. And to her was granted that she should be arrayed in fine linen, clean and white: for the fine linen is the righteousness of saints (Revelation 19:7,8). In addition, those who possess a genuine salvation experience will remain in the book of life eternally. What security! Christ says, I *will not blot out his name...before my Father, and before his angels.*

Verse 6: *He that hath an ear, let him hear what the Spirit saith unto the churches.*

Make sure YOUR experience is real!

Philadelphia

Let's progress to the next church. The sixth letter is written to the church of Philadelphia and covers historically the years from 1750 until the Rapture.

Verse 7: *And to the angel* [or messenger] *of the church of Philadelphia write these things saith he that is holy, he that is true, he that hath the key of David, he that openeth, and no man shutteth; and shutteth, and no man openeth;*

Once again the message is from the Lord Jesus Christ. However, instead of gleaning a picture from chapter 1, as we have in the past, we are now given a new and beautiful fourfold description of the Lord: (1) *He that is holy*: one finds this description of Christ in Hebrews 7:26; (2) *He that is true:* Jesus said, *I am the way, the truth, and the life* (John 14:6); (3) *He that hath the key of David:* Jesus again said, *I am the root and the offspring of David* (chapter 22, verse 16); and (4) *He that openeth, and no man*

44

shutteth; and shutteth, and no man openeth. Christ is not only the One who opens the door, but He is *the door* (John 10:9). Christ's commendation is presented to the local church of Philadelphia in verses 8-10:

Verse 8: *I know thy works: behold, I have set before thee an open door, and no man can shut it: for thou hast a little strength, and hast kept my word, and hast not denied my name.*

Verse 9: *Behold, I will make them of the synagogue of Satan, which say they are Jews, and are not, but do lie; behold, I will make them to come and worship before thy feet, and to know that I have loved thee.*

Verse 10: *Because thou hast kept the word of my patience, I also will keep thee from the hour of temptation, which shall come upon all the world, to try them that dwell upon the earth.*

We immediately realize from this text that the church of Philadelphia is loaded with good works. The open door speaks of missions, and the church covering this era of time undoubtedly has done, and is doing, more than any other group ever attempted to do in the annals of history. Thank God for such vision! *Where there is no vision, the people perish* (Proverbs 29:18).

Although this group does so much, they are still a minority, *for* [they had] *a little strength.* One of their great strengths was that they kept His name. Since the church of Philadelphia extends into our twentieth century and even to the point of the Rapture, the command for each of us today is that we never deny His name, for *if we deny him, he also will deny us* (2 Timothy 2:12). Oh, the tremendous loss some will experience at *the Judgment Seat of Christ* (2 Corinthians 5:10).

Christ also promises these faithful brethren that the members of the synagogue of Satan (false professors of religion as described in chapter 2, verse 9) will be forced to bow and worship the Lord God Almighty, willfully or unwillfully, at a future time (chapter 3, verse 9). This could be at the Judgment Day, for Paul informed the children of God that they would share with Christ in judgment. Hear him: *Do ye know that the saints will judge the world?* (1 Corinthians 6:2). Christ himself spoke of that time when He stated: *As I live, saith the Lord, every knee shall bow to me, and every tongue shall confess to God* (Romans 14:11).

Finally, because of their love for Christ, the Philadelphia-era believers are promised exemption from the day of the Lord's wrath, or the Great Tribulation hour: *I...will keep thee from the hour of temptation* (chapter 3, verse 10). In the Greek, the word *from* is *ek*, meaning "out of." God promises to keep the Philadelphia believers "out of"—not "through" (preservation), but "out of" (evacuation)—the Tribulation. (Order my full-length videocassette entitled "The Great Escape" for a complete study of the pre-Tribulation Rapture.)

Thus, the Church will be gone when the terrible hour of Tribulation judgment comes upon all the world to try the earth dwellers. Praise God, "This world is not my home, I'm only passing through." We believers are not earth dwellers, for our citizenship is in heaven (see Philippians 3:20). In the light of the coming of Christ, an admonition is given in the next verse.

Verse 11: *Behold, I come quickly: hold that fast which thou hast, that no man take thy crown.*

Here the Christian is warned to be faithful, lest all rewards (not salvation, but rewards) be lost—even the loss of one's crown. The promise of verse 12 is to those who are faithful.

Verse 12: *Him that overcometh will I make a pillar in the temple of my God, and he shall go no more out: and I will write upon him the name of my God, and the name of the city of my God, which is new Jerusalem, which cometh down out of heaven from my God: and I will write upon him my new name.*

Three blessings are mentioned for the faithful: (1) They become pillars in the temple of God; (2) they have the name of God written upon them, thus identifying them and allowing them access into the city of God—the New Jerusalem described in Revelation 21 and 22; and (3) they have the new name written upon them. The name of God allows them to enter the Holy City, but the new name of Christ entitles them to be His servants, where they shall see His face (chapter 22, verses 3 and 4). Because the future blessings are so wonderful, the admonition continues.

Verse 13: *He that hath an ear, let him hear what the spirit saith unto the churches.*

Laodicea

The seventh and final letter is to the local church

of Laodicea, which covers the years from 1900 to the Tribulation Hour. The message, as in all previous letters, is from the Lord Jesus Christ.

Verse 14: *And unto the angel of the church of the Laodiceans write; these things saith the Amen, the faithful and true witness, the beginning of the creation of God;*

This threefold description of the Saviour includes: (1) *the Amen.* In Hebrew, this word means "true." The complete meaning is "truth in its finality," which pictures Christ as the final truth; (2) *the faithful and true witness.* This statement links Christ to chapter 1, verse 5, where He is called true, and (3) *the beginning of the creation of God.* Since the Lord is the firstborn of all creation (see Colossians 1:15), we again recognize Him as the speaker.

Verse 15: *I know thy works, that thou art neither cold nor hot: I would thou wert cold or hot.*

The Laodicean church also has works, but her service is rendered in a lukewarm fashion. What a picture of the present age! Some of our churches are so cold that signs above the doors could advertise these religious refrigerators as, "First Church of the Deep Freeze, pastored by Dr. Jack Frost." The situation is so drastic that, whereas parishioners used to quote the verse, "Many are called but few are chosen," they now think the "New Reversed Version" states, "Many are cold and a few are frozen!" God alone knows how serious the present situation literally is.

Verse 16: *So then because thou art lukewarm,*

and neither cold nor hot, I will spue thee out of my mouth.

The condition of the Laodicean church makes God so violently ill that He wants to spue this group out of His mouth. The Greek word is *emeo,* from which we get the word *emetic.* An emetic is given to one who has swallowed poison in order to make him regurgitate. Think of that! A lukewarm church is an emetic to Christ. But what's the reason for this lukewarmness, coldness, indifference, and carnality?

Verse 17: *Because thou sayest, I am rich, and increased with goods, and have need of nothing; and knowest not that thou art wretched, and miserable, and poor, and blind, and naked:*

The Laodicean era is a highly prosperous one. As a result, her people have erected elaborate church structures worth millions of dollars. (Stop a moment and consider the money presently being invested in buildings used one to three hours weekly.) Laodicean pastors often attack the "electronic church" ministries. The command of Jesus is, *Go ye into all the world, and preach the gospel to every creature* (Mark 16:15). However, the "electronic church" ministers, via radio and television, are simply obeying the Saviour. God help each of us to see that although buildings are necessary for worship and service, they should be humble edifices rather than the latest multimillion-dollar architectural monstrosities which glorify men.

God tells the Laodiceans that they are really wretched and miserable, poor (spiritually, though rich materially), blind, and naked. This is true because riches usually make one wretched and miserable. One spends forty years accumulating his wealth and the final thirty years keeping others from getting it. The Laodiceans are also blind because they cannot see the need of the millions who are dying without the Saviour and going into eternal loss. Because of this fact, they are naked both now and in eternity, for they are not clothed with Christ's robe of righteousness (see 2 Corinthians 5:21). His plea to them is...

Verse 18: *I counsel thee to buy of me gold tried in the fire, that thou mayest be rich; and white raiment, that thou mayest be clothed, and that the shame of thy nakedness do not appear; and anoint thine eyes with eyesalve, that thou mayest see.*

Christ instructs the Laodiceans to: (1) *buy of me gold tried in the fire, that thou mayest be rich.* This probably refers to 1 Peter 1:7, where *the trial of* [our] *faith* [is] *...more than of gold;* (2) buy white raiment—undoubtedly, the reference is to the *garments of salvation* and *the robe of righteousness* mentioned in Isaiah 61:10; and (3) *anoint thine eyes with eyesalve, that thou mayest see.* This speaks of illumination which only the saved share: *The natural man receiveth not the things of the spirit of God: for they are foolishness unto him: neither can he know them, because they are spiritually discerned* (1 Corinthians 2:14). Because of the conditions prevalent in the Laodicean church, the Lord states...

Verse 19: *As many as I love, I rebuke and chasten: be zealous therefore, and repent.*

This message reminds us of Hebrews 12:6, which states: *Whom the Lord loveth he chasteneth, and scourgeth every son whom he receiveth.* Spiritual spankings are administered in order that we might be zealous and repent, or "change our minds." He continues...

Verse 20: *Behold, I stand at the door, and knock: if any man hear my voice, and open the door, I will come in to him, and will sup with him, and he with me.*

This verse is actually a picture of Christ standing outside the door of the latter-day church rather than the heart of an individual, as we so often hear stated. Presently, entire churches and denominations are barring the Saviour's entrance. Unbelievable! However, those who listen to His appeal, open the door, and follow Jesus will not be sorry.

Verse 21: *To him that overcometh will I grant to sit with me in my throne, even as I also overcame, and am set down with my Father in his throne.*

Finally, one last time, the Lord proclaims the warning...

Verse 22: *He that hath an ear, let him hear what the Spirit saith unto the churches.*

4

Chapter four begins the prophetical future. Remember chapter 1, verse 19: *Write the things which thou has seen, and the things which are, and the things which shall be hereafter.* That text presented three tenses and informed us that the Book of Revelation is written in chronological order: the *past*—chapter 1; the *present*—chapters 2 and 3 (the history of the seven churches to the present time); and the *future*—chapters 4 through 22.

Now let's take a peek at what's coming.

Verse 1: *After this I looked, and, behold, a door was opened in heaven: and the first voice which I heard was as it were of a trumpet talking with me; which said, come up hither, and I will shew thee things which must be hereafter.*

John states, "After this." After what? After the completion of the history of the seven churches. After this, John sees a door opened in heaven and hears a trumpet-like voice loudly and victoriously crying, *Come up hither.* This is the rapture of the church of Jesus Christ. When it occurs, multitudes from all kindreds, people, tongues, and denominations will meet the Saviour face to face.

What is the Rapture? It is the literal, visible bodily coming of Jesus Christ to call out of this world, literally and bodily, every born-again believer—first the dead, then the living. First we see that Jesus is coming bodily. Remember the cultists of bygone days who said that the Lord was about to return? Clothed in white sheets, they sat on the mountainsides in anxious anticipation—but Christ didn't come. Date-setting is wrong! *But of that day and hour knoweth no man, no, not the angels of heaven, but my Father only* (Matthew 24:36).

Because of their embarrassment, these cultists immediately stated, "Oh, we were right; Christ did come, but it was an invisible manifestation. He came as a spirit." Not so! When Jesus Christ returns, both in the Rapture (chapter 4) and at His Revelation (chapter 19), He will come literally, visibly and bodily. Proof? Acts 1:9-11: *And when* [Jesus] *had spoken these things, while they beheld, he was taken up, and a cloud received him out of their sight. And while they looked stedfastly toward heaven as he went up, behold, two men stood by them in white apparel; Which also said, Ye men of Galilee, why stand ye gazing up into heaven? this same Jesus, which is taken up from you into heaven, shall so come in like manner as ye have seen him go into heaven.* The Lord will return exactly as He left.

How did He leave? Let's see. In Luke 24:39, Christ appeared to His disciples and said, *Behold my hands and my feet, that it is I myself: handle me, and see; for a spirit hath not flesh and bones, as ye see me have.* Then, in verses 41 and 42, He went on to say

Have ye here any meat [food]? *And they gave him a piece of a broiled fish, and of an honeycomb. And he took it, and did eat before them.* The Lord Jesus Christ possessed a new resurrected body—a body that could be seen, a body that could be touched, and a body that could partake of food—a literal body!

Christ died for our sins according to the scriptures; And that he was buried, and that he rose again the third day according to the scriptures: And that he was seen of Cephas, then of the twelve: After that, he was seen of above [or over] *five hundred brethren at once...After that, he was seen of James...And last of all he was seen of me also* (1 Corinthians 15:3-8). No doubt about it, when He returns and the shout, *Come up hither,* is given, we will see Him. At this glorious moment, we, too, shall receive new bodies. The Bible teaches in 1 Thessalonians 4:16 and 17: *For the Lord himself shall descend from heaven with a shout, with the voice of the archangel, and with the trump of God: and the dead in Christ shall rise first: Then we which are alive and remain shall be caught up together with them in the clouds, to meet the Lord in the air: and so shall we ever be with the Lord.*

Notice that the dead in Christ shall rise first. (Perhaps this is because they have six feet further to rise—to the level of the living. Ha!) Then all of us together are caught up into the heavenlies to meet the Lord Jesus Christ in the twinkling of an eye. You don't believe it? Then listen! *Behold, I show you a mystery; We shall not all sleep* [be dead], *but we shall all be changed, in a moment, in the twinkling of an eye, at the last trump: for the trumpet shall sound, and the dead shall be raised incorruptible, and we* [the living] *shall be changed.* Watch it. *For this corruptible* [the dead in Christ] *...must put on immortality* (1 Corinthians 15:51-54). How fast is *the twinkling of an eye?* Close your eyes for a moment. Open them. That's it! General Electric Company tells us that the twinkling of an eye is eleven one-hundredths of a second.

Just that quickly, at that blessed moment, we shall be changed to be like Jesus. David said, *I shall be satisfied, when I awake, with thy likeness* (Psalm 17:15). John adds that when we see Jesus, *we shall be like him; for we shall see him as he is* (1 John 3:2). Then Paul chimes in and states: [He] *shall change our vile body, that it may be fashioned like unto his glorious body* (Philippians 3:21). This, then, is the Rapture.

Some Christians say they do not believe in the term *rapture.* They argue that one cannot find the word *rapture* in the Bible. Interestingly, one cannot find the term *Bible* in the Bible either, but I'm holding one! Listen carefully: The word *rapture*, in English, comes from the Latin, *rapio*, which means "a snatching away." We have just learned from God's Word that all Christians, living and dead, are going to be snatched away in the twinkling of an eye, so whether one knows it or not, one believes in the Rapture.

The Bible also clearly teaches that there is a difference between the Rapture and the Revelation of Christ. We need to fully understand this truth because it is the basis for understanding the Book of Revelation, prophetical truth, and the placement of signs. Simply stated, there are two aspects, or stages, in the process of Christ's second coming, and both begin with the letter "r." We have already designated the first phase as the Rapture. The second phase is called the Revelation. Chapter 4 describes phase one, while phase two is described in chapter 19. The intervening chapters—6 through 18—basically cover a seven-year period called the Tribulation. The Rapture (chapter 4) precedes the Tribulation, and the Revelation (chapter 19) follows the seven-year period of judgment. Chapter 4 is a meeting in the air, whereas chapter 19 is a return to the earth. Chapter 4 removes the believer from the judgments described in chapters 6 through 18, and chapter 19 restores the believer to his earthly sojourn as he returns with Christ to planet earth. The *Come up hither* of Revelation 4:1 is synonymous with the call of 1 Thessalonians 4:16,17: *For the Lord himself shall descend from heaven with a shout, with the voice of the archangel, and with the trump of God: and the dead in Christ shall rise first: then we which are alive and remain shall be caught up together with them in the clouds to meet the Lord in the air: and so shall we ever be with the Lord.*

Immediately following this event, the inhabitants of planet earth experience seven years of incomparable judgment. This judgment ends with the Battle of Armageddon, at which time the door of heaven is again opened (see chapter 19, verses 11 through 16) in order that the believer may exit heaven with Christ for the return trip to earth.

This return of Christ with His saints is called the

Revelation, and comes from the word *revealing*. At that time the Lord will reveal himself to all humanity, so why not call this event the revealing, or revelation, of Christ? Let's not quibble about the labels concerning the Rapture and the Revelation. The truths are there; believe them! The labels only help one organize the teaching systematically.

The question often arises, "Will the church of Jesus Christ be on earth during the Tribulation hour?" The answer is an emphatic, "NO!" The Church is mentioned sixteen times in the first three chapters of the Book of Revelation, but is not found in chapters 6 through 18—the Tribulation period. Why?

First of all, the Tribulation is Israel's time of suffering. *Alas! for that day is great, so that none is like it: it is even the time of Jacob's trouble; but he shall be saved out of it* (Jeremiah 30:7). *And at that time shall Michael stand up, the great prince which standeth for the children of thy people* [Israel]: *and there shall be a time of trouble, such as never was since there was a nation even to that same time: and at that time thy people* [Israelites] *shall be delivered, every one that shall be found written in the book* (Daniel 12:1).

Secondly, the first sixty-nine weeks of Daniel's prophecy involved Israel. Why wouldn't the seventieth week? The Bible is plain: *Seventy weeks are determined upon thy people* [Israelites] *and upon thy holy city* [Jerusalem] (Daniel 9:24). That is why the signs in Matthew 24, Mark 13, and Luke 17 and 21 have to do with Israel and the Middle East.

Third, during the Tribulation hour, the people

involved are instructed to *pray that your flight be not in the winter, neither on the Sabbath day* (Matthew 24:20). Israel is eternally identified with the Sabbath day (see Ezekiel 20:12,20).

Fourth, when Christ returns to Jerusalem (see Zechariah 14:4), all the tribes of the earth mourn (see Matthew 24:30). The mourners are the twelve tribes of Israel, numbering hundreds of thousands of individuals who were brought to repentance by the preaching of the 144,000 Jewish representatives from each of the twelve tribes (12,000 per tribe).

Finally, the persons experiencing the woes of the Church are never called "a synagogue," but rather *the church* (Acts 2:47).

As already stated, the Church cannot be found in Revelation 6 through 18, the portion of the book describing the horrible Tribulation hour. Israel, however, is seen in the midst of the holocaust (see Revelation 12:1-5). This correlates with the elect of Matthew 24:22. Jesus said, *And except those days should be shortened, there should no flesh be saved: but for the elect's sake those days shall be shortened.* This elect group is not the Church but Israel, for God has two elect groups upon earth—the Church and Israel. First, let's look at the Church. *According as he hath chosen us in him before the foundation of the world, that we should be holy and without blame before him in love* (Ephesians 1:4). This chosen group is called the elect in 1 Peter 1:2. However, the Church, the bride of Christ, elected to be His sweetheart and wife for all eternity, is not in view in Matthew 24:22. Instead, this text has Israel, the wife of Jehovah, in mind. What? How can that be? Where was Israel chosen? In Genesis 12:2,3 God said, *And I will make of thee a great nation, and I will bless thee, and make thy name great and thou shalt be a blessing: And I will bless them that bless thee, and curse him that curseth thee: and in thee shall all families of the earth be blessed.*

In Deuteronomy 7:7 and 8, the Israelites were again reminded of their elect status: *The Lord did not set his love upon you, nor choose you, because ye were more in number than any people; for ye were the fewest of all people: But because the Lord loved you, and because he would keep the oath which he had sworn unto your fathers...* [He chose you]. This oath that chooses Israel as an elect group of people has never been abrogated: *For the gifts and calling of God are without repentance*—or without change of mind (Romans 11:29). Because of God's unchanging covenant or oath, Romans 11:26-28 declares, *And so all Israel shall be saved: as it is written, there shall come out of Sion the Deliverer, and shall turn away ungodliness from Jacob: for this is my covenant unto them, when I shall take away their sins...as touching the election* (the elect), *they are beloved for the fathers' sakes.*

When God chose Israel as His elect wife, He chose her forever because the calling of God is without change of mind. Though Jehovah's spouse has often committed spiritual adultery by turning to iniquity and idolatry, still Jehovah loves her because God abides faithful. There is no doubt about it, Israel is the elect group mentioned in the Gospels for whom the days of judgment will be shortened. Israelites are the ones who will pray that their flight for safety will not be on the Sabbath (their day of worship); who will suffer persecution in their own synagogues (only Jews meet in synagogues); and who have the name of Jacob, and who will experience Jacob's time of trouble (see Jeremiah 30:7), for Jacob is Israel (see Romans 11:26).

Hence, a period of seventy weeks is determined upon Israel (see Daniel 9:24). The nation of Israel has seen *Jerusalem compassed* [about] *with armies* (Luke 21:20), and will again observe the armies of the world posed against Jerusalem for the final war as God gathers *all nations against Jerusalem to battle* (Zechariah 14:2). This definitely is not the Church. All Christians slipped out through the open door in the fourth chapter before the judgments of heaven and earth began to be unleashed in the sixth chapter. They were evacuated when the shout, *Come up hither,* was given.

There are those who say that Revelation 4:1 is an exclusive picture of John the Beloved in a vision, being caught away in the presence of God. Therefore, they reason, this has nothing to do with anyone else, including the Church. This argument is fallacious because chapter 4, verse 10 states: *The four and twenty elders fall down before him that sat on the throne, and worship him that liveth for ever and ever, and cast their crowns before the throne.* When will believers be crowned? Immediately after the Rapture. Proof: *Thou shalt be recompensed* [rewarded] *at the resurrection of the just* (Luke 14:14). Again:

61

And when the chief Shepherd shall appear [His coming], *ye shall receive a crown of glory* (1 Peter 5:4). Obviously, the Judgment Seat of Christ must take place before believers are crowned. Then they lay these crowns at Christ's feet, in verses 10 and 11, meaning they were already in His presence. The only way they could have gotten there is through the *Come up hither* of verse 1. We must also remember that John, the representative of all of God's people, is shown the things which must be hereafter and the things that will happen, both in heaven and on earth. Chapters 4 and 5 picture that which takes place in heaven, while chapters 6 through 18 picture that which occurs on earth—the Tribulation.

Verse 2: *And immediately I was in the spirit: and, behold, a throne was set in heaven, and one sat on the throne.*

Again, as in chapter 1, verse 10, the Holy Spirit takes complete control of John in order to give him the most glorious vision in all time or eternity—the Lord Jesus Christ upon His throne. Most of us have not personally met many kings, queens, or presidents, but such introductions will become absolutely meaningless when we see Jesus in His majestic splendor. Praise God, that day will soon be here. We are going home imminently. Amen and amen!

Verse 3: *And he that sat was to look upon like a jasper and a sardine stone: and there was a rainbow round about the throne, in sight like unto an emerald.*

Here we see a comparison of Christ with two precious stones—the jasper and the sardine. The jasper is *clear as crystal* (chapter 21, verse 11) and is likened to the light of the holy Jerusalem which comes from the *glory of God* (chapter 21, verse 23). Imagine, glory is that which first strikes our eyes as we see the Lord Jesus Christ. The sardine is red, the color of fire. This undoubtedly speaks of the righteous wrath of God and the judgment that is to fall in chapters 6 through 18. The rainbow, resembling an emerald, proves that the impending judgment will not come through a flood (because of God's promise to Noah in Genesis 9:13), but that it will be a holocaust of fire. After describing the throne and its occupant, John indicates the presence of another group situated in the very presence of the Lord...

Verse 4: *And round about the throne were four and twenty seats; and upon the seats I saw four and twenty elders sitting, clothed in white raiment; and they had on their heads crowns of gold.*

These are not angels, for elders always depict members of the human race. What members? The redeemed. They are also in resurrection bodies, as is the Lord, for they sit down. An immaterial spirit cannot sit, for a material body is necessary in order to sit on a material throne. Christ possesses such a new glorified body (see Luke 24:39), and when we see Jesus *we shall be like him* (1 John 3:2). The elders are also clothed in white raiment. One could not put a coat on a spirit very readily, for it would continually fall to the floor! The Book of Revelation cannot be spiritualized. These are real people! In fact, since the Judgment Seat took place immediately after the *Come up hither* of verse 1, these individuals are already wearing the crowns which they will place at the Master's feet in verse 11.

Who are these twenty-four elders? Some believe they represent the twenty-four groups or orders within the Levitical priesthood. This, in turn, represents all believers in Christ for, through Him as High Priest, every Christian is a member of the *royal priesthood* (1 Peter 2:9). Others believe the twenty-four elders represent the twelve tribes of Israel and the twelve apostles—for a total of twenty-four. In other words, they say the elders represent God's people of all ages. This is a good possibility since Revelation 21 describes the New Jerusalem, the names of the twelve tribes inscribed on the gates, and the names of the twelve apostles found upon the twelve foundations (see verses 12-14). Regardless of the view one holds, the four and twenty elders represent the children of God in the presence of the Lord, before the horrible Tribulation begins in chapter 6. A preview of the judgment about to be unleashed upon the entire globe is found in the following verse.

Verse 5: *And out of the throne proceeded lightnings and thunderings and voices: and there were seven lamps of fire burning before the throne, which are the seven spirits of God.*

Lightning, thunder, and voices speak of judgment. Rumblings resound through the heavens as the saints are informed of what is about to occur on earth.

The present hour is so late, prophetically speaking, that this very scene could happen soon. We may go home momentarily to become the very participants around the throne! Jesus is coming and His appearing is at the door (see Matthew 24:33). But wait! The *seven lamps of fire burning before the throne, which are the seven Spirits of God,* picture the Holy Spirit in all His perfection, for seven always denotes flawlessness in the Bible. (Note the seven characteristics of the Holy Spirit in Isaiah 11:2.) This blessed Holy Spirit is also involved in the impending judgment. Each member of the Trinity is righteously indignant over earth's inundation with wickedness and participates unitedly in the twenty-one seal, trumpet, and bowl judgments which occur in chapters 6 through 18.

Verse 6: *And before the throne there was a sea of glass like unto crystal: and in the midst of the throne, and round about the throne, were four beasts full of eyes before and behind.*

Although thunderous judgment will soon be released upon earth, perfect peace surrounds God's throne. The glassy sea pictures calmness, a sea untroubled by winds and storms. This is the Church at rest in heaven before the storm occurs upon earth. Hallelujah!

Verse 7: *And the first beast was like a lion, and the second beast like a calf, and the third beast had a face as a man, and the fourth beast was like a flying eagle.*

Verse 8: *And the four beasts had each of them six wings about him; and they were full of eyes within: and they rest not day and night, saying, Holy, holy, holy, Lord God Almighty, which was, and is, and is to come.*

These verses are symbolic. Always take every

word of the Bible literally unless God specifically indicates that it is figurative. In these texts we find the words, "like a" and "as a," expressing symbolism. The term *beast* is *Zoon* in the Greek, and means "a living creature." These are literal, created beings. At this point, the symbolic and figurative expressions depict their strength and knowledge. Thus, they have eyes before and behind to see all things clearly and accurately. By comparing the characteristics of these living creatures with Isaiah 6:1-3, we see they are undoubtedly seraphim—angels of God—created to praise, exalt, and adulate the Lord. These beings are not monstrosities. Instead, they are a picture of beauty. Within each species there is always a leader—the lion among wild beasts, the calf among domestic animals, the eagle among birds, and man among all creatures. This is the portrait set before us—angels in all their magnificence praising the Lord, saying, *Holy, holy, holy, Lord God Almighty, which was, and is, and is to come.* This threefold adulation of holiness is for the Father, the Son, and the Holy Spirit—the three in One (see 1 John 5:7). The description—*which was, and is, and is to come*—is the title of the Father (chapter 1, verse 4), the Son (verse 8), and also the Holy Spirit who always *was, and is, and is to come,* for the Trinity works unitedly. The praising of God by these living creatures is contagious and the entire group of God's people, pictured by the twenty-four elders, joins them.

Verse 9: *And when those beasts give glory and honour and thanks to him that sat on the throne, who liveth for ever and ever,*

Verse 10: *The four and twenty elders fall down before him that sat on the throne, and worship him that liveth for ever and ever, and cast their crowns before the throne, saying,*

Verse 11: *Thou art worthy, O Lord, to receive glory and honour and power: for thou hast created all things, and for thy pleasure they are and were created.*

This is one of the most glorious moments in heaven. The crowned saints lay their rewards at the feet of Jesus. They lay aside their rewarded glory to add to His glory, thereby ascribing all glory to Him. They know that their victories came only because of His power working within them. (My full-length audio cassette, "The Judgment Seat of Christ," contains detailed teaching on this subject.) The praise session is concluded with the words, *Thou art worthy, O Lord, to receive glory and honour and power: for thou hast created all things, and for thy pleasure they are and were created.* Imagine, both the angels and the elders praise God for creating them! This proves there will be no evolutionists in heaven. Instead, they will join with Darwin in singing songs about their ancestors—the monkeys—in a place where air conditioning does not exist. Jesus is coming! Prepare! Be with the blessed host when the greatest praise festival in the entire universe and heaven occurs.

5

Here is an important statement to consider: Bible chapters and verses came into existence 500 years ago. They are not inspired, but greatly assist one in finding texts. Sometimes, however, they break the continuity of a study. Such is the case at this point. Because John continues describing the heavenly scene, there should not have been a break between chapters 4 and 5.

Verse 1: *And I saw in the right hand of him that sat on the throne a book written within and on the backside, sealed with seven seals.*

The book in the right hand of the Lord Jesus Christ is actually a scroll of either sheepskin, papyrus, or vellum. Its subject is redemption, and its contents unlock the remainder of this chapter. The message is contained on the inside and outside, and is enclosed by seven seals.

Verse 2: *And I saw a strong angel proclaiming with a loud voice, Who is worthy to open the book, and to loose the seals thereof?*

The search for a member of the human race, past or present, or any rank of angel to open the book proves fruitless. None is worthy!

Verse 3: *And no man in heaven, nor in earth, neither under the earth, was able to open the book, neither to look thereon.*

John is heartbroken!

Verse 4: *And I wept much, because no man was found worthy to open and to read the book, neither to look thereon.*

John's lament has to do with the fact that this scroll is also the title deed to the earth. As long as it remains sealed, Satan will be in complete control of the planet.

Verse 5: *And one of the elders saith unto me, Weep not: behold, the Lion of the tribe of Juda, the root of David, hath prevailed to open the book, and to loose the seven seals thereof.*

John's weeping ends at the place where all tears are dried. He is pointed to Christ where tears are turned to joy. Christ is the Lion of the tribe of Judah, the Root of David. Since Judah is the leading tribe of Israel and a lion is the king of the beasts, Christ is thus pictured when He comes as Israel's King (see chapter 19, verse 16). It is at this same moment that the Lord God gives *unto him the throne of his father David* (Luke 1:32). Let's go further in proving that our Saviour is the One John sees.

Verse 6: *And I beheld, and, lo, in the midst of the throne and of the four beasts, and in the midst of the elders, stood a Lamb as it had been slain, having seven horns and seven eyes, which are the seven spirits of God sent forth into all the earth.*

As mentioned previously, the seven-sealed scroll is the title deed to the earth and its subject is redemp-

70

tion. The *Lamb of God* (John 1:29), who earned the right by redemption to the title deed of the earth, is the only One worthy to open the seals. This is the Lamb who died for you and for me. Yes, *Christ died for our sins* (1 Corinthians 15:3). He shed His precious blood to purchase our redemption, for *the blood of Jesus Christ* [God's] *son cleanseth us from all sin* (1 John 1:7). John, who recorded the fact that Jesus was the *Lamb of God* when He walked upon the earth, now says that no one can overcome but *by the blood of the Lamb* (chapter 12, verse 11). "Have you been to Jesus for the cleansing power? Are you washed in the blood of the Lamb?" There is no other way! Without the shedding of blood, there is no remission for sins (see Hebrews 9:22). This Lamb is worthy because of the sacrifice He paid for your sin and mine. Yes, worthy is the Lamb to be praised for time and eternity.

The Lamb's seven horns picture strength. Jesus said, *All* [authority] *is given unto me in heaven and in earth* (Matthew 28:18). The seven eyes picture the fact that He sees everything each of us does: *All things are naked and opened unto the eyes of him with whom we have to do* (Hebrews 4:13). Since "seven" means perfection, there will be no mistakes made as the judgment is meted out, because the seven spirits of God—a picture of the Holy Spirit in all of His fullness—rest upon Christ without measure. Coupling His power (seven horns), His all-seeing vision (seven eyes), along with His filling of the Spirit of God in a sevenfold way (see Isaiah 11:1,2), not one

71

mistake will be made during the Tribulation hour. The One found worthy now acts.

Verse 7: *And he came and took the book out of the right hand of him that sat upon the throne.*

Verse 8: *And when he had taken the book, the four beasts and four and twenty elders fell down before the lamb, having every one of them harps, and golden vials full of odours, which are the prayers of saints.*

The twenty-four elders, representatives of all of God's saved people, share in this glorious moment. The praise is so spectacular that the redeemed break out in song. What a heavenly choir—the largest ever assembled! Listen to them!

Verse 9: *And they* [sang] *a new song, saying, thou art worthy to take the book, and to open the seals thereof: for thou wast slain, and hast redeemed us to God by thy blood out of every kindred, and tongue, and people, and nation;*

Verse 10: *And hast made us unto our God kings and priests: and we shall reign on the earth.*

The song is in appreciation of the fact that Christ was slain on Calvary's cross, that His precious blood was shed (see 1 Peter 1:19), and that it was shed for the entire world. This includes Presbyterians, Lutherans, Methodists, Catholics, and Baptists. Some Christians think they are going to have their own little corner, all alone, in heaven. Not so! Christ's sacrifice was for all kindreds, all tongues, and all people, all nations. God loves the world! The choir also sings about their soon return with Him when He comes as *King of kings* (chapter 19, verse 11). At that time they—the armies of heaven—will follow Him upon white horses. At this point the angels also join in praising the Lamb...

Verse 11: *And I beheld, and I heard the voice of many angels round about the throne and the beasts and the elders: and the number of them was ten thousand times ten thousand, and thousands of thousands;*

Verse 12: *Saying with a loud voice, worthy is the Lamb that was slain to receive power, and riches, and wisdom, and strength, and honour, and glory, and blessing.*

Notice that this passage is not a song. Nowhere does the Bible teach that angels sing. They recite their praise, whereas the Church Triumphant sings her glorious message. The angels, associated with the Lord since their creation, know Him as few know Him—for they have lived with Him for thousands of years. They praise the Lamb for seven reasons: (1) His power; (2) His spiritual riches; (3) His wisdom; (4) His might; (5) His honor; (6) His glory; and (7) His blessing. Carnal Christians who will not bow in worship to Christ here on earth, soon will!

Verse 13: *And every creature which is in heaven, and on the earth, and under the earth, and such as are in the sea, and all that are in them, heard I saying, Blessing, and honour, and glory, and power, be unto him that sitteth upon the throne, and unto the Lamb for ever and ever.*

At this point Philippians 2:9-11 will be fulfilled: *Wherefore God also hath highly exalted him, and given him a name which is above every name: That at the name of Jesus every knee should bow, of things in heaven, and things in earth, and things under the earth; And that every tongue should confess that Jesus Christ is Lord, to the glory of God the Father.*

What is the response as the heavenly hosts envision this future hour?

Verse 14: *And the four beasts said, Amen. And the four and twenty elders fell down and worshipped him that liveth for ever and ever.*

Notice they get a head start. They cannot wait to begin their worship of the Lamb—the Lord Jesus Christ!

6

As we begin chapter six, which introduces the Tribulation hour upon earth, a word of explanation is in order concerning the placement of signs. Some sincere Christians say, "Matthew 24:14 states that the gospel of the kingdom shall be preached in all the world for a witness unto all nations and then shall the end come. Since there are some tribes who have not yet heard, Jesus Christ cannot return." Such people have their signs in the wrong place, because the Rapture is a signless, timeless event. Let's investigate this statement further.

What relationship exists between the Rapture and prophetic signs? None. Are you shocked? The Rapture is only an evacuation of believers before the great judgment of the Tribulation hour. It is a meeting in the heavenlies and not Christ's return to the earth. Since His first coming was to earth, His second coming must also be to earth. The Rapture, then, is not a coming to earth, but a meeting in the clouds. Seven years later we return with Him, and all the signs point to this coming when He returns to earth.

Watch the simplicity of this next statement unfold. Take two Bibles and place them side by side.

Open one to the Book of Revelation, chapter 6, where the signs begin. Then open the other to Matthew 24, Mark 13, Luke 17 or Luke 21. Compare the signs in these chapters with those found in the Book of Revelation. The inescapable conclusion? They are identical! The texts are practically the same. The Church is raptured in chapter 4, verse 1, and believers—represented by the twenty-four elders in verses 10 and 11—are placing crowns at the Saviour's feet before the signs and judgments of the Tribulation hour begin in chapters 6 through 18. The signs, then, are post-Rapture and pre-Revelational. In other words, they are fulfilled after the Rapture and before the Revelation—after Christ calls His saints home to heaven and before He returns with them to earth. Not one sign needs to be fulfilled prior to the Rapture, because all the signs point to the Revelation, or the revealing of Christ to the earth. Thus, there is a period of seven years following the Rapture during which every sign can be adequately fulfilled. This, of course, is the Tribulation hour, after we Christians have been raptured.

At this point every believer should praise the Lord, because the next statement is utterly fantastic. Since the signs point to Christ's return to earth, and since we believers return with Him, then the logical deduction is that all signs point to our return with Christ. Presently the signs are casting their shadows. They are all beginning to be fulfilled. Imagine! The prophecies that take place after we believers are gone and which indicate that we will return with Him are already beginning. If the signs indicate that we are coming back with Jesus soon, and we are still on earth, how very, very soon must the Rapture then occur to take us out of this earth so that, seven years later, we can return with Him!

Presently a number of the sealed judgments contained in this chapter deserve special emphasis. Each will be discussed thoroughly later. First, in verse 2, we discover a rider on a white horse. This coincides with Jesus' statement in Matthew 24:3-5, when His disciples asked Him, *What shall be the sign of thy coming, and of the end of the world? And Jesus answered and said unto them, Take heed that no man deceive you. For many shall come in my name, saying, I am Christ.* This rider on the white horse, depicting the first seal judgment, is a counterfeit. Satan always attempts to do everything that the Lord Jesus Christ is going to do. The Lord is seated on a white horse in chapter 19, verse 11, when He returns with you and me to the earth. Thus, seven years before Christ returns, the Antichrist also mounts a white horse. This event is identical to the sign of Matthew 24:3.

Next one should note verses 3 and 4: *And when he had opened the second seal, I heard the second beast say, Come and see. And there went out another horse that was red: and power was given to him that sat thereon to take peace from the earth, and that they should kill one another: and there was given unto him a great sword.* This is the second sign Jesus mentioned: that there would be wars and rumors of wars (see Matthew 24:6).

Verses 5 and 6 state: *And when he had opened*

the third seal, I heard the third beast say, Come and see. And I beheld, and lo a black horse; and he that sat on him had a pair of balances in his hand. And I heard a voice in the midst of the four beasts say, A measure of wheat for a penny, and three measures of barley for a penny; and see thou hurt not the oil and the wine. This is a picture of mass starvation and agrees with Christ's third sign: There shall be famines (Matthew 24:7).

In verses 7 and 8 we are told, And when he had opened the fourth seal, I heard the voice of the fourth beast say, Come and see. And I looked, and behold a pale horse: and his name that sat on him was Death, and Hell followed with him. And power was given unto them over the fourth part of the earth, to kill with sword, and with hunger, and with death, and with the beasts of the earth. The fourth seal judgment agrees with Christ's statement: [There shall be] pestilences, and earthquakes, in divers places, destroying thousands, yea millions (Matthew 24:7).

Verse 9 states: And when he had opened the fifth seal, I saw under the altar the souls of them that were slain for the word of God, and for the testimony which they held. This is the fifth sign Jesus gave in Matthew 24:8 and 9: These are the beginning of sorrows. Then shall they deliver you up to be afflicted, and shall kill you: and ye shall be hated of all nations for my name's sake.

Finally in verses 12-16, John tells us, And I beheld when he had opened the sixth seal, and, lo, there was a great earthquake; and the sun became black as sackcloth of hair, and the moon became as blood;

And the stars of heaven fell unto the earth, even as a fig tree casteth her untimely figs, when she is shaken of a mighty wind. And the heaven departed as a scroll when it is rolled together; and every mountain and island were moved out of their places. And the kings of the earth, and the great men, and the rich men, and the chief captains, and the mighty men, and every bondman, and every free man, hid themselves in the dens and in the rocks of the mountains; And said to the mountains and rocks, Fall on us, and hide us from the face of him that sitteth on the throne, and from the wrath of the Lamb. The sixth seal is the sixth sign Jesus mentioned in Matthew 24:29: *Immediately after the tribulation of those days shall the sun be darkened, and the moon shall not give her light, and the stars shall fall from heaven.*

Thus, it is evident that Matthew, Mark, and Luke contain the same signs as the Book of Revelation. However, one must realize that each sign is completed or fulfilled *after* chapter 4, verse 1, where the Church is called to heaven in the twinkling of an eye through the phrase, *Come up hither.* As previously stated, these signs that are to be fulfilled after we are gone are *already* transpiring. We see them before our eyes daily in world events. Todays "Bible Headlines" indicate that you and I will soon return with Jesus. However, we must first go home via the Rapture in order to return soon. Surely this momentous event is at the door!

I think you know that the foregoing discussion of prophetic signs in relationship to the Rapture and the Revelation has given us a panoramic view of chapter

6. Now let's delve into this portion of God's Word more deeply.

In chapters 6 through 18, we witness firsthand the events which take place upon the earth during the Tribulation. The presentation occupies nearly two-thirds of the Book of Revelation—a total of thirteen chapters. One should also note that three additional Bible verses graphically describe this hour of horrendous judgment: (1) Jeremiah 30:7: *Alas! for that day is great, so that none is like it: it is even the time of Jacob's trouble; but he shall be saved out of it*; (2) Daniel 12:1: *And at that time shall Michael stand up, the great prince which standeth for the children of thy people: and there shall be a time of trouble, such as never was since there was a nation even to that same time: and at that time thy people shall be delivered, every one that shall be found written in the book*; and (3) Matthew 24:21: *For then shall be great tribulation, such as was not since the beginning of the world to this time, no, nor ever shall be.*

These texts inform us of the fact that the Tribulation will constitute earth's bloodiest hour. There will not have been anything in past centuries to equal it, neither will there be any event in the future to match the judgment unleashed upon our planet. The catastrophic calamities arrive through a series of twenty-one judgments which are described as seven seals, seven trumpets, and seven bowls. At the outpouring of each bowl, a new judgment is released. The seal judgments are found in Revelation 6:1 through 8:1. The first six are located in chapter 6. Chapter 7 is a parenthesis, and the seventh seal judgment takes place in chapter 8, verse 1.

First seal

Verse 1: *And I saw when the Lamb opened one of the seals, and I heard, as it were the voice of thunder, one of the four beasts saying, Come and see.*

At this command, the apostle sees the One who is worthy to take the book and open the seals thereof, the blessed Lamb of God, the Lord Jesus, beginning the work of judgment. Immediately John hears the noise of thunder—a sign of impending catastrophe— as well as one of the living creatures (angels) saying, *Come and see.* The words, *and see*, are not in the original, just the word *Come.* It is a command given to the rider on the white horse, the infamous Antichrist. His time has arrived!

Verse 2: *And I saw, and behold a white horse: and he that sat on him had a bow; and a crown was given unto him: and he went forth conquering, and to conquer.*

Satan has always tried to duplicate the works of God. Back in the day of Moses, the demon-possessed magicians of Pharaoh were able to accomplish the same miracles as Aaron. This has always been Satan's ploy. He is not the creator—God is. All he can do is imitate or fake the works of the Almighty.

This rider appears at the outset, or beginning, of the Tribulation period. There can be no such hour without him. Since he is the master counterfeiter, who is he imitating? The answer is found in chapter 19, verses 11 through 16, which describe Christ's return at the conclusion of the Tribulation. The fake begins it and the Saviour ends it. John says, *And I saw heaven opened.* This is the second time an opening appears in heaven (see Revelation 19:11) to provide an exit for Christ and His bride as they return to earth. As heaven is opened, John beholds *a white horse; and he that sat upon him was called Faithful and True, and in righteousness he doth judge and make war. His eyes were as a flame of fire, and on his head were many crowns; and he had a name written, that no man knew, but he himself. And he was clothed with a vesture dipped in blood; and his name is called The Word of God. And the armies which were in heaven followed him upon white horses, clothed in fine linen, white and clean. And out of his mouth goeth a sharp sword, that with it he should smite the nations: and he shall rule them with a rod of iron: and he treadeth the winepress of the fierceness and wrath of Almighty God. And he hath on his vesture and on his thigh a name written, KING OF KINGS, AND LORD OF LORDS.*

This is the coming of the true Christ. Since our Christ is God, the Antichrist also proclaims himself as God. *Who opposeth and exalteth himself above all that is called God, or that is worshipped; so that he as God sitteth in the temple of God, showing himself that he is God* (2 Thessalonians 2:4). We will study this hypocritical creep later. Presently let's just skim the surface.

The Antichrist comes to power through an international peace pact (see Daniel 9:27). This is why the horse's rider has a bow but no arrows. The Antichrist conquers through diplomacy as a king, hence, the crown. In fact, when he takes control over the nations via a world government, *power* [is] *given him over all kindreds, and tongues, and nations* (Revelation 13:7).

The Antichrist is rapidly followed by three additional riders of judgment. Together, these four horsemen of the apocalypse bring heartache upon the globe such as has never been experienced in the annals of history. The Antichrist is called *the Beast* because of his character (chapter 13, verses 2 and 3), because he ascends out of the abyss (chapter 17, verse 8) and because he receives his power, his throne, and his authority from Satan (chapter 13, verse 2). The Antichrist's ascendancy to world leadership signals the unleashing of the remaining twenty judgments.

The peace that was made by the first rider is broken by the one who mounts the red horse. This, of course, is in harmony with the first rider's—or Antichrist's—program. Daniel 9:27 outlines the peace package as well as its failure: *And he* [the Antichrist] *shall confirm the covenant with many for one week: and in the midst of the week he shall cause the sacrifice and the oblation to cease.* When peace is confirmed, the Jews will feel at ease to conduct sacrifices without fear of war. However, in the midst of the week, or literally in the middle of the *heptad*, the contract is broken. The term *heptad* in the original means "seven years." As *decade* means "ten years" in English, so *heptad* means "seven years" in Hebrew. Now we understand more fully why the Tribulation covers a timetable of seven years—simply because Daniel 9:27 states that the Antichrist will make his proposal for a *heptad*—seven years—and then break it in the midst of the *heptad*, or after three and one-half years.

Second seal

Verse 3: *And when he had opened the second seal, I heard the second beast say, Come and see.*

Verse 4: *And there went out another horse that was red: and power was given to him that sat thereon to take peace from the earth, and that they should kill one another: and there was given unto him a great sword.*

One of the nations that marches during this period of time is Red Russia. How interesting that a rider on a red horse takes peace from the earth! Could Red Russia play such a major role during this hour?

In Ezekiel 38:2, the terms *Magog, Meshech, Tubal,* and *Rosh* are mentioned in connection with a march to the Middle East for the battle of battles, before Armageddon. Listen to the message God gave Ezekiel: *Son of man, set thy face against Gog, the land of Magog, the chief prince of Meshech and Tubal, and prophesy against him* (Ezekiel 38:2). Each of these names can be located within the present-day Soviet Union. Tobolsk, the eastern capital of the USSR, is the ancient "Tubal" mentioned in the text. It is southwest of Siberia on modern maps—the place where U-2 pilot Gary Powers was gunned down years ago. Meshech is Moscow. The historical names for Moscow begin with "Meshech," then "Moshoch," then "Moschi," then "Moscoty," then "Moscovy" and finally, Moscow. "Rosh" is Russia herself.

This "great bear" invades Israel from the north:

And thou shalt come up from thy place of the north parts, thou, and many people with thee, all of them riding upon horses, a great company, and a mighty army: And thou shalt come up against my people of Israel, as a cloud to cover the land; it shall be in the latter days, and I will bring thee against my land, that the heathen may know me, when I shall be sanctified in thee, O Gog, before their eyes (Ezekiel 38:15,16). The Soviet Union is directly north of Israel and moves against her in the latter days (see Ezekiel 38:8). The attack centers around the Holy Land. In fact, the name Israel is used eighteen times to identify the nation being invaded in Ezekiel, chapters 38 and 39. Such information attests to the divine inspiration of the Bible, for there was no nation in modern history called Israel until 1948.

This war of the future undoubtedly occurs close to or during the Tribulation hour because the facts presented in this Book of Revelation tie in harmoniously with Ezekiel's prophecy. In fact, the eighth and ninth chapters contain two unusual predictions concerning the woes of the Tribulation hour which point to such a mid-East war. Chapter 8, verse 7, mentions the burning of one-third of the earth as the first angel sounded. I quote: *The first angel sounded, And there followed hail and fire mingled with blood, and they were cast upon the earth: and the third part of trees was burnt up, and all green grass was burnt up.* In turn, Revelation 9:18 depicts the extinction of one-third of the world's inhabitants, for, *by these three was the third part of men killed, by the fire, and by the smoke, and by the brimstone, which issued out of their mouths.*

The *Life Pictorial Atlas,* which lists land areas and population figures for every country of the world, contains shocking proof that these prophecies and astronomical figures are capable of being fulfilled at the present time. According to this statistical survey, Africa, Antarctica, Asia, Australia, Europe, North America, and South America incorporate a total of 56,889,581 square miles. Dividing this figure by three, one arrives at the sum of 18,963,194 square miles—the amount of land area that will burn during the Tribulation period according to Revelation 8:7. Comparing this figure with the combined land areas of the nations predicted to align themselves for the Middle East confrontations (Daniel 2:7 and 11 and Ezekiel 38 and 39), one discovers that the two sums are identical—one-third of the globe to the exact mile, believe it or not! Is this startling? Let's go one step further. The *Atlas* also lists the population figures for the nations of earth. The same alignment of pro- and anti-Russian nations for the war of wars totals one-third of earth's inhabitants! Revelation 8:7 and 9:18 could become factual events, fulfilling verse 4 very, very soon!

(To study this subject thoroughly, order my full-length videocassette entitled "Russia, World War III, and Armageddon.")

Third seal

Verse 5: *And when he had opened the third seal, I heard the third beast say, Come and see. And I* *beheld, and lo a black horse; and he that sat on him had a pair of balances in his hand.*

Verse 6: *And I heard a voice in the midst of the four beasts say, A measure of wheat for a penny, and three measures of barley for a penny; and see thou hurt not the oil and wine.*

Famine and inflation usually follow war. The rider on the black horse produces these tragic twin sorrows upon earth. Ezekiel prophesied this hour: *And thy meat which thou shalt eat shall be by weight, twenty shekels a day: from time to time thou shalt eat it. Thou shalt drink also water by measure...behold, I will break the staff of bread in Jerusalem: and they shall eat bread by weight, and with care* (Ezekiel 4:10,11,16). Leviticus 26:26 states: *Ye shall eat, and not be satisfied.* This is pictured by the pair of balances in our text. The angel in Revelation 6:6 also cries, *A measure of wheat for a penny, and three measures of barley for a penny.* In Bible times laborers received a *denarious*, or one penny, as an entire day's wages (see Matthew 20:2). A measure would be sixteen of our American ounces. Think of it! An entire day's wages for a loaf of bread! No wonder Moses said, *Ye shall eat, and not be satisfied.* A man will have to spend everything he has just for the necessities of life. What about the oil and wine? These items were luxuries in Bible times, and we find that there are those who still possess them during the Tribulation. Nevertheless, the general picture is that of hunger stalking the world. Why?

Inflation, the leading economic culprit, becomes so bad during the Tribulation that precious metals actually become worthless. Those who think that it will help to hoard diamonds, gold, or silver should beware! During this period of time, inflation will skyrocket and the Antichrist's numerical program, 666, will replace gold, silver, and paper money. Because of the situation, *they shall cast their silver in the streets, and their gold shall be removed: their silver and their gold shall not be able to deliver them in the day of the wrath of the Lord* (Ezekiel 7:19). James adds in chapter 5, verses 1 and 3, *Go to now, ye rich men, weep and howl for your miseries that shall come upon you...your gold and silver is cankered; and the rust of them shall be a witness against you, and shall eat your flesh as it were fire. Ye have heaped treasure together for the last days.*

Earthly treasure, then as now, brings nothing but sorrow and tears in the last days. One had better do what he can for the Lord while he can. Why leave it behind for the Tribulation hour or keep it until it becomes valueless? Every Christian should serve God with material blessings, winning souls to Him for all eternity. Jesus said, *Lay not up for yourselves treasures upon earth, where moth and rust doth corrupt, and where thieves break through and steal: But lay up for yourselves treasures in heaven, where neither moth nor rust doth corrupt, and where thieves do not break through nor steal: For where your treasure is, there will your heart be also* (Matthew 6:19-21). One can either let go—give it to God and store it up on the other side—or hang on, keep it, and let greedy, unsaved relatives share it, losing it both here and forever. One must make his choice—either for the here and now, or for eternity.

Fourth seal

Let's move on to the next rider, on a pale horse, who aggravates the conditions begun by the rider on the black horse. The third seal unleashes hunger and inflation upon the earth, but the fourth seal produces mass starvation.

Verse 7: *And when he had opened the fourth seal, I heard the voice of the fourth beast say, Come and see.*

Verse 8: *And I looked, and behold a pale horse: and his name that sat on him was Death, and Hell followed with him. And power was given unto them over the fourth part of the earth, to kill with sword, and with hunger, and with death, and with the beasts of the earth.*

This horse is described as *pale*. The Greek word is *chloros* from which we get the term chlorine gas. In other areas of the New Testament, we find that *chloros* is translated "green" (see Mark 6:39 and Revelation 9:4).

The fourth rider is the deadliest. This is why his name is *Death* and why *Hell* follows with him. He destroys the body, then Hell swallows up the souls and spirits of those he kills with sword, hunger, and the beasts of the earth—probably AIDS, produced by the green monkey virus. One-fourth of the world's population dies through his brutality—more than one billion, two hundred fifty million people at today's population figures. This could easily happen given the capability of mankind's atomic, hydrogen, and neutron bombs. Today's armies have the means to reduce population figures by tens of millions within hours. Their arsenals include chemical warfare and test tubes filled with germs for the greatest biological and bacteriological attack ever. The aftereffects of such a battle could easily dwindle earth's population by twenty-five percent. God help us when it happens!

Fifth seal

Next, the opening of the fifth seal brings forth the cries of slain martyrs. Jesus spoke of this hour in Matthew 24:9,10. Hear Him: *Then shall they deliver you up to be afflicted, and shall kill you: and ye shall be hated of all nations for my name's sake. And then shall many be offended, and shall betray one another, and shall hate one another.*

Please read chapter 4 again. Rediscover that this reference is to Tribulation saints composed of elect Israelites and those Gentiles converted by the preaching of the 144,00 Jewish evangelists. These persecuted saints and martyrs are not part of the Church—the body of Christ and the bride of the Saviour—already in glory (chapter 4, verse 1).

Verse 9: *And when he had opened the fifth seal, I saw under the altar the souls of them that were slain for the word of God, and for the testimony which they held:*

Verse 10: *And they cried with a loud voice, saying, How long, O Lord, holy and true, dost thou* *not judge and avenge our blood on them that dwell on the earth?*

Verse 11: *And white robes were given unto every one of them; and it was said unto them, that they should rest yet for a little season, until their fellowservants also and their brethren, that should be killed as they were, should be fulfilled.*

These martyred saints are seen under the altar. In the Old Testament, the altar always referred to the place where blood had been sacrificed. Souls will be saved during the Tribulation hour the same way souls are saved today—through the precious shed blood of the Lord Jesus Christ. Because the believers of the Tribulation hour proclaim Christ crucified, they lose their lives. At this point every twentieth-century believer should ask himself the question, "Would there be enough evidence to convict me as a Christian during this period of time were I present?" However, in this age of grace, we also will be the losers if we attempt to be secret disciples, never testifying of our faith in Christ Jesus. The Saviour said, *Whosoever therefore shall confess me before men, him will I confess also before my Father which is in heaven. But whosoever shall deny me before men, him will I also deny before my father which is in heaven* (Matthew 10:32,33).

Please listen to this next statement carefully. These slain martyrs are crying. They are not in an unconscious state. The doctrine of "soul sleep" is not taught in the Bible. Some denominations teach that all believers sleep until the resurrection morning. Not so! Paul said in 2 Corinthians 5:8, *To be absent from the body* [is] *to be present with the Lord.* The "soul sleep" adherents can never find a time when they are absent from their bodies. If the soul remains in a state of sleep in that body until the morning of Christ's return, the two are never together. The *Bible* teaches that they are *separated.* The body is asleep in one place (the grave), whereas the soul is alive in another place (heaven or hell). For the Christian, *to be absent from the body* means *to be present with the Lord.* That is why Paul said, *To die is gain* (Philippians 1:21).

It is also the reason that, when Christ returns at the Rapture, He brings those who sleep (the dead) with Him: *For if we believe that Jesus died and rose again, even so them also which sleep in Jesus will God bring with him* (1 Thessalonians 4:14). Now, how can the Lord bring the dead with Him and still come after the dead in 1 Thessalonians 4:16? Simple. It's because the dead are in two places! The souls and spirits are with the Lord (absent from the body and present with the Lord), but their bodies are in the grave. Hence, Christ brings the dead—the souls and spirits already in His presence—with Him, so they may come to get their bodies. That's why the dead in Christ rise first. But all this pictures the Rapture. The text under investigation describes a later time—the Tribulation hour.

It is then that the spirits of the martyred Tribulation saints cry. They also wear white robes. Lifeless spirits cannot cry or wear white robes. The solution? The spiritual being has a temporary covering. Proof: *For we know that if our earthly house of this taberna-*

cle were dissolved [dead], *we have a building of God, an house not made with hands, eternal in the heavens* (2 Corinthians 5:1). We may not understand everything about the spirit world, but one thing is certain—being in spirit form does not mean unconsciousness. Spirits move, talk, cry, and even wear white robes. Demons also are spirits. They spoke on many occasions in the Gospels. Why? Spirits live! Away with the doctrine of "soul sleep" in any dispensation! Our loved ones are with Jesus if they died trusting in the merits of the shed blood. They are also under the altar, just as these Tribulation saints will be. Soon they will come forth for their eternal covering, their bodies.

Now, since we have learned that it is possible for the dead to cry because the spirit never ceases to exist, we next discover that their cry is one of vengeance. Why? They are not under grace, the love covenant. Instead, they want blood. Stephen, under grace, cried, *Lord, lay not this sin to their charge* (Acts 7:60). But this is a different dispensation—the fulfillment of the hour mentioned by David when he spoke of the actions of Jehovah, saying, *He maketh inquisition for blood* (Psalm 9:12). This group of saints knows that prophecy is being fulfilled, and they wonder how much longer their loved ones, still alive, must suffer. The Lord speaks to them about having a little more patience. There will be one more wave of persecution in chapter 20, verse 4. Then they will live and reign with Him for 1,000 years.

Sixth seal

Verse 12: *And I beheld when he had opened the sixth seal, and, lo, there was a great earthquake; and the sun became black as sackcloth of hair, and the moon became as blood;*

Verse 13: *And the stars of heaven fell unto the earth, even as a fig tree casteth her untimely figs when she is shaken of a mighty wind.*

Verse 14: *And the heaven departed as a scroll when it is rolled together; and every mountain and island were moved out of their places.*

Verse 15: *And the kings of the earth, and the great men, and the rich men, and the chief captains, and the mighty men, and every bondman, and every free man, hid themselves in the dens and in the rocks of the mountains;*

Verse 16: *And said to the mountains and rocks, Fall on us, and hide us from the face of him that sitteth on the throne, and from the wrath of the Lamb:*

Verse 17: *For the great day of his wrath is come; and who shall be able to stand?*

In verse 12, we see a great earthquake. There are three quakes in the Book of Revelation—the one mentioned here plus two others in chapter 11, verse 13, and chapter 16, verses 18 and 19. It is interesting to note that the judgments of the first four seals were under the jurisdiction of the Antichrist. The opening of the sixth seal, however, begins the administration of supernatural judgment from heaven. One cannot conscientiously interpret these events figuratively. The judgments occurring in this portion of Scripture are to be taken literally. And why not? Do you know that earthquakes have accompanied the judgment of God throughout history? Mount Sinai quaked when God descended upon it in fire: *And mount Sinai was altogether on a smoke, because the Lord descended upon it in fire: and the smoke thereof ascended as the smoke of a furnace, and the whole mount quaked greatly* (Exodus 19:18). Rocks were smashed to smithereens through earthquakes in Elijah's day: *For, behold, the Lord passed by, and a great and strong wind rent the mountains, and brake in pieces the rocks before the Lord* (1 Kings 19:11).

There was also a great earthquake when Christ died at Calvary: *Behold, the veil of the temple was rent in twain from the top to the bottom; and the earth did quake, and the rocks rent; And the graves were opened; and many bodies of the saints which slept arose* (Matthew 27:51,52). If all these quakes were real, why wouldn't the scene before us be literal? It is exactly what Jesus predicted for the Tribulation hour. He said, *And there shall be signs in the sun, and in the moon, and in the stars; and upon the earth distress of nations, with perplexity; the sea and the waves roaring; men's hearts failing them for fear, and for looking after those things which are coming on the earth: for the powers of heaven shall be shaken* (Luke 21:25,26).

At this time the earthquakes and convulsions upon earth are so great that the stars of heaven fall like figs being shaken out of a tree prematurely. Strong winds, possible tornados, and hurricanes also wreak great havoc. The devastating quakes cause mountains and islands to be moved from their foundations. No wonder one-half of the world's population dies through the manifold catastrophes that bombard the earth. The scene is so terrifying that kings, great men, rich men, chief captains, mighty men, bondmen, and all free men hide in dens and mountains for safety. Now we understand Christ's statement: *Men's hearts failing them for fear, and for looking after those things which are coming on the earth* (Luke 21:26). The situation becomes so unbearable that humanity pleads to die, begging for obliteration and annihilation by crying to the mountains and rocks saying, *Fall on us, and hide us from the face of him that sitteth on the throne, and from the wrath of the Lamb: For the great day of his wrath is come; and who shall be able to stand?* (Revelation 6:16,17).

Thank God, the Church is in heaven during this calamitous hour!

7

The seventh seal is discussed in chapter 8. However, before we get there, God has a parenthesis for us in this chapter. Chapter 7 may be divided into two portions dealing with two groups—verses 1 through 8—the 144,000 Israelites, and verses 9 through 17—the multitudinous Gentiles. This chapter also portrays God as compassionate, merciful, and loving. This is right, for *God is love* (1 John 4:8). In fact, *God so loved the world, that he gave his only begotten Son, that whosoever believeth in him should not perish, but have everlasting life. For God sent not his son into the world to condemn the world; but that the world through him might be saved* (John 3:16,17).

It's mankind's wickedness, rebellion, and sin that produce judgment: *For the wages of sin is death* (Romans 6:23), and *they that plow iniquity, and sow wickedness, reap the same* (Job 4:8). The judgments already described were unleashed because of the hardness of men's hearts. They rebelled—and continue to rebel—for thousands of years. God, however, is so great that, at this point, He declares a "time out." He still loves the human race and longs to save mankind. He desires for men everywhere to open their minds and hearts and come unto Him. The result is this chapter, which deals with the mercy of God in the midst of Tribulation. God, in love, creates a lull before the storm in order to call men to salvation and revival.

The 144,000 Israelites

Verse 1: *And after these things I saw four angels standing on the four corners of the earth, holding the four winds of the earth, that the wind should not blow on the earth, nor on the sea, nor on any tree.*

The fact that the angels are standing on the four corners of the earth does not signify that the earth is square. God knows the world He made is round: *He ...sitteth upon the circle of the earth* (Isaiah 40:22). This statement was in the Bible when Christopher Columbus allegedly was making a fool of himself by claiming, contrary to public opinion, that the world was round. The God who made it and sits upon the circle of it knows it is not square. Therefore, the term "the four corners of the earth" is but a Bible expression depicting north, south, east, and west—the four points of the compass. The four angels, standing at these four positions administering judgment, are commanded to relent so there might be a time of great revival as the servants of God are sealed in their foreheads.

Verse 2: *And I saw another angel ascending from the east, having the seal of the living God: and he cried with a loud voice to the four angels, to whom it was given to hurt the earth and the sea,*

Verse 3: *Saying, Hurt not the earth, neither the*

sea, nor the trees, till we have sealed the servants of our God in their foreheads.

The wicked get their seal—666—under the super-deceiver, the great imitator, the Antichrist (chapter 13, verses 17 and 18). The genuine believers receive their seal from the angel of God at this point in time.

Verse 4: *And I heard the number of them which were sealed: and there were sealed an hundred and forty and four thousand of all the tribes of the children of Israel.*

Verse 5: *Of the tribe of Juda were sealed twelve thousand. Of the tribe of Reuben were sealed twelve thousand. Of the tribe of Gad were sealed twelve thousand.*

Verse 6: *Of the tribe of Aser were sealed twelve thousand. Of the tribe of Nepthalim were sealed twelve thousand. Of the tribe of Manasses were sealed twelve thousand.*

Verse 7: *Of the tribe of Simeon were sealed twelve thousand. Of the tribe of Levi were sealed twelve thousand. Of the tribe of Issachar were sealed twelve thousand.*

Verse 8: *Of the tribe of Zabulon were sealed twelve thousand. Of the tribe of Joseph were sealed twelve thousand. Of the tribe of Benjamin were sealed twelve thousand.*

This group cannot be the Church, for the Church is already in heaven (chapter 4, verse 1). Also, the Church is not Jewish, but is composed of all races, people, and tongues. Again, this group does not picture the Seventh Day Adventists or the Jehovah's

Witnesses. Both have claimed this in their theological writings. The Seventh Day Adventists say that the 144,000 are not Englishmen or Americans either, as the advocates of British Israelism teach. They make the Israelites forerunners of the Anglo-Saxons. Come on now, Armstrongites and Garner Ted. Surely you cannot be that foolish! These are Jewish tribes with Jewish names. Do the names Juda, Reuben, Gad, Aser, Nepthalim, Manasses, Simeon, Levi, Issachar, Zabulon, Joseph and Benjamin sound British? Had they been named Heathcliff, Sir Winston, or Sherlock Holmes you might have had reason to propose such nonsense. Under the circumstances, however, you had better allow Jews with Jewish names to head up Jewish tribes in a Jewish nation—Israel.

Presently the Jews are not certain of their tribal heritage. However, the omniscient, all-knowing God will untangle this condition at the appointed time. Actually, no one today really knows what his stock is. As a result of migrations, most people are a hodgepodge of differing nationalities. Perhaps it is best not to know or trace one's ancestry. We might be embarrassed to discover our roots! One might learn that he is a descendant of Attilla the Hun! Persons planning to study their family tree should beware. They might find some of their relatives hanging by the neck, while the evolutionists find theirs hanging by the tail!

The 144,000 Jewish evangelists are anointed by the Spirit. Joel 2:28,29 describes the situation as these Spirit-filled preachers proclaim the gospel of the kingdom. *And it shall come to pass afterward, that I will pour out my spirit upon all flesh; and your*

100

sons and your daughters shall prophesy, your old men shall dream dreams, your young men shall see visions: and also upon the servants and upon the handmaids in those days will I pour out my spirit.

We need to pause here briefly because there is a great deal of confusion concerning the presence of the Holy Spirit during the Tribulation hour. This has resulted from a faulty understanding and interpretation of 2 Thessalonians 2:7: *For the mystery of iniquity doth already work: only he who now letteth will let, until he be taken out of the way.* The term *letteth* is the Old English word for *hinders.* The picture being painted here is the rise of the Antichrist. Second Thessalonians 2:6 states: *Ye know what withholdeth that* [the Antichrist] *might be revealed in his time.* Then verse seven makes it clear that the Hinderer—the Holy Spirit—continues to hinder the Antichrist's rise until He—the Holy Spirit—is taken out of the way.

Here is another reason millions believe in the pre-Tribulation Rapture. Why? The Hinderer lives in the hearts of His people: *If any man have not the Spirit of Christ, he is none of his* (Romans 8:9). Also, 1 Corinthians 3:16: *Know ye not that ye are the temple of God, and that the Spirit of God dwelleth in you?* Because of this truth, God's Spirit cannot be taken unless those in whom He lives are taken. Hallelujah! One should note, however, that the Spirit's removal only speaks of His restraining power.

Let me prove this assertion: The Holy Spirit is God, the third member of the Trinity. As God, He is omniscient (all knowing), omnipotent (all powerful), and omnipresent (everywhere at all times). There-fore, the Holy Spirit cannot be removed from the earth because He, as God, is in all places constantly. David states in Psalm 139:7-10: *Whither shall I go from thy spirit? or whither shall I flee from thy presence? If I ascend up into heaven, thou art there: if I make my bed in hell, behold, thou art there. If I take the wings of the morning, and dwell in the uttermost parts of the sea; even there shall thy hand lead me, and thy right hand shall hold me.* Since the Holy Spirit is everywhere at all times, only His restraining influence over sin is removed during the Tribulation hour.

Presently Christians are *the salt of the earth* and the light of the world (see Matthew 5:13-16). The evacuation of Christians, in whose hearts the Holy Spirit lives, is the way—the only way—His restraining influence on sin is removed, ridding the world of salt and light. Christians are God's preservative forces, as well as the dispellers of darkness. Imagine what happens when the Spirit's restraining influence (the Church) is removed via the Rapture. Quite literally, all hell will break loose upon earth. Still, even during this time, His continuing personal presence on earth produces one of the greatest revivals in the history of mankind.

The message of the 144,000 centers on the person and work of the Lord Jesus Christ. This was the emphasis of the Old Testament preachers: *To* [Jesus] *give all the prophets witness, that through his name whosoever believeth in him shall receive remission of sins* (Acts 10:43).

In addition to preaching the message of the shed blood of Jesus, the 144,000 proclaim the advent of the King: *And this gospel* [or good news] *of the kingdom shall be preached in all the world for a witness unto all nations; and then shall the end come* (Matthew 24:14). This is not the message of His first coming—the Rapture (chapter 4, verse 1) but the Revelation or revealing of Christ as King (chapter 19, verse 16).

In order to get a picture of the complete message the kingdom messengers proclaim, one must study the life of John the Baptist. John's message was: (1) Repentance: He said, *Repent ye: for the kingdom of heaven is at hand* (Matthew 3:2); (2) the blood: again, He *saith, behold the Lamb of God, which taketh away the sin of the world* (John 1:29). This message of repentance and the blood was to prepare the hearts of the people for the third part of His message—the coming of the King. Though Christ was rejected in the days of John the Baptist, He will be accepted when the 144,000 Jews preach the identical message.

At this time a worldwide revival ensues, for one of the elders asks, *What are these which are arrayed in white robes? and whence came they? And I said unto him, Sir, thou knowest. And he said to me, These are they which came out of great tribulation, and have washed their robes, and made them white in the blood of the Lamb* (chapter 7, verses 13 and 14). Let's study this God-sent, Holy Spirit-empowered revival, step by step.

The Multitudinous Gentiles

Verse 9: *After this I beheld, and, lo, a great*

multitude, which no man could number, of all na-
tions, and kindreds, and people, and tongues, stood
before the throne, and before the Lamb, clothed with
white robes, and palms in their hands;

John states: *After this.* After what? After the
144,000 Jewish evangelists are sealed by the Spirit of
God. God's message is always to the Jew first, then
to the Gentile. That's why Romans 1:16 declares, *I*
am not ashamed of the gospel of Christ: for it is the
power of God unto salvation to every one that be-
lieveth; to the Jew first, and also to the Greek. Since
the Jews have heard, John sees a great multitude
standing before the throne which no man could count,
from every race and nationality. Their white robes
prove that they have trusted in the message of the
blood and are clothed in the righteousness of Christ.
The waving of the palms in their hands signifies
victory. They have overcome the world, the flesh,
and the devil. They are joyous because they have
survived the first six seals of judgment and their joy
leads to praise.

Verse 10: *They cried with a loud voice, saying,*
Salvation to our God which sitteth upon the throne,
and unto the Lamb.

This multitude recognizes the source of their
salvation and victory. They cannot be kept silent.
Who can be silent when the grace of God does its
mighty work of salvation in one's heart? Immediately the angels join with them in praise to the Father and
to the Son.

Verse 11: *And all the angels stood round about*
the throne, and about the elders and the four beasts,

and fell before the throne on their faces, and wor-
shipped God,

Verse 12: *Saying, Amen: Blessing, and glory,*
and wisdom, and thanksgiving, and honour, and
power, and might, be unto our God for ever and ever.
Amen.

What a glorious scene as the angels surrounding
the throne and God's people (represented by the elders) fall on their faces in worship, praise, and adoration!

Their sevenfold praise session to God centers
around: (1) blessing, (2) glory, (3) wisdom, (4) thanksgiving, (5) honour, (6) power, and (7) might...forever
and forever! No wonder they say, "Amen!" Then
one of the elders asks a question.

Verse 13: *And one of the elders answered, say-*
ing unto me, What are these which are arrayed in
white robes? and whence came they?

The answer?

Verse 14: *And I said unto him, Sir, thou know-*
est. And he said to me, These are they which came out
of great tribulation, and have washed their robes,
and made them white in the blood of the Lamb.

This is another proof that the Church is in heav-
en, not upon earth. Why? John does not recognize
this group. He knows the raptured Church in heaven
(chapter 4, verse 1), but not the ones on earth in this
text. These are Tribulation saints who have *washed*
their robes, and made them white in the blood of the
Lamb. Please hear God once again: *These are they*
which came out of great tribulation. That settles it
and explains why John—who recognized the Church

in heaven—is in a fog concerning these individuals. They are new brothers and sisters in Christ, though unknown to John. They have been saved in a different period of time—a time when he and the Church were in heaven. The Church was not on earth to make their acquaintance.

The next scene is exciting. Each group saved during different dispensations of time has different duties to perform. The Church is the bride of Christ and enjoys the 1,000-year honeymoon upon earth (chapter 20, verse 4). They reign as rulers, kings, and priests (1 Peter 2:9 and Revelation 1:6). The 144,000 serve as bodyguards of the Lamb and His bride (chapter 14, verse 4). The Gentiles saved during the Tribulation will be Temple servants, waiting on Christ and His bride. They serve in the glorious Temple (described in Ezekiel chapters 40 through 48) which is set up immediately after Russia—under the names of Gog, Magog, Meshech, Tubal, and Rosh—is destroyed (Ezekiel 38 and 39). Everything is so near. Russia could march soon, then Antichrist would be smashed and the Lord would return with His bride. At that time the millennial Temple is erected and the Gentiles serve.

Verse 15: *Therefore are they before the throne of God, and serve him day and night in his temple: and he that sitteth on the throne shall dwell among them.* Because God is dwelling among them, the depravations they suffered under the Antichrist are now abolished. Under the reign of the world dictator, there was little food and one had to take the mark of the beast, 666, to obtain sustenance. These believers

106

who refused the number had to eke out an existence day by day. Now, with the Lord in their midst, the picture changes.

Verse 16: *They shall hunger no more, neither thirst any more; neither shall the sun light on them, nor any heat.* This refers to the scorching effects of the sun during the Tribulation hour: [As] *the fourth angel poured out his vial upon the sun; and power was given unto him to scorch men with fire* (chapter 16, verse 8). In addition, the word *heat* refers to the fires of persecution as described in 1 Peter 1:7. Such trials are finished forever.

From this point onward the people of God from all dispensations enjoy the presence of God. Their days of suffering, heartache, and abuse by an ungodly world are finished. Tears are wiped way as every remembrance of past sorrow is obliterated from their minds.

Verse 17: *For the Lamb which is in the midst of the throne shall feed them, and shall lead them unto living fountains of waters: and God shall wipe away all tears from their eyes.*

8

Seventh seal

We now witness the opening of the seventh seal. This seal includes the seven trumpet judgments. They are so terrifying that, as they are opened, all the heavenly host becomes silent.

Verse 1: *And when he had opened the seventh seal, there was silence in heaven about the space of half an hour.*

Bob Ripley, in his "Believe It or Not" newspaper column, stated: "This verse proves there will be no women in heaven." Ha! Seriously, what causes this breathtaking silence among angels and men? Answer—the contemplation of the forthcoming trumpet blasts.

Verse 2: *And I saw the seven angels which stood before God; and to them were given seven trumpets.*

These trumpet judgments were prophesied by Enoch as recorded in the Book of Jude, verses 14 and 15, and were anticipated by the psalmist as well. That's why Psalm 96:13 states: *He cometh to judge the earth: he shall judge the world with righteousness, and the people with his truth.* Paul also confirmed these judgments in Acts 17:31, mentioning a time when *the wrath of God is revealed from heaven against all ungodliness and unrighteousness of men* (Romans 1:18). Before the first trumpet sends forth its blast in verse 7, however, we witness an unusual prayer meeting in the next three verses.

Verse 3: *And another angel came and stood at the altar, having a golden censer; and there was given unto him much incense, that he should offer it with the prayers of all saints upon the golden altar which was before the throne.*

This angel is obviously the Lord Jesus Christ himself, because He ministers both to God and man (see 1 Timothy 2:5). The Saviour also appeared as the angel of the Lord in the Old Testament in many instances: He wrestled with Jacob, walked among Shadrach, Meshach, and Abednego in the fiery furnace, and made numerous other Old Testament visits to His people. This Mediator between God and men *ever liveth to make intercession* (Hebrews 7:25) and now stands at the altar adding incense (efficacy) to the prayers being offered by the saints of God on earth. They are imprecatory prayers for judgment, as in Revelation 6:10. They cry, *How long, O Lord, holy and true, dost thou not judge and avenge our blood on them that dwell on the earth?* At this point their prayers have reached the throne of God!

Verse 4: *And the smoke of the incense, which came with the prayers of the saints, ascended up before God out of the angel's hand.*

Now prayers are answered, and judgment is prepared.

Verse 5: *And the angel took the censer, and*

110

filled it with fire of the altar, and cast it into the earth: and there were voices, and thunderings, and lightnings, and an earthquake.

What a contrast from the solemn silence of verse 1. Now every noise imaginable is heard as judgment is prepared.

Verse 6: *And the seven angels which had the seven trumpets prepared themselves to sound.*

At this moment the heavenly military says, "Ready! Aim! Fire!" This is it!

First Trumpet

Verse 7: *The first angel sounded, and there followed hail and fire mingled with blood, and they were cast upon the earth: and the third part of trees was burnt up, and all green grass was burnt up.*

We have no difficulty understanding this verse literally. The same kind of judgment occurred in Exodus 9:22,23: *And the Lord said unto Moses, Stretch forth thine hand toward heaven, that there may be hail in all the land of Egypt...And Moses stretched forth his rod toward heaven: and the Lord sent thunder and hail, and the fire ran along upon the ground; and the Lord rained hail upon the land of Egypt. So there was hail, and fire mingled with the hail, very grievous, such as there was none like it in all the land of Egypt since it became a nation.* It happened then; now it happens again!

Second trumpet

Verse 8: *And the second angel sounded, and as it were a great mountain burning with fire was cast* *into the sea: and the third part of the sea became blood;*

This judgment is undoubtedly a giant meteor falling into the sea. Notice the phrase, *as it were a mountain.* This, again, is a symbolic description. Always take every word of the Bible literally unless God tells you to take it figuratively. This passage is an example of the latter. Something gigantic, *as* or *like* a mountain, is *cast into the sea* and causes *a third part of the sea to become blood.* A similar occurrence was experienced in Moses' day: *And the Lord spake unto Moses, Say unto Aaron, Take thy rod, and stretch out thine hand upon the waters of Egypt, upon their streams, upon their rivers, and upon their ponds, and upon all their pools of water, that they may become blood; and that there may be blood throughout all the land of Egypt, both in vessels of wood, and in vessels of stone. And Moses and Aaron did so, as the Lord commanded; and he lifted up the rod, and smote the waters that were in the river, in the sight of Pharaoh, and in the sight of his servants; and all the waters that were in the river were turned to blood. And the fish that* [were] *in the river died* (Exodus 7:19-21).

Verse 9: *And the third part of the creatures which were in the sea, and had life, died; and the third part of the ships were destroyed.*

God's second trumpet blast is so horrendous that one-third of the creatures in the sea die and a third part of the ships are destroyed. God only knows what horrendous plagues will result when nuclear war under, upon, and above the oceans takes place.

Third trumpet

Verse 10: *And the third angel sounded, and there fell a great star from heaven, burning as it were a lamp, and it fell upon the third part of the rivers, and upon the fountains of waters;*

Verse 11: *And the name of the star is called Wormwood: and the third part of the waters became wormwood; and many men died of the waters, because they were made bitter.*

Strange that *Chernobyl* in the Ukraine Bible means "Wormwood." This judgment also occurred in Moses' day: *Behold, I will smite with the rod that is in mine hand upon the waters which are in the river, and they shall be turned to blood* (Exodus 7:17). Now the phenomenon is repeated. A star, or meteor, soaring through space, speeds toward earth. When it strikes, one-third of our planet's water supply becomes a deadly poison. Rivers, springs, and wells are affected. Something similar happened in decades past. A volcanic explosion in the Aleutian Islands on March 21, 1823, caused the waters in that area to become bitter and unfit for human consumption. This could easily happen again.

God created every star, knows their locations, and has named them. Job 9:9 states: [He] *maketh Arcturus, Orion, and Pleiades, and the chambers of the south.* He also knows where the star, *Wormwood,* meaning "bitterness," is located, because Jeremiah 9:15 reports, *Therefore thus saith the Lord of hosts, the God of Israel; behold, I will feed them, even this people, with wormwood, and give them water of gall to drink* (Jeremiah 9:15). It will happen!

113

Fourth trumpet

Verse 12: *And the fourth angel sounded, and the third part of the sun was smitten, and the third part of the moon, and the third part of the stars; so as the third part of them was darkened, and the day shone not for a third part of it, and the night likewise.*

Verse 13: *And I beheld, and heard an angel flying through the midst of heaven, saying with a loud voice, Woe, woe, woe, to the inhabiters of the earth by reason of the other voices of the trumpet of the three angels, which are yet to sound!*

This fourth judgment has to do with earth's luminaries—the sun, moon, and stars. We note with interest that, on the fourth day of creation, God said, *Let there be lights in the firmament of the heaven* (Genesis 1:14). Now, at the blast of the fourth trumpet, one-third of the light produced by these bodies is extinguished. This, too, happened in Moses' day: *And the Lord said unto Moses, Stretch out thine hand toward heaven, that there may be darkness over the land of Egypt, even darkness which may be felt. And Moses stretched forth his hand toward heaven; and there was a thick darkness in all the land of Egypt three days: They saw not one another, neither rose any from his place for three days* (Exodus 10:21-23). It happened once; it will happen again!

The worst, however, is yet to come. An angel flying through the midst of heaven cries, *Woe, woe, woe!* This correlates with Daniel, chapter 9, where the Seventieth Week (discussed in Revelation, chapter 6) is described. The first three and one-half years of the Tribulation are not nearly as severe as the final

114

three and one-half years. In Matthew 24:8, our Lord described the first half of this time period as the *beginning of sorrows*. However, He referred to the final three and one-half years as the *great tribulation* (Matthew 24:21). As the Tribulation hour approaches its climax, the judgments become more severe and the loss of life greater. This is especially noticed as one observes that two verses cover the scope of each of the first four trumpets. However, trumpet five requires twelve verses and trumpet six necessitates nine verses.

9

Chapter 9 contains the lengthy portion of Scripture covering trumpet judgments five and six. We will investigate both in depth.

Fifth trumpet

Verse 1: *And the fifth angel sounded, and I saw a star fall from heaven unto earth: and to him was given the key of the bottomless pit.*

The star John sees—a male personage—is without a doubt the devil of verse 11. The Greek tense in verse 1 is not *fall*—present tense, but *fallen*—past tense. Isaiah describes this *fall* in chapter 14, verses 12 through 14: *How art thou fallen from heaven, O Lucifer, son of the morning! how art thou cut down to the ground, which didst weaken the nations! For thou hast said in thine heart, I will ascend into heaven, I will exalt my throne above the stars of God: I will sit also upon the mount of the congregation, in the sides of the north: I will ascend above the heights of the clouds; I will be like the most high.* Satan's fall came through pride. He wanted to be coequal with God. Jesus, in eternity past, beheld this fall and said to His seventy disciples, *I beheld Satan as lightning fall from heaven* (Luke 10:18). This fallen one is presented with a key to the bottomless pit, and he uses it.

Verse 2: *And he opened the bottomless pit; and there arose a smoke out of the pit, as the smoke of a great furnace; and the sun and the air were darkened by reason of the smoke of the pit.*

The term *bottomless pit* does not refer to one who has a voluminous appetite! Instead, the literal Greek renders it "the pit of the abyss." The term is found nine times in the New Testament. In each case, it is a place to restrain or hold certain beings which have come under the judgment of God. For instance, when Christ went into the country of Gadarenes, He met a certain man who had a legion of demons. The demons within the man besought the Lord *that he would not command them to go out into the deep* [or abyss] (Luke 8:31). Their dread and terror of the pit (or abyss) was so great that they would rather become incarnated in swine. Oh, the pit of the abyss must be a terrible place!

How frightful, then, is the hour when the prison house of fallen angels is finally opened. The smoke ascending out of the pit darkens the sun and the air. Talk about pollution! The environmentalists had better get saved or they will be around for the greatest soot inundation in history. Then they will have a steady job picketing the portals of hell—but it will be too late.

Verse 3: *And there came out of the smoke locusts upon the earth: and unto them was given power, as the scorpions of the earth have power.*

These are not literal locusts. Their power is too great. They are most likely fallen angels who have been restrained and imprisoned in the bottomless pit since their fall (described in Genesis 6). These wicked beings, chained in darkness all of these centuries (see 2 Peter 2:4), can hardly wait to begin their acts of evil. They are told what they can and cannot do:

Verse 4: *And it was commanded them that they should not hurt the grass of the earth, neither any green thing, neither any tree; but only those men which have not the seal of God in their foreheads.*

In chapter 7, we saw multitudes sealed. The locusts, or fallen angels, are not allowed to touch the sealed, only the unsealed—those who have worshipped the Beast and accepted his number, 666. Note also that the locusts are not allowed to kill the unsealed (the unsaved). They are permitted only to torture them.

Verse 5: *And to them it was given that they should not kill them, but that they should be tormented five months: and their torment was as the torment of a scorpion, when he striketh a man.*

What an agonizing period of time this will be!

Verse 6: *And in those days shall men seek death, and shall not find it; and shall desire to die, and death shall flee from them.*

The next four verses give us a vivid description of these locusts, or fallen angels.

Verse 7: *And the shapes of the locusts were like unto horses prepared unto battle* [this speaks of strength and speed]; *and on their heads were as it were crowns like gold* [this speaks of royalty; a picture of conquerors], *and their faces were as the faces of men* [denoting intelligence].

Verse 8: *And they had hair as the hair of women* [picturing attractiveness], *and their teeth were as the teeth of lions* [portraying cruelty].

Verse 9: *And they had breastplates, as it were breastplates of iron* [picturing invincibility]*; and the sound of their wings was as the sound of chariots of many horses running to battle* [denoting calamity].

Verse 10: *And they had tails like unto scorpions, and there were stings in their tails: and their power was to hurt men five months.*

These facts reinforce the gruesome portrait of life upon earth as the pit of the abyss is opened and the convicts of the ages—the fallen angels—are released. The next verse clearly identifies the fallen star who is the leader of these perverted angels.

Verse 11: *And they had a king over them, which is the angel of the bottomless pit, whose name in the Hebrew tongue is Abaddon, but in the Greek tongue hath his name Apollyon.*

This king is named in both Hebrew and Greek. *Abaddon* is Hebrew. The term, found only this one time in our English Bible, is found six times in the Hebrew Bible: Job 26:6; 28:22; 31:12; Psalm 88:11; Proverbs 15:11; and 27:20. The Greek form, *Apollyon,* means "the destroyer"—a word that certainly describes Satan.

Verse 12: *One woe is past; and, behold, there come two woes more hereafter.*

Sixth trumpet

Verse 13: *And the sixth angel sounded, and I heard a voice from the four horns of the golden altar which is before God,*

Verse 14: *Saying to the sixth angel which had the trumpet, Loose the four angels which are bound in the great river Euphrates.*

As the sixth angel sounds, John hears a voice from the four horns of the golden altar which is in the presence of God. Isn't it strange that many of the judgments are directly linked with God's program of atonement? Perhaps this is because so many have rejected the message of the altar which speaks of the shed blood of Jesus. Paul warned the human race of the danger of refusing this teaching: *He that despised Moses' law died without mercy under two or three witnesses: Of how much sorer punishment, suppose ye, shall he be thought worthy, who hath trodden under foot the Son of God, and hath counted the blood of the covenant, wherewith he was sanctified, an unholy thing, and hath done despite unto the spirit of grace?* (Hebrews 10:28,29). The rejection of God's Word always brings serious consequences. Before us is a scene wherein even the altar (the only place where sin can be forgiven) and the horns of the altar (actually touched by the blood) unitedly cry out to God for judgment. Never treat the message of the precious shed blood of Christ lightly. Those who do will be sorry!

Now, because of rejecting the message, the voice from the altar tells the sixth angel to loose the four angels which are bound in the great river Euphrates.

The fact that they are bound proves that they are the fallen angels who rebelled and fell with Lucifer at the time of his revolt (see Isaiah 14:12-14). Once the Church is safely in heaven, four denizens from the pit of the abyss are released upon earth. Earlier we saw four unfallen angels holding back the judgment of God (chapter 7, verse 1). Now four wicked angels are set free to wreak havoc upon planet earth. They are commanded to execute their judgment in the area of the Euphrates River. This body of water runs through Iraq and Syria and will become the point of origin for the battle of the ages in the future.

I have repeatedly said that the Gulf War of 1991 was not the fulfillment of this prophecy but was simply the beginning of the end, as the final pieces of the puzzle were being assembled for the future. This is the part of the world where Satan performed his destructive work against our first parents, Adam and Eve (Genesis 2:10-14). It is the area where Cain murdered his brother Abel (Genesis 4:8), and where mankind made its first united move against God (Genesis 11:1-4). Later God made His unconditional covenant with Abraham in this location, saying, *Unto thy seed have I given this land, from the river of Egypt unto the great river, the river Euphrates* (Genesis 15:18).

This land area belongs to Israel and no one but Israel. God will see that they get it. Proof? *And I will set thy bounds from the Red sea of the Philistines, and from the desert unto the river: for I will deliver the inhabitants of the land into your hand; and thou shalt drive them out before thee* (Exodus 23:31). *Every*

122

place whereon the soles of your feet shall tread shall be yours: from the wilderness and Lebanon, from the river, the river Euphrates, even unto the uttermost sea shall your coast be (Deuteronomy 11:24). Again God says, *From the wilderness and this Lebanon even unto the great river, the river Euphrates, all the land of the Hittites, and unto the great sea toward the going down of the sun, shall be your coast* (Joshua 1:4).

At one point in history, the Euphrates River became the boundary of the old Roman Empire—which is being restored and will fall under the rule of the Antichrist (chapter 13, verse 1). This area will surely become the sore spot as history progresses, for it serves as both the frontier of the promised land and the boundary of the ten-toed, ten-horned, western federation of nations that produces the Antichrist (Daniel 2:40,41; 7:23,24; and Revelation 13:1). The destruction unleashed upon the earth by the four evil emissaries is described in the next verse.

Verse 15: *And the four angels were loosed, which were prepared for an hour, and a day, and a month, and a year, for to slay the third part of men.*

The population of earth is presently five billion souls. In our study, we have seen one-fourth of this number die under the rider of the fourth, or pale horse (chapter 6, verse 8). Thus, at this point in time, earth's population is three billion, seven hundred fifty million. Now an additional one-third—or one billion, two hundred fifty million—perish as the four fallen angels are released. These four executioners are undoubtedly waiting in the wings to begin the drama of the ages. They are prepared and eagerly anticipating their scheduled timetable. Remember, the Euphrates River is Middle East territory—the location of present-day Iraq and Syria. This is the world's present and future tinderbox.

The holocaust will also include the Soviet Union and her allies posed against Israel (Ezekiel 38 and 39). The barbaric troops come against the nation of Israel from the north: *Thou shalt come from thy place out of the north parts, thou, and many people with thee, all of them riding upon horses, a great company, and a mighty army: And thou shalt come up against my people of Israel, as a cloud to cover the land; it shall be in the latter days, and I will bring thee against my land* (Ezekiel 38:15,16). Russia is north of Israel. This is why Joel declared in chapter 2, verse 20, *I will remove far off from you* [Israel] *the northern army, and will drive him into a land barren and desolate* [Siberia], *with his face toward the east sea, and his hinder part toward the utmost sea.* Geographically, Russia alone meets the qualifications of this text.

As stated previously, Israel is mentioned as the battlefield of the world on eighteen occasions in Ezekiel 38 and 39. There is no doubt that the Holy Land becomes the site of the greatest war in the annals of history. Now Russia marches toward the middle of the Tribulation hour, but is driven back to Siberia (see Ezekiel 39:1,2 and Joel 2:20). She strengthens her forces and then returns to the land of Israel once again. The scope and intensity of the offensive continues to increase until all nations become involved and are finally gathered together against Israel at Jerusalem. God says, *I will gather all nations against Jerusalem to battle* (Zechariah 14:2). At that point the Battle of Armageddon takes place: *He gathered them together into a place called in the Hebrew tongue Armageddon* (Revelation 16:16).

This Mid-east war numbers the largest armies in the history of mankind.

Verse 16: *And the number of the army of the horsemen* [was] *two hundred thousand thousand: and I heard the number of them.*

Think of it! Two hundred million soldiers! No wonder the ancient prophet said, *And thou shalt come up against my people of Israel, as a cloud to cover the land* (Ezekiel 38:16). This army advances in the latest and best of equipment: *For the chariots shall be with flaming torches in the day of his preparation ...The chariots shall rage in the streets, they shall justle one against another in the broad ways: they shall seem like torches, they shall run like the lightnings* (Nahum 2:3,4).

Many Bible scholars associate the army of two hundred million with Red China and her oriental allies by tying this text concerning the Euphrates together with chapter 16, verse 12: *And the sixth angel poured out his vial upon the great river Euphrates; and the water thereof was dried up, that the way of the kings of the east* [or the kings of the sunrising] *might be prepared.* Such an assembly of military might is quite feasible considering China's present population of nearly one billion. Other Bible

125

commentators believe this army is a supernatural one in light of the three verses which follow:

Verse 17: *And thus I saw the horses in the vision, and them that sat on them, having breastplates of fire, and of jacinth, and brimstone: and the heads of the horses were as the heads of lions; and out of their mouths issued fire and smoke and brimstone.*

Verse 18: *By these three was the third part of men killed, by the fire, and by the smoke, and by the brimstone, which issued out of their mouths.*

Verse 19: *For their power is in their mouth, and in their tails: for their tails were like unto serpents, and had heads, and with them they do hurt.*

The advocates of literalism believe that these same verses portray the latest inventions stockpiled in the military arsenals of the world. Either way, it will be a devastating period of time as the remaining third of earth's inhabitants are destroyed by fire, smoke, and brimstone—a sulfurous, poisonous gas.

At this point several verses predicting the final war of fire should be considered: *A fire goeth before him* (Psalm 97:3). *For, behold, the Lord will come with fire (*Isaiah 66:15*). The whole land shall be devoured by the fire of his jealousy* (Zephaniah 1:18). *A fire devoureth before them* (Joel 2:3). Who! The Russian army coming from the north. Then God states: *I will remove far off from you* [Israel] *the northern army, and will drive him into a land barren and desolate, with his face toward the east sea, and his hinder part toward the utmost sea, and his stink shall come up, and his ill savour shall come up, because he hath done great* [or terrible] *things* (Joel

2:20). This is the point at which the Soviets are pushed back to Siberia. Joel continues in verse 30 of chapter 2: *And I will show wonders in the heavens and in the earth, blood, and fire, and pillars of smoke.*

This sounds similar to the report mentioned in Malachi 4:1: *For, behold, the day cometh, that shall burn as an oven.* And *the third part of trees was burnt up, and all green grass was burnt up* (Revelation 8:7). Again—whether the means are natural or supernatural—it is catastrophic. Personally, I believe that both the natural and the supernatural—men and demons—will be involved in the Tribulation woes. Now, what about the remaining sixty-five percent of the population?

Verse 20: *And the rest of the men which were not killed by these plagues yet repented not of the works of their hands, that they should not worship devils, and idols of gold, and silver, and brass, and stone, and of wood: which neither can see, nor hear, nor walk:*

Verse 21: *Neither repented they of their murders, nor of their sorceries, nor of their fornication, nor of their thefts.*

We have now witnessed the release of thirteen judgments—seven seals and six trumpets. One would think that after experiencing such devastation, mankind would begin considering eternity. Not so! Those who are still alive continue to rebel. Wicked sinners do not give in or give up easily. In fact, God's Word tells us that men won't repent even after they have been in the regions of the doomed and the damned for centuries. Even then they continue gnashing their teeth in an expression of their hatred toward God. Proof? *The Son of man shall send forth his angels, and they shall gather out of his kingdom all things that offend, and them which do iniquity; And shall cast them into a furnace of fire: there shall be wailing and gnashing of teeth* (Matthew 13:41,42).

Verses 20 and 21 present five major sins which permeate the Tribulation scene—and for which men would rather die than switch: (1) occultism, (2) murder, (3) drug abuse, (4) fornication (sexual orgies), and (5) stealing. Let's investigate them further.

Occultism

The Tribulation will be a time of pronounced devil worship. Anton LaVey began the church of Satan movement in San Francisco. Estimates reveal that tens of thousands in California alone are connected to this or some other type of occult organization. Stores where satanic objects may be purchased are presently springing up everywhere nationally and internationally. God hates this sin!

Listen to the Almighty: *Regard not them that have familiar spirits, neither seek after wizards, to be defiled by them: I am the Lord your God* (Leviticus 19:31). *And the soul that turneth after such as have familiar spirits, and after wizards, to go a whoring after them, I will even set my face against that soul, and will cut him off from among his people* (Leviticus 20:6). Anything that smacks of demonic-related practices has the *anathema* of God upon it. Look at the listing found in Deuteronomy 18:10-12: *There shall not be found among you any one that maketh his son or his daughter to pass through the fire, or that useth divination, or an observer of times* [astrology], *or an enchanter, or a witch, Or a charmer, or a consulter with familiar spirits, or a wizard, or a necromancer. For all that do these things are an abomination unto the Lord.*

In addition to worshipping devils, earth dwellers of the Tribulation hour also use idols made of gold, silver, brass, stone, and wood. God hates idolatry! This practice breaks His holy law—the second commandment—given to Moses in Exodus 20:4,5 which declares, *Thou shalt not make unto thee any graven image...Thou shalt not bow down thyself to them, nor serve them: for I the Lord thy God am a jealous God.*

There are those today who, knowingly or unknowingly, break God's commandment by worshipping lifeless, man-made idols. Their worship, however, is meaningless to God. The psalmist says in Psalm 115:4-8, *Their idols are silver and gold, the work of men's hands. They have mouths, but they speak not: eyes have they, but they see not: They have ears, but they hear not: noses have they, but they smell not: They have hands, but they handle not: feet have they, but they walk not: neither speak they through their throat. They that make them are like unto them* [helpless and hopeless]; *so is every one that trusteth in them.* God condemns idolatry—past, present, and future!

During the Tribulation hour, the world—steeped in occultism and idolatry—progresses to the worship of the image of the beast, or Antichrist, who proclaims himself as God (see 2 Thessalonians 2:4).

This image, made in his likeness (see Revelation 13:15), is undoubtedly the *abomination of desolation* spoken of in Matthew 24:15, which is placed in the Temple in Jerusalem and which brings great heartache to the Jews of that day. One can see that the world's present surge of occultism is paving the way for the coming of the greatest religious imposter in history.

Murder

During this same time, murder becomes a sport and judgment does not change the situation. The wicked refuse to turn from their brutalistic manner of living. They find pleasure in killing people, perhaps because terrorism is rampant. Jesus said, *But as the days of Noe were, so shall the coming of the Son of man be* (Matthew 24:37). Noah's day was characterized by violence: *The earth also was corrupt before God, and the earth was filled with violence* (Genesis 6:11). Our twentieth century is certainly leading us to this terrifying hour.

Drugs, fornication, and stealing

The final three sins prevalent during the end time are interrelated and have to do with sorceries—drug abuse, fornication (the practice of every conceivable sex sin), and theft. These sins indicate that bodies are being sold (through prostitution) and burglaries are being committed in order to support the drug kick. Present news headlines indicate that this day is already dawning! Surely our time as the Church upon earth is about to end and we must *prepare to meet*

[our] *God* (Amos 4:12). In concluding this chapter, let's spend some time on the matter of drugs.

There are a number of words used in the Bible to describe the subject of sorcery. Altogether there are at least twenty-seven references to sorcery, sorceries, sorcerers, witches, witchcraft, and the art of bewitching. Of these, at least five in the New Testament are especially pertinent, for they have a direct bearing on the day in which we live—the present day of drugs and drug addiction.

In the books of the Old Testament and the Book of Acts the term *sorcery* always means "witchcraft" or "magic"—and one should note that the practice is continually and constantly condemned! Five occurrences of the word *sorcery* in the New Testament, however, have to do with drug addiction. In these instances, the original Greek word is *pharmakeia*—from which we get our English term *pharmacy* or *drugstore*. The literal meaning of the Greek is an "enchantment with drugs," or to "get high on" or "get a kick out of" drugs. Medications prescribed by doctors are not part of this condemnation. The literal rendering of verse 21, then, is that men repent not of their enchantment with drugs during the Tribulation hour. Each of the five references must be carefully considered in the light of its context. Collectively, they clearly reveal: (1) the present world condition as foretold in the prophetic scriptures; (2) the inevitable result of drug addiction; (3) the certain and definite judgment upon the drug pusher as well as (4) the drug victim; and finally (5) the appraisal of this terrible sin in the sight of God Almighty.

As previously stated, we can already see the dawning of the day of drugs in the spread of drug use throughout all levels of society. Such a widespread use of drugs cannot help but bring its own destruction. Even amid all the trips in mind expansion propaganda, not one user has ever been able to actually do more or be more efficient than he was before experimenting with drugs. This steady downward retrogression will be climaxed at the close of the Great Tribulation, when the full cup of its own judgment is measured.

The closing chapters of the Book of Revelation graphically portray the terrible consequences of mankind's enchantment with drugs. What we are presently witnessing is only the beginning of the coming disintegration of society during the Tribulation period. Revelation 18:23 states: *For by thy sorceries were all nations deceived.* The Greek word for *sorceries*, as already mentioned, is *pharmakeia*. Thus, "by their enchantment with drugs, or getting high on drugs, were all nations deceived." This is the result of mankind's first mass usage of drugs.

Now there is a change in the next occurrence of the word translated *sorcerers*. This change reveals a class of people who are doomed and is found in chapter 21, verse 8: *But the fearful, and unbelieving, and the abominable, and murderers, and whoremongers, and sorcerers, and idolaters, and all liars, shall have their part in the lake which burneth with fire and brimstone: which is the second death.* The Greek word for *sorcerers* in this text is *pharmakeus*. Whereas the word *pharmakeia* meant "enchantment with drugs," *pharmakeus* means "the enchanter with drugs"—the pusher or the seller of drugs. This text plainly declares that eight distinct groups of people will never get into heaven but will rather be assigned to the lake of fire (a description of a literal hell). One of these groups is composed of those who are enchanters, or pushers of drugs. What a solemn warning against having anything to do with the soul-damning drug traffic of the present hour!

But wait! There is another reference to sorcerers in this book of the Bible—chapter 22, verse 15: *For without are dogs, and sorcerers, and whoremongers, and murderers, and idolaters, and whosoever loveth and maketh a lie.* Here again the word is *pharmakeus.* Although the word is the same as the one found in chapter 21, verse 8, it has a deeper meaning in this context. By extension, it includes both the drug pusher and user! Take notice—these individuals are kept out of heaven. (Heaven would not be heaven very long if they were admitted.) There is only one place to which they can go and that is the place of eternal separation from the presence of God— the place prepared for Satan and his angels (see Matthew 25:41).

The Bible is explicit in stating that there is no heaven for those who refuse to repent of their sins. In hell, they will keep on sinning forever. They never repent or get saved there. Notice also that of the six groups named in chapter 22, verse 15, sorcerers (drug pushers and users) occupy second place—immediately following the term which describes outlaws as wild dogs. Oh, God hates this sin!

An additional word, *witchcraft*, with the same meaning is found in Galatians 5:19-21: *Now the works of the flesh are manifest, which are these; Adultery, fornication, uncleanness, lasciviousness, Idolatry, witchcraft, hatred, variance, emulations, wrath, strife, seditions, heresies, envyings, murders, drunkenness, revellings, and such like: of the which I tell you before, as I have also told you in time past, that they which do such things shall not inherit the kingdom of God.* The word *witchcraft* in our English Bible is again *pharmakeia* in the Greek. We also see that this sin is number six in this listing of seventeen kinds of sinners who shall not—*shall not*—inherit the kingdom of God. The drug user and the drug pusher are both excluded from heaven!

Is there no hope or escape from the clutches of this binding habit? Praise God, there is a source of liberation—it is the Lord Jesus Christ: *For this purpose the son of God was manifested, that he might destroy the works of the devil* (1 John 3:8). Beloved, it is by the way of the cross of Calvary that Jesus has broken Satan's grip. Now, when any—*any*—guilty sinner calls upon Him for salvation, Jesus Christ immediately frees that person from the shackles of sin and death which bind him. Try Him. There is no limit to the saving power of the Lord Jesus Christ.

10

In chapter 10, we again discover a parenthesis similar to the one in chapter 7. Between the sixth and seventh seal judgments, there was a lull before the storm. Now we experience a break between the sixth and the seventh trumpet blasts. The study of this parenthetical period continues through chapter 11, verse 14.

Verse 1: *And I saw another mighty angel come down from heaven, clothed with a cloud: and a rainbow was upon his head, and his face was as it were the sun, and his feet as pillars of fire.*

This angel is Christ. Remember, Christ was and is eternal. In fact, He was before the angels because He created them. *For by him were all things created, that are in heaven, and that are in earth, visible and invisible, whether they be thrones, or dominions, or principalities, or powers: all things were created by him, and for him* (Colossians 1:16). Thus, I believe that such Theophanies and Christophanies were appearances of Christ throughout the Old Testament, usually in the form of angelic manifestations. This angel of Jehovah has always acted and worked as a deity. Proof? Isaiah 63:9: *In all their affliction he was afflicted, and the angel of his presence saved them: in his love and in his pity he redeemed them; and he bare them, and carried them all the days of old.*

On three occasions to this point in time, we have observed this angelic messenger in action. In chapter 7, verses 2 and 3, He holds back the tides of judgment for a special hour of grace. In chapter 8, verse 5, He stands as the messenger of the covenant, pouring out the fire of judgment upon the earth. Now He appears again in the text before us. In the first appearance, He is a prophet, in the second, a priest, and now, in the third, He appears as a King. This is the threefold ministry of the Saviour. Hence, this angel is Jesus. As He comes down from heaven, He is clothed with a cloud, has a rainbow upon His head, exhibits a countenance that shines like the sun, and has feet like unto pillars of fire. What do these attributes signify?

First, Christ, in His deity, is usually surrounded by a cloud: *Clouds and darkness are round about him: righteousness and judgment are the habitation of his throne* (Psalm 97:2). Bickering Israel witnessed *the glory of the Lord* [appearing] *in the cloud* (Exodus 16:10). When God gave Moses the Ten Commandments of judgment, He descended in a thick cloud, and immediately *the Lord said unto Moses, Lo, I come unto thee in a thick cloud...And it came to pass on the third day in the morning, that there were thunders and lightnings, and a thick cloud upon the mount* (Exodus 19:9,16). At the completion of the tabernacle, *a cloud covered the tent of the congregation, and the glory of the Lord filled the tabernacle*

(Exodus 40:34). This was *the cloud of the Lord* (Exodus 40:38). On the Mount of Transfiguration, *a bright cloud overshadowed them: and behold a voice out of the cloud, which said, This is my beloved Son, in whom I am well pleased; hear ye him* (Matthew 17:5). When Christ ascended to heaven, *a cloud received him out of their sight* (Acts 1:9). And as He departed He said, they shall *see the Son of man coming in a cloud with power and great glory* (Luke 21:27). When He returns, He will come *with clouds; and every eye shall see him* (Revelation 1:7).

Second, the God of all eternity made a covenant with Noah, placing a rainbow in the sky as a symbol of His mercy. The rainbow pictures mercy in the midst of judgment. Ah! Who but the Lord could wear it?

Third, Christ is often pictured as One who has a shining face as unto the sun. In fact, Saul of Tarsus met this One whose countenance was and is light: *And as* [Saul] *journeyed, he came near Damascus: and suddenly there shined round about him a light from heaven: And he fell to the earth, and heard a voice saying unto him, Saul, Saul, why persecutest thou me? And he said, Who art thou, Lord? And the Lord said, I am Jesus* (Acts 9:3-5).

Finally Christ's feet as pillars of fire picture judgment, as we saw in chapter 1, verse 15.

Verse 2: *And he had in his hand a little book open: and he set his right foot upon the sea, and his left foot on the earth,*

This verse pictures Christ preparing to take control of the earth and sea, which have always been rightfully His. He created them, for *all things were made by him; and without him was not any thing made that was made* (John 1:3). When Christ came to take control 1,900 years ago, He was rejected, crucified, and buried, but He rose again. Since then He has been at the right hand of the Father, making intercession for His people (see Hebrews 7:25). At a given moment He will rise from the throne and make a request. The picture is presented in Psalm 2:6-8. God says, *Yet have I set my king upon my holy hill of Zion. I will declare the decree.* Then Christ says, *The Lord hath said unto me, Thou art my Son; this day have I begotten thee.* Immediately the Father asks His Son to make a request, saying, *Ask of me, and I shall give thee the heathen for thine inheritance, and the uttermost parts of the earth for thy possession.* At the granting of the request, the Lord Jesus sets His right foot upon the sea and His left foot on the earth, and He unrolls the scroll (or book) which contains the record of the judgments He plans to unleash.

Verse 3: *And* [he] *cried with a loud voice, as when a lion roareth: and when he had cried, seven thunders uttered their voices.*

This is the cry of the Lion of the tribe of Judah (see Hebrews 7:14). Immediately prior to executing the judgments listed in the book, He cries loudly (or roars as a lion) to warn of impending danger. Other portions of Scripture also speak of His roaring when He comes as the Judge of the universe. Hosea 11:10 states: *They shall walk after the Lord: he shall roar like a lion: when he shall roar, then the children shall tremble from the west.* Joel 3:16 adds: *The*

Lord also shall roar out of Zion, and utter his voice from Jerusalem; and the heavens and the earth shall shake: but the Lord will be the hope of his people, and the strength of the children of Israel. Again, Amos 1:2: *The Lord will roar from Zion, and utter his voice from Jerusalem.*

When the Lord roars, seven thunders utter their voices. Though thunder is usually associated with judgment, no attempt will be made to explain the meaning, since God forbids it in verse 4.

Verse 4: *And when the seven thunders had uttered their voices, I was about to write: and I heard a voice from heaven saying unto me, Seal up those things which the seven thunders uttered, and write them not.*

Well, someday we will know! For the present, however, God commands that this one portion of Scripture be kept secret.

Verse 5: *And the angel which I saw stand upon the sea and upon the earth lifted up his hand to heaven,*

Verse 6: *And sware by him that liveth for ever and ever, who created heaven, and the things that therein are, and the earth, and the things that therein are, and the sea, and the things which are therein, that there should be time no longer* [or literally no waiting period].

Here we see our God taking an oath. Though this is forbidden in our dispensation of grace, it was not under the Law age of Moses and will not be during the Tribulation and Kingdom periods. This oath is by the eternal Creator, based upon His creation of heaven, the earth, the sea, and all things contained within them. The oath is that time should be no longer or, more accurately, that there should be no more delay. The time has come for the seventh trumpet blast and nothing can stop it or hinder its execution. There will be no further waiting.

Verse 7: *But in the days of the voice of the seventh angel, when he shall begin to sound, the mystery of God should be finished, as he hath declared to his servants the prophets.*

The seventh angel does not sound at this point, but rather in Revelation 11:15. When he does, all the warnings of the prophets concerning judgment will be fulfilled. Then the mystery of God will be finished, and the Tribulation hour will end. At that time *the earth shall be full of the knowledge of the Lord, as the waters cover the sea* (Isaiah 11:9). When this knowledge floods the land, the mystery disappears.

The Old Testament prophets could not understand all the scriptures concerning this mystery. They could not see God's timetable as we can. First Peter 1:10,11 describes their situation. The text states: *Of which salvation the prophets have inquired and searched diligently, who prophesied of the grace that should come unto you: Searching what, or what manner of time the Spirit of Christ which was in them did signify, when [he] testified beforehand the sufferings of Christ, and the glory that should follow.* This glory has to do with the return of Christ to earth to establish His millennial kingdom. Though the prophets knew this would happen—as evidenced by their many predictions—they did not clearly foresee the

2,000-year interval between the time of Christ's rejection and the establishment of His kingdom. Still their writings reflected the fact that a suffering Saviour preceded a ruling King, as can be seen in Psalm 22:14-16. This is Christ, speaking prophetically concerning His suffering and crucifixion: *I am poured out like water, and all my bones are out of joint: my heart is like wax; it is melted in the midst of my bowels. My strength is dried up like a potsherd; and my tongue cleaveth to my jaws; and thou hast brought me into the dust of death. For dogs have compassed me: the assembly of the wicked have enclosed me: they pierced my hands and my feet.*

Again Isaiah mentions a cross preceding the crown in chapter 53, verses 4 through 6: *Surely he hath borne our griefs, and carried our sorrows: yet we did esteem him stricken, smitten of God, and afflicted. But he was wounded for our transgressions, he was bruised for our iniquities: the chastisement of our peace was upon him; and with his stripes we are healed. All we like sheep have gone astray; we have turned every one to his own way; and the Lord hath laid on him the iniquity of us all.*

The centuries have now passed and, in our study, we are presently at the moment in history when the mystery of God is finished. The final pieces of the puzzle have now fallen into place. The prophetic time clock has struck midnight, or the "zero hour." There will be no further delay. The final trumpet is ready to sound and the Tribulation hour is about to come to an end. There is great rejoicing as the heavenly host proclaims the joyous news. Listen to

141

them: *The kingdoms of this world are become the kingdoms of our Lord, and of his Christ; and he shall reign for ever and ever* (Revelation 11:15).

Some may find it strange that the Tribulation hour ends in chapter 11—especially in light of the facts that chapters 18 and 19 contain seven more bowl judgments and the Lord Jesus Christ does not return until chapter 19, verses 11-16. The answer? Chapters 12 through 19:15 run concurrently with the judgments already discussed. They are a repeat of chapters 6 through 11. Actually, the simplistic outline of the Book of Revelation should be as mentioned in chapter 1, verse 19: the *past*—chapter 1; the *present*—chapters 2 and 3; the *future*—chapters 4 through 22, with chapters 5 through 11 and 12 through 19:15 running neck and neck.

Verse 8: *And the voice which I heard from heaven spake unto me again, and said, Go and take the little book which is open in the hand of the angel which standeth upon the sea and upon the earth.*

At this point John is told to take the book out of the hand of Christ, who stands upon the sea and upon the earth. This he does.

Verse 9: *And I went unto the angel, and said unto him, Give me the little book. And he said unto me, Take it, and eat it up; and it shall make thy belly bitter, but it shall be in thy mouth sweet as honey.*

The little book John is commanded to take is either all or a portion of the Word of God dealing with the judgments. John obeys.

Verse 10: *And I took the little book out of the angel's hand, and ate it up; and it was in my mouth* *sweet as honey: and as soon as I had eaten it, my belly was bitter.*

This verse pictures a devouring of God's Word—assimilating it through study and personal application. At times it is both sweet and bitter. The Prophet Jeremiah stated: *Thy words were found, and I did eat them; and thy word was unto me the joy and rejoicing of mine heart* (Jeremiah 15:16). The psalmist also declared in Psalm 119:103, *How sweet are thy words unto my taste! yea, sweeter than honey to my mouth!* Now John, following the angel's instructions, also finds the Word of God sweet as honey. This is because he can see the light at the end of the tunnel. As he reads the prophecies, he envisions the established kingdom, the Bride sitting beside the Bridegroom, and the peace and prosperity prevalent in the land with Satan bound and sin abolished. What sweetness! What blessing! Yet, as John learns of the remaining judgments still to be released, the Word becomes bitter in his digestive tract.

How true for us today! How precious is the good news of the gospel. Jesus loves sinners. He shed His blood for the remission of sins. By trusting in Christ, one obtains eternal life, yea, *he that believeth on the Son hath everlasting life* (John 3:36). However, this message becomes a bitter pill to swallow when one realizes that the rejection of the beautiful gospel appeal brings judgment, for *he that believeth not shall be damned* (Mark 16:16). Get in on the honey! Believe and be saved! It's for all! *For whosoever shall call upon the name of the Lord shall be saved*

(Romans 10:13). This bittersweet message is now about to be propagated by John.

Verse 11: *And he said unto me, Thou must prophesy again before many peoples, and nations, and tongues, and kings.*

John does this, as we will discover in the remaining chapters. He is faithful unto the end, proclaiming both the good news and the bad, presenting both the sweet and the bitter. He warns of the remaining judgments—the seven bowls or vials, the Great White Throne Judgment, and the dissolution of the present heavens and earth. May we be found as faithful in proclaiming all of God's Holy Word. For God commands that we preach the Word: *Be instant in season, out of season; reprove, rebuke, exhort with all long-suffering and doctrine* (2 Timothy 4:2).

11

Chapter 11 deals with the spiritual life of Israel while chapter 12 describes her persecution. Since one needs a place for communication with God, we see that a Temple has been erected.

Verse 1: *And there was given me a reed like unto a rod: and the angel stood, saying, Rise, and measure the temple of God, and the altar, and them that worship therein.*

The measuring reed, like unto a rod, is most likely from the brakes of the Jordan Valley and is probably about ten feet in length. Through the angel, John is told to measure the temple of God and the altar, as well as the people of Israel (concerning their spirituality).

The first place of worship ever built was called Solomon's Temple and is discussed in 1 Chronicles, chapters 22, 28, and 29, and 2 Chronicles, chapters 2 through 7. This temple was destroyed by King Nebuchadnezzar of Babylon in approximately 590 B.C. Seventy years later it was rebuilt under Zerubbabel and Joshua. This second temple was desecrated by Antiochus Epiphanes, a Greco-Syrian ruler. He stuck a pig in the temple—an act which prefigured the final desecration to occur under Antichrist as he sets up *the abomination of desolation* in the Tribulation temple (Matthew 24:15).

Now we find that a third temple has been erected. It is probably not the final millennial Temple of Ezekiel 40 through 48, but one which is built during the Tribulation hour and used sacrilegiously by the beast who claims to be God (see 2 Thessalonians 2:4). This temple, its altar, and the attendants are Jewish. There is no outer court for Gentiles as there was in past temples.

Verse 2: *But the court which is without the temple leave out, and measure it not; for it is given unto the Gentiles: and the holy city shall they tread under foot forty and two months.*

Notice that this temple has nothing to do with the Church which is already in heaven (chapter 4, verse 1). It is for Jews and Gentiles, not Jews, Gentiles, and the church of God. In the second temple, rebuilt and enlarged by Herod the Great in 20 or 21 B.C., the outer court was marked off from the inner one where only Israel was permitted to enter. The courts were separated by *the middle wall of partition* (Ephesians 2:14), and no Gentile was allowed beyond that point. When the Apostle Paul broke this rule, angry Jews almost killed him. *Crying out, Men of Israel, help: This is the man, that teacheth all men every where against the people, and the law, and this place: and further brought Greeks also into the temple, and hath polluted this holy place* (Acts 21:28).

So as John measures the Tribulation temple, he is told to omit the outer court, undoubtedly because

Gentiles will trample the Holy City (Jerusalem) under their feet for forty-two months.

There is no doubt about the literalness of this seven-year period. Daniel's first sixty-nine weeks (see Daniel 9:24-26) totaled 483 years. We recall from our discussion in Chapter 6 that the term *week* is *heptad* in the original Hebrew, and means "seven years." Thus, sixty-nine multiplied by seven equals 483 years to the day. If this be so, why wouldn't Daniel's final, or seventieth, week also consist of seven years—or 2,520 days—as well? The formula is so clear that a child can grasp it. One half of 2,520 is 1,260 days—or forty-two months of thirty days each—or three and one-half years. Conversely, two times three and one-half years equals seven years— or eighty-four months of thirty days each—or 2,520 days. Don't forget to take into account that the old Jewish calendar contained twelve months of thirty days each, not the 365 days of modern calendars. Is a seven-year plan scriptural then? We can check for ourselves because the days are mentioned in chapter 11, verse 3, and chapter 12, verse 6 as 1,260. Likewise, the months are mentioned in chapter 11, verse 2, and chapter 13, verse 5, as forty-two. Again we can easily see that 1,260 days multiplied by two equals 2,520 days, and that forty-two multiplied by two equals eighty-four months—one *heptad*, or seven years. One does not have to be a mathematical wizard or a calculus genius to discover that the Tribulation is a full seven years in duration. Take it literally!

147

During the final half of the seven years, two witnesses appear.

Verse 3: *And I will give power unto my two witnesses, and they shall prophesy a thousand two hundred and threescore days, clothed in sackcloth.*

These two witnesses are God's prophets, sent to proclaim His message of doom. They are clothed in sackcloth. In the Bible, sackcloth and ashes always picture repentance—and repentance is demanded when sin stalks a nation. Repentance is God's call to either turn or burn. The witnesses are described in the next verse.

Verse 4: *These are the two olive trees, and the two candlesticks standing before the God of the earth.*

Olive trees exude oil. Oil is a symbol of the Holy Spirit. Candlesticks are light bearers. Thus, we have a beautiful picture of two chosen witnesses, anointed by the power of the Holy Spirit, proclaiming the message of light in the midst of a sin-blackened world. There is no other way to do God's service. Oh! *Be filled with the Spirit* (Ephesians 5:18).

There has been a great deal of discussion concerning the identity of these two witnesses. Most Bible scholars believe they are either Elijah and Moses, or Elijah and Enoch. Malachi is explicit in predicting Elijah's future appearance upon earth. He states: *Behold, I will send my messenger, and he shall prepare the way before me: and the Lord, whom ye seek, shall suddenly come to his temple, even the messenger of the covenant, whom ye delight in: behold, he shall come, saith the Lord of hosts. Behold, I will send you Elijah the prophet before the coming of the great and dreadful day of the Lord* (Malachi 3:1 and 4:5). Thus, there is no doubt about Elijah being one of the witnesses.

This prediction is corroborated by the fact that Elijah did not die a physical death but was taken up into heaven by a whirlwind and a chariot of fire (see 2 Kings 2:9-11). Likewise, Enoch was taken to heaven without experiencing death (see Genesis 5:24 and Hebrews 11:5). He also prophesied the coming day of God's judgment and the return of Christ with His church (see Jude 14,15). Since Enoch's earthly ministry predated the establishment of the Jewish race, he is considered by some as God's first prophet to the Gentiles. Elijah, on the other hand, was God's prophet to Israel. Thus, since God's witness during the Tribulation hour is to both groups, many believe the two witnesses to be Elijah and Enoch.

Personally, I believe that Moses will be the other witness because he appeared with Elijah on the Mount of Transfiguration (see Matthew 17:1-8)—a preview of the glory to come in that day when the Lord Jesus Christ will be the only important one. The preview indicates that, when the day finally arrives, Moses and Elijah (also called Elias)—representatives of the law and of the prophets—will be present, undoubtedly as the two witnesses.

Concerning Moses: *The Lord thy God will raise up unto thee a Prophet from the midst of thee, of thy brethren, like unto me; unto him ye shall hearken...and he shall speak unto them all that I shall command him. And it shall come to pass, that whosoever will not hearken unto my words which he shall speak in*

149

my name, I will require it of him (Deuteronomy 18:15,18,19). One should also keep in mind that the body of Moses was preserved by God. Jude 9 declares: *Yet Michael the archangel, when contending with the devil he disputed about the body of Moses, durst not bring against a railing accusation, but said, The Lord rebuke thee.*

These witnesses, dressed in sackcloth and proclaiming the message of judgment, will be hated. Latter-day terrorists will attempt to destroy them. God, however, forbids it and offers sovereign protection.

Verse 5: *And if any man will hurt them, fire proceedeth out of their mouth, and devoureth their enemies: and if any man will hurt them, he must in this manner be killed.*

This can be nothing but supernatural power and intervention. The fact that the two witnesses have superhuman anointing is evident from the next verse.

Verse 6: *These have power to shut heaven, that it rain not in the days of their prophecy: and have power over waters to turn them to blood, and to smite the earth with all plagues, as often as they will.*

One of these two witnesses, Elijah (or Elias), performed this very miracle in earlier days: *Elias ...prayed earnestly that it might not rain: and it rained not on the earth by the space of three years and six months. And he prayed again, and the heaven gave rain, and the earth brought forth her fruit* (James 5:17,18).

Moses, the second witness, had power (along with Aaron his brother) to turn the waters into blood and smite the earth with diversified plagues (see Exodus 7-10). Thus, the Tribulation ministry of these two supernaturally anointed prophets will be but a repeat performance. During the entire period of their witness they cannot be killed. Their death must be at God's appointed time.

Verse 7: *And when they shall have finished their testimony, the beast that ascendeth out of the bottomless pit shall make war against them, and shall overcome them, and kill them.*

Isn't it wonderful to know that nothing can happen to any child of God without the Lord's divine permission? "What have I to dread, what have I to fear; leaning on the everlasting arms? I have blessed peace, with my Lord so near; leaning on the everlasting arms." That's right, no one can take a believer's life without the permissive will of God: *Is there not an appointed time to man upon earth?* (Job 7:1). *It is appointed unto men once to die* (Hebrews 9:27). This is why Christians should always say, *If the Lord will, we shall live, and do this, or that* (James 4:15). At this point the time of the witnesses' testifying ends. God's purpose for His two servants has been completed. Soon they will be called home. The method of their release from the body is death at the hands of the beast. His conduct is identical to that of the now deceased Ayatollah Khomeini of Iran, who had the bodies of America's brave servicemen displayed in the streets of Tehran following the April 1980 hostage rescue attempt. His action was one of the most repulsive, repugnant sights ever witnessed. The An-

151

tichrist commits the same dastardly deed with the bodies of Moses and Elijah.

Verse 8: *And their dead bodies shall lie in the street of the great city, which spiritually is called Sodom and Egypt, where also our Lord was crucified.*

Since the Lord was crucified in this city, we know it to be Jerusalem. The term *great city* is the Holy City (Jerusalem) of verse 2. Why, then, is it called Sodom and Egypt? Because the moral and spiritual conditions that existed in Sodom before its destruction, and the idolatrous iniquities that abounded in Egypt before God judged the land, are found inundating Jerusalem during this period of time. All the preaching of repentance by the two witnesses in sackcloth does not change the wicked complexion of the city.

The death of the two witnesses is observed by the entire world, as evidenced by the next verse.

Verse 9: *And they of the people and kindreds and tongues and nations shall see their dead bodies three days and an half, and shall not suffer their dead bodies to be put in graves.*

Satellite television, beaming the identical image to every nation on earth, and into every home equipped with a receiver, allows the spectacle to be observed internationally. The action constitutes a victory celebration by the Antichrist, similar to Khomeini's televised production. In response, the world rejoices. The two "gloom and doom" preachers are gone! No longer will two hellfire advocates spoil their tea parties. No longer will their beer and salami festivals be hindered. The two witnesses are dead.

Verse 10: *And they that dwell upon the earth shall rejoice over them, and make merry, and shall send gifts one to another; because these two prophets tormented them that dwelt on the earth.*

Wait! The party is coming to an end! Their food will soon stick in their throats. A miracle of spectacular proportion is about to occur!

Verse 11: *And after three days and an half the Spirit of life from God entered into them, and they stood upon their feet; and great fear fell upon them which saw them.*

Verse 12: *And they heard a great voice from heaven saying unto them, Come up hither. And they ascended up to heaven in a cloud; and their enemies beheld them.*

Elijah and Moses receive the same treatment as the raptured saints in Revelation 4:1. Hallelujah! They depart for glory in a twinkling of an eye. As this awe-inspiring sight is being observed, God sends judgment for all the sacrilegious acts the violent, drug-crazed crowds perpetrated on these two servants.

Verse 13: *And the same hour was there a great earthquake, and the tenth part of the city fell, and in the earthquake were slain of men seven thousand: and the remnant were affrighted, and gave glory to the God of heaven.*

Talk about a television spectacular! Two men come to life again and then vanish in a cloud! Next an unprecedented earthquake hits the city and 7,000 celebrities (the interpretation of many scholars)—yes, big names among the elite—are killed. This video extravaganza will make the nightly news seem like child's play.

Those who live through the experience become exceedingly frightened and begin to praise God. However, it is not from converted hearts that they exalt Him. Instead, their praise is the result of astonishment and alarm. Their reaction is similar to that of the scribes and the Pharisees who witnessed the miracle of the healed paralytic and were all amazed, and glorified God, and were filled with fear (see Luke 5:26). They did not get saved, just scared! Some people develop a spiritual vocabulary in a hurry. Wait until atomic bombs begin flying. Prayer and praise will become the order of the day!

We come now to the third woe. Remember the angel in chapter 8, verse 13 who cried, "Woe, woe, woe?" Each woe depicted a different judgment. Each, in turn, became more severe. The first woe was the fifth trumpet blast, the second woe the sixth trumpet blast. At this point the final woe, or seventh trumpet, is about to sound.

Verse 14: *The second woe is past; and, behold, the third woe cometh quickly.*

Seventh trumpet

Verse 15: *And the seventh angel sounded; and there were great voices in heaven, saying, The kingdoms of this world are become the kingdoms of our Lord, and of his Christ; and he shall reign for ever and ever.*

The picture before us is the same as the one in chapter 19, verses 11 through 16—the return of the

154

King. If one remembers that chapters 6 through 11 and 12 through 19:15 run concurrently, or side by side, during the Tribulation hour, he will understand why the King returns both in chapter 11, verse 15 and in chapter 19, verse 16. Chapters 12 through 19, verse 15 are but a repeat of the events described in chapters 6 through 11. Now, as the King returns, a praise and worship service begins.

Verse 16: *And the four and twenty elders, which sat before God on their seats, fell upon their faces, and worshipped God.*

This is an act of gratitude. Remember that the twenty-four elders represent all believers—Old and New Testament—who have lived on this earth and who have been raptured to heaven in chapter 4, verse 1. They know firsthand that Satan has been the God of this world system (see 2 Corinthians 4:4). They understand fully that the nations of this world have been under his control (see Matthew 4:8,9). But now, praise God, Satan's reign has finally ended—the King has come! There is great rejoicing in heaven among the raptured saints as the midnight newscast is shared. They unitedly pray...

Verse 17: *Saying, We give thee thanks, O Lord God Almighty, which art, and wast, and art to come; because thou hast taken to thee thy great power, and hast reigned.*

Their prayer is to Christ, the One who used the title, *which art, and wast, and art to come.* The power that was always His has now been embraced, and He has begun His reign. The wicked are upset over the King's return.

Verse 18: *And the nations were angry, and thy wrath is come, and the time of the dead, that they should be judged, and that thou shouldest give reward unto thy servants the prophets, and to the saints, and them that fear thy name, small and great; and shouldest destroy them which destroy the earth.*

Notice the number of happenings which transpire at the King's return.

First, the nations are angry. This is also observed in the other text describing the King's descent to earth: *And I saw the beast, and the kings of the earth, and their armies, gathered together to make war against him that sat on the horse, and against his army* (chapter 19, verse 19).

Second, the day of God's wrath has come as the King returns. This is the period of time when *out of his mouth goeth a sharp sword, that with it he should smite the nations: and he shall rule them with a rod of iron: and he treadeth the winepress of the fierceness and wrath of Almighty God* (chapter 19, verse 15).

Third, at the conclusion of the King's 1,000-year reign, the wicked are judged. The setting is chapter 20, verses 11 through 15.

Fourth, the faithful prophets and saints, small and great, are rewarded at the end of the 1,000 years. This is not a picture of the Judgment Seat of Christ (see 2 Corinthians 5:10). Then believers were raptured (chapter 4, verse 1), investigated (chapter 4, verse 2), coronated (chapter 4, verse 4), and exalted as they laid their crowns at Jesus' feet (chapter 4, verse 10), long before the Tribulation hour ended.

The rewards presented at this time are for those who were faithful during the kingdom age—those who did not rebel and follow Satan at its conclusion (chapter 20, verses 7, 8).

Fifth, those who destroyed the earth are destroyed. This refers to spirit beings who followed the destroyer, Satan. Their destruction is separate from that of the nations, hence the division between the two in verse 18. Satanic beings receive their judgment at this hour as well as the earth dwellers. In the midst of all of this, Israel is spared.

Verse 19: *And the temple of God was opened in heaven, and there was seen in his temple the ark of his testament: and there were lightnings, and voices, and thunderings, and an earthquake, and great hail.*

The temple of God and the Ark of the Testament, both connected with Jewish worship, picture Israel. Thus, in the midst of *lightnings, and voices and thunderings, and an earthquake, and great hail,* God spares His covenant people.

12

As noted previously, chapters 12 through 19 constitute a rerun of the Tribulation hour as presented in chapters 6 through 11. Thus, at this point we come once again to the middle of the Tribulation—and to the worst wave of anti-Semitism the world has ever observed. This is truly what Jeremiah had in mind in chapter 30, verse 7, when he said, *Alas! for that day is great, so that none is like it: it is even the time of Jacob's trouble.* Jacob, as one discovers in Romans 11:26, is Israel.

A number of great signs and occurrences are witnessed in this chapter, each having to do with the horrendous judgment that is enveloping the earth, including the persecution being directed against Israel. These include a *great wonder* (verse 1), *a great red dragon* (verse 3), *great wrath* (verse 12), and *two wings of a great eagle* (verse 14).

Verse 1: *And there appeared a great wonder in heaven; a woman clothed with the sun, and the moon under her feet, and upon her head a crown of twelve stars:*

In total, the Book of Revelation pictures four different women: (1) Jezebel, the high priestess of paganism (chapter 2, verse 20);(2) the scarlet woman, the high priestess of apostasy (chapter 17); (3) the Lamb's wife, the representative of the true, blood-bought Church (chapter 19, verse 7); and (4) Israel, in the text before us.

This woman of chapter 12 is a picture of Israel. Mary Baker Eddy Glover Patterson presented herself as this woman, but her claim was absurd, to say the least. The woman's offspring could not possibly be the Christian Science movement. Who, then, is this woman, and why does she appear? The term *wonder* in our text comes from the same Greek word *sign*. Thus, we see that the woman is a sign. What sign? The sign of Israel. Let's prove this assertion.

The woman of Revelation 12:1 was pictured in the dream of Joseph centuries ago: *And he dreamed yet another dream, and told it* [to] *his brethren, and said, Behold, I have dreamed a dream more; and, behold, the sun and the moon* [representing father and mother] *and the eleven stars* [representing Joseph's eleven brothers] *made obeisance to me* [the twelfth star]. *And he told it to his father, and to his brethren: and his father rebuked him, and said unto him, What is this dream that thou hast dreamed? Shall I and thy mother and thy brethren indeed come to bow down ourselves to thee to the earth? And his brethren envied him; but his father observed the saying* (Genesis 37:9-11).

Clearly, the woman clothed with the sun and wearing a crown of twelve stars upon her head, just like in Joseph's dream, is Israel. The birth of this woman's (Israel's) son is predicted in Isaiah 66, verses 7 and 8: *Before she travailed, she brought forth; before her pain came, she was delivered of a man child. Who hath heard such a thing? who hath seen such things? Shall the earth be made to bring forth in one day? or shall a nation be born at once? for as soon as Zion travailed, she brought forth her children* [or her son]. Isaiah's prediction finds its fulfillment in the next verse.

Verse 2: *And she being with child cried, travailing in birth, and pained to be delivered.*

Here we have the mother, Israel, bringing forth a man-child who is none other than the blessed Lord Jesus Christ, as one discovers in verse 5. This truth harmonizes with many New Testament texts. For instance, Romans 9:4,5 states; [They] *are Israelites; to whom pertaineth the adoption, and the glory, and the covenants, and the giving of the law, and the service of God, and the promises; Whose are the fathers, and of whom as concerning the flesh Christ came, who is over all, God blessed for ever. Amen.*

Christ, in His flesh, came forth from Israel; and, at this point in our text, Christ's adversary, Satan—the one who rebelled centuries ago against the authority of God (see Isaiah 14:12-14)—is about to strike another blow.

Verse 3: *And there appeared another wonder in heaven; and behold a great red dragon, having seven heads and ten horns, and seven crowns upon his heads.*

Verse 4: *And his tail drew the third part of the stars of heaven, and did cast them to the earth: and the dragon stood before the woman which was ready*

161

to be delivered, for to devour her child as soon as it was born.

The red dragon is conclusively proven to be Satan in verse 9. The number seven speaks of completeness, and therefore, the dragon's seven heads picture his wisdom. It is written that Satan is *full of wisdom* (Ezekiel 28:12). God created him that way when he was *the anointed cherub* [or angel] *that covereth* (Ezekiel 28:14). His ten horns speak of universal power, just as the ten toes of Daniel's image do. Satan's international control, of course, is possible because millions of demons jump at his command. Remember, he is *the god of this world* system (2 Corinthians 4:4). He is also *the prince of the power of the air* (Ephesians 2:2) and *the prince of this world* (John 12:31). However, since he is not omniscient (all knowing), or omnipresent (in all places at all times), Satan must rely on demonic hosts (fallen angels) in diversified places to administer his power. This explains why Christians are not fighting against flesh and blood only but *against spiritual wickedness in high places* as well (Ephesians 6:12). Satan probably enlisted the angels who fell at the time of his rebellion when *his tail drew the third part of the stars of heaven* [a reference to angels] *and did cast them to the earth.* A similar reference is found in Jude 13.

At this point, one may ask why we use these texts to discuss past, present, and future history. The answer is simple. The scene we are about to witness speaks of the entire age-long conflict from beginning to end. Its details are squeezed into these few verses before us. The same devil who attempted to destroy the woman's (or Israel's) son in centuries past (see Genesis 3:15) is now about to strike out against the woman herself via the greatest anti-Semitic purge in history. Hitler's murderous and barbaric attempt at Jewish annihilation will seem like a Sunday school picnic compared to this holocaust! That's why Daniel stated: *There shall be a time of trouble, such as never was since there was a nation even to that same time: and at that time thy people shall be delivered, every one that shall be found written in the book* (12:1). Jesus himself said in Matthew 24:21,22, *For then shall be great tribulation, such as was not since the beginning of the world to this time, no, nor ever shall be. And except those days should be shortened, there should no flesh be saved: but for the elect's sake those days shall be shortened.* The elect, as spoken of here, are the Israelites of Romans 11:28.

Verse 5 proves my earlier statement that the verses before us cover the age-long conflict—past, present, and future.

Verse 5: *And she brought forth a man child* [1,900 years ago], *who was to rule all nations with a rod of iron* [future]: *and her child was caught up unto God, and to his throne* [the present age of grace].

Verse 6: *And the woman fled into the wilderness, where she hath a place prepared of God, that they should feed her there a thousand two hundred and threescore days.*

During this final forty-two-month period, described as the Great Tribulation (see Revelation 7:14), because of its intensity and immensity, the Children of Israel are protected by their God. He took care of

163

them for forty years as they wandered through the wilderness, and now He again proves His love to His ancient people by delivering them. Yes, they *shall be saved out of it* (Jeremiah 30:7). *And at that time thy people shall be delivered* (Daniel 12:1). Matthew 24:22 adds, *For the elect's sake those days shall be shortened.* In the next few verses, a shocking space war takes place.

Verse 7: *And there was war in heaven: Michael and his angels fought against the dragon; and the dragon fought and his angels,*

Verse 8: *And prevailed not; neither was their place found any more in heaven.*

Verse 9: *And the great dragon was cast out, that old serpent, called the Devil, and Satan, which deceiveth the whole world: he was cast out into the earth, and his angels were cast out with him.*

Some Bible authorities believe that this war in heaven began at the time of the Rapture in chapter 4, verse 1. Since a war involves a number of skirmishes or battles, this is a distinct possibility. The assumption is based on Daniel 12:1 and 2.

These scholars reason that since those who are caught up in the rapture of the Church must pass through the areas where Satan reigns—the aerial and stellar heavens—Satan becomes aroused and attempts to hinder this evacuation of the saints from the earth. However, as he attempts to interfere in this glorious event, angels—ministers of the saints (see Hebrews 1:14)—rush to the rescue, and the space confrontation and conflagration begins. This happened in the past—why could it not occur again? Where did it happen in the past? Consider Daniel 10:13 as we are introduced to Michael, the commander in chief of heaven's armies. Daniel says, *But the prince of the kingdom of Persia withstood me one and twenty days: but, lo, Michael, one of the chief princes* [an angelic name and title], *came to help me.* God tells Daniel that He had every intention of answering His prayers, but that for twenty-one days the devil tried to hinder the response. Finally God had to send Michael to battle the devil in the area of his domain (the first and second heavens) in order to make the answer a reality. Thus, it is possible that Michael will again battle God's adversary at the time of the Rapture in order to allow Christians their entrance into glory in the twinkling of an eye, as promised in 1 Corinthians 15:51-54.

Michael is mentioned five times in God's Word, beginning with Daniel 10:13. We find him again in Daniel 10:21 where he is described to the Children of Israel as Michael, *your prince.* His third mention is in Daniel 12:1: *And at that time shall Michael stand up, the great prince which standeth for the children of thy people.* In Jude 9, we find Michael, the archangel, contending with the devil over the body of Moses. Notice that every time Michael appears, he is connected with the Children of Israel—making it very plausible that he is at war with Satan in our present and fifth text, defending the Jewish people.

The war is on, and it is the greatest aerial combat in history: *Michael and his angels fought against the dragon* [Satan]*; and the dragon fought and his angels.* Are you shocked to discover Satan in heaven?

165

Most people (including most Christians) imagine him as a little creature dressed in a red uniform, running around in a place called hell, jabbing his victims with a pitchfork. This is all a lot of mythological nonsense.

Satan is a magnificent creature to behold. In fact, his beauty brought his ruin. Ezekiel 28:17 states: *Thine heart was lifted up because of thy beauty, thou hast corrupted thy wisdom by reason of thy brightness: I will cast thee to the ground, I will lay thee before kings, that they may behold thee.* Not only is it a lie to picture Satan as a grotesque monstrosity, but it is equally false to place him in hell. He has never been there. He is the *god of this world* system, the *prince of the power of the air,* and the *prince of this world,* as we have already observed. He has been in heavens one and two (the aerial and stellar heavens) since his fall—and he will remain there until he is cast to the earth in verse 9. It is also important to note that he is not cast into eternal hell (the lake of fire) to join those he has duped until after the Millennium (chapter 20, verse 10). Now, as this battle is fought, Satan is defeated. Praise God! Satan is mighty, but God is Almighty! Satan can destroy, but God can destroy the destroyer! That is why the Christian should never fear the events of daily life. He has victory in Jesus. Yes, *greater is he that is in you, than he that is in the world* (1 John 4:4).

Satan's demise began when he was cast out of the third heaven (see Isaiah 14:12-14), continues until Revelation 12:9 when he is cast out of the first and second heavens, and is completed when he is cast into the lake of fire (chapter 20, verse 10). John foresaw that hour and said, *The prince of this world* [shall] *be cast out* (John 12:31) and *the prince of this world is judged* (John 16:11). To the eternal Christ, Satan's doom was as good as accomplished, but for you and me, time had to pass. Now, in our text, the moment has arrived: (Satan and his angels) *prevailed not* (verse 8.) Michael's gunners zero in, and Satan's place—an abiding location for centuries—is found no longer. Instead, the dragon (Satan) *which deceiveth the whole world:* [is] *cast out into the earth, and his angels* [are] *cast out with him.* This signals the end of Satan's rule in the aerial and stellar heavens, and the victory celebration begins. All heaven rejoices over that which Michael's defeat of Satan has accomplished.

Verse 10: *And I heard a loud voice saying in heaven, Now is come salvation, and strength, and the kingdom of our God, and the power of his Christ: for the accuser of our brethren is cast down, which accused them before our God day and night.*

The spontaneous praise session within this verse occurs because (1) salvation from Satan's atmospheric control has taken place; (2) God's strength has crushed Satan's might; (3) the kingdom is about to arrive; and (4) the power of Christ will be seen as He comes to set up His kingdom. Think of it! The united power of Father and Son casts the accuser of the brethren out of the heavens.

Did you know that accusing the brethren is Satan's present ministry? He also uses some ministers and holier-than-thou church members to accomplish this goal. Listen carefully. Every bit of slander against another brother or sister in Christ is simply the devil using an individual's mind and vocal cords. In fact, *devil* means "slanderer." The term *false accuser* in the English Bible is translated from the word *diabolos* or *devil*. Thus, Titus 2:3 states: *The aged women likewise, that they be in behaviour as becometh holiness, not false accusers.* Literally rendered, this verse states: "That the aged women be not she devils." A woman who gossips is a "she devil," and a male gossip is a "macho devil." Both are controlled by the power of the vile one. No wonder lying is one of the seven sins God hates (see Proverbs 6:16-19).

When Satan is cast out into the earth (verse 9), the hot spot will be our *terra firma* where men walk and breathe. At that time there will be only one place of safety and victory—in the arms of the Lord Jesus through His shed blood.

Verse 11: *And they overcame him by the blood of the Lamb, and by the word of their testimony; and they loved not their lives unto the death.*

These wise saints resisted Satan by the blood of Jesus and by the Word of God. There is no other way to win a spiritual battle (see Hebrews 4:12). They also overcame Satan by their testimony and loved not their own lives unto death. What a crown awaits them—and you, if you're true blue! Thus, John states in Revelation 2:10: *Be thou faithful unto death, and I will give thee a crown of life.*

Though there is rejoicing in the heavenlies, the picture is quite different for earth dwellers.

Verse 12: *Therefore rejoice, ye heavens, and ye that dwell in them. Woe to the inhabiters of the earth and of the sea! for the devil is come down unto you, having great wrath, because he knoweth that he hath but a short time.*

At this point Satan unleashes all his fury for he knows that within forty-two months (three and one-half years), his reign will be ended. Thus, the great anti-Semitic purge now begins.

Verse 13: *And when the dragon saw that he was cast unto the earth, he persecuted the woman which brought forth the man child.*

Immediately God intervenes.

Verse 14: *And to the woman were given two wings of a great eagle, that she might fly into the wilderness, into her place, where she is nourished for a time, and times, and half a time, from the face of the serpent.*

This verse describes God in His sovereignty and love, protecting His chosen people for three and one-half years. The eagle's wings probably indicate an airlift or some other miraculous speedy escape. God is probably reminding the Children of Israel of His act of preservation in Pharoah's day, and uses the picture of wings to show them His goodness. He declares, *Ye have seen what I did unto the Egyptians, and how I bare you on eagles' wings, and brought you unto myself* (Exodus 19:4). Safety is promised to His people.

Verse 15: *And the serpent cast out of his mouth water as a flood after the woman, that he might cause her to be carried away of the flood.*

The flood undoubtedly portrays a volume of propaganda—anti-Semitic insinuations, slanders, and slurs—released internationally. Yet, God promises: *When the enemy shall come in like a flood, the Spirit of the Lord shall lift up a standard against him* (Isaiah 59:19).

Verse 16: *And the earth helped the woman, and the earth opened her mouth, and swallowed up the flood which the dragon cast out of his mouth.*

This verse, too, is reminiscent of the miraculous deliverance God provided the Children of Israel during their exodus from Egypt, when the Red Sea closed in over Pharaoh and his army. *The enemy said, I will pursue, I will overtake, I will divide the spoil; my lust shall be satisfied upon them; I will draw my sword, my hand shall destroy them. Thou didst blow with thy wind, the sea covered them: they sank as lead in the mighty waters. Who is like unto thee, O Lord, among the gods? who is like thee, glorious in holiness, fearful in praises, doing wonders? Thou stretchedst out thy right hand, the earth swallowed them* (Exodus 15:9-12). At this point Satan reaches the height of his anger.

Verse 17: *And the dragon was wroth with the woman, and went to make war with the remnant of her seed, which keep the commandments of God, and have the testimony of Jesus Christ.*

170

13

This chapter introduces us to two beasts. The first one, commonly known as the Antichrist, is unveiled in verses 1 through 10, while the second beast, known as the false prophet, is revealed in verses 11 through 18. The first beast is political; the second is religious. Both, however, are energized by the power of Satan, and thus constitute an unholy trinity—the devil, the Antichrist, and the false prophet. Remember, Satan is the great imitator. The incarnation of himself in these two villains is his final attempt to wreak havoc upon earth. Knowing that he has but a short time left, he makes an all-out move to usurp God's position and authority through his two allies—the beasts of this chapter.

Verse 1: *And I stood upon the sand of the sea, and saw a beast rise up out of the sea, having seven heads and ten horns, and upon his horns ten crowns, and upon his heads the name of blasphemy.*

As stated earlier in our study, Bible chapters and verses came into existence in the 1500s. They are very helpful in locating passages, but they are not inspired. At times they even cloud the information being presented. Actually, verse 1 of chapter 13 should have been part of chapter 12, for the subject is Satan and his persecution of earth dwellers. Therefore, according to the original Greek manuscript, the personal pronoun should be *he* instead of *I*, because *he* pictures Satan standing upon the sand of the sea. Accordingly, this portion of Scripture should read, "And the dragon was wroth with the woman...and Satan stood upon the sand of the sea."

Satan standing upon the sand of the sea pictures his control over earth's teeming millions at an appointed time (chapter 17, verse 5, and chapter 20, verse 8). This control is established through the two satanically-inspired beasts who come out of the sea and the earth. The first beast (the Antichrist) rises out of the sea and has seven heads and ten horns, and upon his horns ten crowns. He is a literal man, but demon-possessed, for he (or his power) comes out of the abyss, for *the beast that thou sawest was, and is not; and shall ascend out of the bottomless pit* (chapter 17, verse 8).

The seven heads, loaded with blasphemy, also portray the five kings who had ruled up to John's day; the sixth king who was in power at that time; and the seventh king who will reign as the Antichrist during the Tribulation hour.

Chapter 17, verse 10 confirms this: *And there are seven kings: five are fallen, and one is, and the other is not yet come; and when he cometh, he must continue a short space.* Likewise, the ten horns also picture ten nations over whom the beast or Antichrist rules. The scene before us pictures the final, or

seventh, world leader ruling over a confederation of
ten nations during the end time.

In order to understand that the ten horns are
actually ten western nations—each of which was part
of the old Roman Empire—one must study the prophecy of Daniel in chapters 2 and 7 of the book bearing
his name. Let's digress for a moment and investigate.

Nebuchadnezzar, the king of Babylon in Daniel's
day, had a dream. When he awakened, however, he
could not recall the dream. Therefore, he called his
magicians, astrologers, and soothsayers together, re-
questing that they both recall the dream and explain
its meaning. Not one of them was able to do so, even
under the sentence of death: *And the decree went
forth that the wise men should be slain; and they
sought Daniel and his fellows to be slain. Then
Daniel went in, and desired of the king that he would
give him time, and that he would shew the king the
interpretation. Then was the secret revealed unto
Daniel in a night vision. Then Daniel blessed the
God of heaven* (Daniel 2:13,16,19).

Next we find Daniel in the presence of the king,
explaining God's vision to him in verses 27 through
36. This is one of the most important texts in the
entire Bible because it reveals the history of the world
from that time to our present day. *Daniel answered in
the presence of the king, and said, The secret which
the king hath demanded cannot the wise men, the
astrologers, the magicians, the soothsayers, show
unto the king; But there is a God in heaven that
revealeth secrets, and maketh known to the king Nebuchadnezzar what shall be in the latter days. Thy*

dream, and the visions of thy head upon thy bed, are these; As for thee, O king, thy thoughts came into thy mind upon thy bed, what should come to pass hereafter: and he that revealeth secrets maketh known to thee what shall come to pass. But as for me, this secret is not revealed to me for any wisdom that I have more than any living, but for their sakes that shall make known the interpretation to the king, and that thou mightest know the thoughts of thy heart. Thou, O king, sawest, and behold a great image. This great image, whose brightness was excellent, stood before thee; and the form thereof was terrible. This image's head was of fine gold, his breast and his arms of silver, his belly and his thighs of brass, His legs of iron, his feet part of iron and part of clay. Thou sawest till that a stone was cut out without hands, which smote the image upon his feet that were of iron and clay, and brake them to pieces. Then was the iron, the clay, the brass, the silver, and the gold, broken to pieces together, and became like the chaff of the summer threshing floors; and the wind carried them away, that no place was found for them: and the stone that smote the image became a great mountain, and filled the whole earth. This is the dream.

Nebuchadnezzar was astonished as his dream was revealed, and shocked as its interpretation was given. Daniel told the king that he (Nebuchadnezzar), as the leader of the Babylonian empire, was the head of gold and that the two arms of silver (representing the Medes and the Persians) would soon overthrow him. Next the stomach and thighs of brass (Greece) would defeat the Medes and the Persians.

174

Eventually the two legs of iron (the Roman Empire, headquartered at Rome and Constantinople) would conquer the Greco empire. These events occurred exactly as God had revealed them to Daniel and as he, in turn, told Nebuchadnezzar.

Now notice something extremely important. The ten toes of iron and clay never destroyed the legs of iron—the Roman Empire! Why? Rome fell through internal corruption.

This historical fact is the subject of Edward Gibbon's great book, *The History of the Rise and Fall of the Roman Empire.* Therefore, we see that the final world power is a union of ten western nations represented by the ten toes of the great image. The iron tells us these nations were part of the old Roman Empire, whereas the clay speaks of a deterioration as the empire weakened over the centuries. Thus, the final world power will not be communism but a confederation of ten western nations under the first beast, or the Antichrist.

The ten toes also coincide with the ten horns of the beast in the verse under consideration. In the interpretation of Nebuchadnezzar's dream (2:36-44), Daniel described the toes as kingdoms, concluding with the statement, *And in the days of these kings* [ten of them, as pictured by the ten toes] *shall the God of heaven set up a kingdom, which shall never be destroyed: and the kingdom shall not be left to other people, but it shall break in pieces and consume all these kingdoms, and it shall stand for ever.*

For centuries Christians have prayed Matthew 6:10: *Thy kingdom come.* During the Tribulation

175

hour, the 144,000 Jewish evangelists of Revelation 7:3-8 will preach the gospel of the kingdom—the good news that the King is about to return. Can you hear them shouting this exciting information in the streets? "The King is coming! The King is coming!" Finally the King is seen returning in chapter 11, verse 15, and chapter 19, verse 16, and this event of the ages takes place when a final confederation of ten western nations has been established upon earth. Could the present European Economic Community or Common Market be a part of this picture? I believe it could be! Oh, Jesus is coming soon!

At this point we need to consider another extremely important fact. Ireland and Denmark—present Common Market members—were never part of the old Roman Empire. This apparent problem, however, is quickly resolved when one considers the information presented in Daniel, chapter 7. Here we discover that, following the establishment of a ten-nation confederacy, another world leader arises. He takes control, ousts three nations, and replaces them with two others and his own. Specifically, Daniel says, *I considered the horns* [ten of them], *and, behold, there came up among them another little horn, before whom there were three of the first horns* [original members] *plucked up by the roots* (7:8). This coincides perfectly with Revelation 13:5.

Daniel continues in verses 24 and 25: *And the ten horns out of this kingdom are ten kings that shall arise: and another shall rise after them; and he shall be diverse from the first, and he shall subdue three kings. And he shall speak great words against the*

176

most High. Here we not only see the world leader overpowering three kings and replacing them with original members of the old Roman Empire—we also observe him fulfilling the prediction of blasphemy described in our text.

There is no doubt about it. A confederacy of ten western nations will be formed. Then another leader will appear, remove three nations, replace them, and rule as the Antichrist until the King of kings returns to earth and destroys his evil empire. Thus, the Common Market will grow to thirteen nations, and these thirteen could eventually control all nations and finally be reduced to ten at the end when this ten-toed, ten-horned confederacy is destroyed. This is the event described by Daniel as a *stone cut out without hands* [breaking] *in pieces the iron, the brass, the clay, the silver, and the gold.*

Then Daniel 2:44,45 occurs: *And in the days of these kings shall the God of heaven set up a kingdom, which shall never be destroyed: and the kingdom shall not be left to other people, but it shall break in pieces and consume all these kingdoms, and it shall stand for ever. Forasmuch as thou sawest that the stone was cut out of the mountain without hands, and that it brake in pieces the iron, the brass, the clay, the silver, and the gold; the great God hath made known to the king what shall come to pass hereafter: and the dream is certain, and the interpretation thereof sure.*

Yes, King Nebuchadnezzar's dream has come to pass throughout hundreds of years of history, and the present alignment of western nations in the form of the European Economic Community may well be the final piece in the puzzle. *Prepare to meet thy God* (Amos 4:12).

Verse 2: *And the beast which I saw was like unto a leopard, and his feet were as the feet of a bear, and his mouth as the mouth of a lion: and the dragon gave him his power, and his seat, and great authority.*

We have already discovered that (1) Babylon, (2) Medo-Persia, (3) Greece, and (4) Rome constitute the four empires of world history. We have also learned that the revived Roman Empire, in the form of a final ten-nation confederation, becomes the end-time power block. Daniel 7 pictures these four empires as (1) a lion, (2) a bear, (3) a leopard, and (4) a beast who is a combination of the previous world powers he has conquered. The beast's empire contains a portion of each preceding empire. Actually, the only difference between the descriptions of John and Daniel is that the order is reversed in the Book of Revelation. The reason for this is simple: John is looking back to the beginning while Daniel is looking forward to the conclusion. Putting it all together, the message of the ten horns, the ten toes, and the four beasts is one and the same from different vantage points—and all picture a world dictator governing ten nations at the time of the end! This ten-nation confederacy constitutes the revival of the fourth power— the old Roman Empire—as typified by the fourth monstrous animal or beast.

Verse 3: *And I saw one of his heads as it were wounded to death; and his deadly wound was healed: and all the world wondered after the beast.*

The wounding of the beast is mentioned three

times in this chapter—verse 3, 12, and 14. The wound produces death, but restoration to life follows. Some commentators think that this statement represents the fall of the old Roman Empire and its restoration through the ten-nation confederacy. Others believe that it speaks of the resurrection of Judas Iscariot, for he and the Antichrist are the only ones ever called the *son of perdition* (John 17:12 and 2 Thessalonians 2:3). God alone knows.

A third possibility would be that the Antichrist is assassinated midway through the Tribulation hour, perhaps in retaliation for overthrowing three members of the original ten-nation federation. Such an event would give the great counterfeiter, Satan, the opportunity to perform a resurrection. This would prove invaluable to the prestige of the Antichrist, since the deity of the Lord Jesus was affirmed by His resurrection 2,000 years before (see Matthew 12:39,40). Remember that the Antichrist proclaims himself God and even sits in the Temple in Jerusalem during the Tribulation (see 2 Thessalonians 2:4 and Matthew 24:15). Thus, a counterfeit resurrection would assure the world that he is all he claims to be. I personally believe this to be the correct solution, because when it happens, *all the world* [wonders] *after* [him]. Mankind is literally overwhelmed by the Antichrist's power and authority.

Verse 4: *And they worshipped the dragon which gave power unto the beast: and they worshipped the beast, saying, Who is like unto the beast? who is able to make war with him?*

Another reason that verse 3 may speak of an

179

actual resurrection is that millions who previously would not believe in the Antichrist now begin to worship him—and Satan.

In the second half of this chapter, we will see that the false prophet or religious leader of the Tribulation period actually enforces the worship of the Antichrist! Since the people think of him as God, they cry, *Who is like unto the beast? who is able to make war with him?* Yes, who can combat this self-proclaimed god and be victorious?

Verse 5: *And there was given unto him a mouth speaking great things and blasphemies; and power was given unto him to continue forty and two months.*

The Antichrist's blasphemy during the final three and one-half years of the Tribulation hour most likely has to do with his mockery of the Almighty. One of the reasons God hates idolatry (the use of images in worship) is that He wants no rivals. Hear Jehovah in Exodus 20:4 and 5: *Thou shalt not make unto thee any graven image, or any likeness of any thing that is in heaven above, or that is in the earth beneath, or that is in the water under the earth: Thou shalt not bow down thyself to them, nor serve them: for I the Lord thy God am a jealous God.* Think of the insult to the Eternal One when the Antichrist says, "I am God," and teeming millions bow to him, to Satan, to the false prophet, and to the image—the abomination of desolation—erected in his honor. This blasphemy continues.

Verse 6: *And he opened his mouth in blasphemy against God, to blaspheme his name, and his tabernacle, and them that dwell in heaven.*

Jesus, the true God, was accused of blasphemy in His day because He claimed to be God (see Matthew 9:3). Ironically, the world accepts the Antichrist's claim to deity, and this perpetrated lie is blasphemy to God. The blasphemy is undoubtedly intensified because Satan himself is speaking.

Now, here is a thought-provoking theory: during the first forty-two months of the Tribulation, the Antichrist acts under the influence of Satan. However, after Satan is cast out of heaven (in chapter 12) and comes to earth, he may actually incarnate himself in the dead body of the Antichrist who had the wound by a sword, and did live (chapter 14). Thus, the beast is raised from the dead by the counterfeiter (Satan), who dwells in that body for the final forty-two months, claiming deity. As a result, he is able to experience that which he sought when he was cast out of heaven, crying, *I will be like the most high* (see Isaiah 14:12-14). Satan's ultimate desire is now realized—he is worshipped as God. The blasphemy is unspeakable! He desecrates everything his filthy hands touch, including the Tabernacle and its worshipers.

Verse 7: *And it was given unto him to make war with the saints, and to overcome them: and power was given him over all kindreds, and tongues, and nations.*

The fight is on for the saints of the Tribulation hour. Remember, this is not the Church. Satan battles the Church as they return with Christ (chapter 19, verse 14). In the scene before us, he is attempting to destroy the millions who *washed their robes, and made them white in the blood of the Lamb* (chapter 7,

181

verse 14) and who also refused the mark of the beast (chapter 20, verse 4). Instead of experiencing defeat, they overcome (Satan) *by the blood of the Lamb, and by the word of their testimony* (chapter 12, verse 11).

During this time, the Antichrist controls the entire world. He is an international despot exercising power over all kindreds, tongues, and nations. Such a one-world government is almost upon us. Consider for a moment the global organizations which have become existent in our day: (1) the International Atomic Energy Agency, (2) the International Labor Organization, (3) the Food and Agricultural Organization, (4) the International Bank for Reconstruction and Development, or World Bank, (5) the International Development Association, (6) the United Nations Educational, Scientific, and Cultural Organization, commonly called UNESCO, (7) the World Health Organization, (8) the International Finance Corporation, (9) the International Monetary Fund, (10) the International Civil Aviation Organization, (11) the Universal Postal Union, (12) the International Telecommunications Union, (13) the World Meteorological Association, (14) the Intergovernmental Maritime Consultive Organization, and (15) the General Agreement on Tariffs and Trades Organization. The formation of such international alliances has led outstanding thinkers to state that "a New World Order" is on the horizon.

Presently we may be witnessing mankind's final approach to the much-publicized New World Order, or one-world government, of the Antichrist. At this point in history, all the world will be amazed as this self-styled deity takes control, and the majority will submit to his authority. However, God always has a remnant who will not bow to Baal or other deities.

Verse 8: *And all that dwell upon the earth shall worship him, whose names are not written in the book of life of the Lamb slain from the foundation of the world.*

The true believers of the Tribulation hour will have nothing to do with this satanic monster, even though they will not be able to buy or sell without his approval (chapter 13, verse 17). Their love for Christ will mean more than life, shelter, and food. They will love Christ to the end, for John declares, *I saw thrones, and they sat upon them, and judgment was given unto them: and I saw the souls of them that were beheaded for the witness of Jesus, and for the word of God, and which had not worshipped the beast, neither his image, neither had received his mark upon their foreheads, or in their hands; and they lived and reigned with Christ a thousand years* (chapter 20, verse 4).

Is the Tribulation hour approaching? Will a demon-possessed or devil-incarnate human claim deity and be accepted as world leader and be worshipped as God? I believe so. Why? Henry Spaak, a spokesman for the Society for Worldwide Interbank Financial Telecommunications (SWIFT) in Brussels, Belgium, headquarters for the Common Market, made a profound statement relevant to that organization's goals and operations a few years ago. He said, "We do not want another committee. We have too many already. What we want is a man of sufficient stature to hold the allegiance of the people and lift us out of the economic morass into which we are sinking. Send us such a man, and be he God or devil, we will accept him." Mr. Spaak, your wish will soon become a reality! The life-and-death matter of verses 1 through 8 is so important that God repeats the warning He so often presented to the seven churches.

Verse 9: *If any man have an ear, let him hear.*
Beware! Take heed! Think seriously! Why?

Verse 10: *He that leadeth into captivity shall go into captivity: he that killeth with the sword must be killed with the sword. Here is the patience and the faith of the saints.*

This is the exact caution Paul stressed in Galatians 6:7: *For whatsoever a man soweth, that shall he also reap.*

Verse 11: *And I beheld another beast coming up out of the earth; and he had two horns like a lamb* [identifying him with Christianity], *and he spake as a dragon* [tying him in with Satan].

Verses 11 through 18 introduce us to the second beast (the religious fake, or false prophet) who is the third member of the satanic trinity. The devil imitates the Father, the Antichrist imitates the Son, and the false prophet imitates the Holy Spirit. This religious hypocrite fulfills the prediction of the Saviour who said in Matthew 24:24, *For there shall arise false Christs, and false prophets, and shall shew great signs and wonders; insomuch that, if it were possible, they shall deceive the very elect.*

Verse 12: *And he exerciseth all the power of the first beast before him, and causeth the earth and them* *which dwell therein to worship the first beast, whose deadly wound was healed.*

Clearly, the power of the false prophet is in the realm of religion. He is coequal in power with the Antichrist. One heads up the secular world, while the other controls the religious scene. These two work closely together. The Antichrist shares his authority with the false prophet, protecting him and his religious colossus in return for a promise of loyalty and devotion. Thus, as head of the world church, the false prophet sees to it that the Antichrist—who was wounded and resurrected—is worshipped. What a team! This second beast is also one of the greatest miracle workers in history.

Verse 13: *And he doeth great wonders, so that he maketh fire come down from heaven on the earth in the sight of men.*

These great wonders are called *lying wonders* in 2 Thessalonians 2:9. They are not magical, "sleight of hand" manipulations, but the result of supernatural power from the dragon that enables these men to even produce fire. Since God often revealed himself by fire (see Genesis 19:24, Leviticus 10:1,2, and 1 Kings 18:38), the false prophet also uses fire. Satan shares his supernatural power for one reason:

Verse 14: *And deceiveth them that dwell on the earth by the means of those miracles which he had power to do in the sight of the beast; saying to them that dwell on the earth, that they should make an image to the beast, which had the wound by a sword, and did live.*

The sole purpose of all these miracles is to prepare the people for idolatry. The false prophet actually entices mankind to build the greatest statue in history in the very image of the Antichrist. This monstrosity will be erected in Jerusalem and will be placed in the Jewish Temple. Such a blasphemous act is against the city conscience and is forbidden by the second commandment (see Exodus 20:4). This is why the image is such an obnoxious, hateful, and abominable thing and is labeled the abomination of desolation by the Lord Jesus Christ in Matthew 24:15.

Verse 15: *And he had power to give life unto the image of the beast, that the image of the beast should both speak, and cause that as many as would not worship the image of the beast should be killed.*

Since the image is able to speak, it might well be the ultimate achievement of our present-day computer systems, already capable of conducting intelligent conversations.

Professor Seymour Wolfson, of Wayne State University in Detroit, is an expert in the field of computers. He states: "Already there is a report of computer systems that have the storage capability of ten trillion human beings." Personally, I believe that the Antichrist will enslave and control earth's four billion inhabitants through such an all-knowing, monstrous computer. Such a system is absolutely essential to his having all the facts on every member of the human race at his fingertips. As a result, he will, with unerring precision, be able to know who receives his orders, obeys his commands, and honors his laws. His computer will also tell him who earth's rebels are!

How efficient are modern computers? *Computer Digest* states: "In one-half second, today's computers can debit 2,000 checks to 300 different bank accounts, or can examine 1,000 electrocardiograms, or score 150,000 answers on 3,000 exams or figure the company payroll for 1,000 employees." Amazing!

The Antichrist will most certainly use such a computer—and it will be fashioned in his own image.

Verse 16: *And he causeth all, both small and great, rich and poor, free and bond, to receive a mark in their right hand, or in their foreheads:*

Verse 17: *And that no man might buy or sell, save he that had the mark, or the name of the beast, or the number of his name.*

Verse 18: *Here is wisdom. Let him that hath understanding count the number of the beast: for it is the number of a man; and his number is Six hundred threescore and six.*

As we have seen, the Antichrist will undoubtedly use a computer to enslave earth's population during the Tribulation hour. Also we discover that he will effect and maintain this control through commerce—the buying and selling of products. In order to make his plan operable, the Antichrist will also introduce an international identification system in the form of a mark (possibly a laser tattoo) placed in the right hand or forehead of every individual participant. Without this mark, no man—*no man*—will be permitted to purchase or sell even the smallest item of merchandise.

According to verses 17 and 18, this identification

mark will be—or will include as a prefix—the digits "666." The use of "666" as a prefix appears most plausible, as this is the only way one person could be differentiated from another. If all numbers were identical, mass confusion would ensue. Therefore, prefixes preceding the "666" or using the "666" as the prefix code are essential for marketing purposes.

With specific reference to verse 18, one should be aware of the fact that there have always been, and always will be, individuals who claim to know the identity of the Antichrist. They take the number "666" and, through all kinds of mathematical formulations, attempt to come to a conclusion. Their efforts, however, can amount to no more than mere speculation because we cannot know who the Antichrist is until he arrives on the scene, and he cannot arrive until the Church is raptured. Still, God's Word admonishes the Christian to be wise (see Matthew 10:16) and watchful (see Matthew 24:42), especially as the day of Christ's return approaches (see Hebrews 10:25).

As shocking as the information presented in this chapter may seem, such a day is at hand. A cashless, checkless society is in the planning stages and a number of countries are already experimenting. To be sure, "It's later than you think!" The reign of the Antichrist is upon the horizon. This new Hitler, with a monstrous computer which will enslave millions, may soon control the earth. Unbeliever, *Seek ye the Lord while he may be found, call ye upon him while he is near* (Isaiah 55:6).

14

Chapter 14 deals with the seven visions, each complete in itself. They are not presented in a chronological sequence of events but rather panoramically with details following later. Let me illustrate this point. The pronouncement of doom upon Babylon, for instance, is uttered in verse 8. However, the details are presented in chapter 16, verses 17-21. With this point in mind, let's investigate.

Verse 1: *And I looked, and, lo, a Lamb stood on the mount Sion, and with him an hundred forty and four thousand, having his Father's name written in their foreheads.*

The Lamb, as we already know, is the Lord Jesus Christ. John the Baptist called Him by this name as he saw the Lord walking upon earth saying, *Behold the Lamb of God, which taketh away the sin of the world* (John 1:29). Also, John sees the Tribulation saints overcoming Satan *by the blood of the Lamb* (Revelation 12:11). This same Lamb and His bride are the honored participants at a marriage feast conducted in chapter 19, verse 7 which states: *Let us be glad and rejoice, and give honour to him: for the marriage of the Lamb is come, and his wife hath made herself ready*. The wedding occurs in heaven but the feast probably takes place on earth as the Lamb returns to Mount Sion (or Zion) for His millennial reign as King of kings and Lord of lords. This would fulfill scores of Old Testament prophecies.

Did you know that Zion, or Jerusalem, is the place God seems to love most? Today's anti-Zionists should take heed. They are opposing the Almighty himself as they rebel against His city and His people because—I repeat—Jerusalem is closest to God's heart. *For the Lord hath chosen Zion; he hath desired it for his habitation. This is my rest for ever: here will I dwell; for I have desired it* (Psalm 132:13,14). While the first verse of chapter 14 is the only place where Zion is mentioned in the Book of Revelation, it nevertheless authenticates an unlimited number of Old Testament passages that point to Jerusalem as the headquarters of Christ's earthly kingdom. Seemingly, God is saying through this text, "I know that millions are following the Antichrist. I see that the false prophet is scoring many victories as he, through lying wonders and deceits, turns the hearts of multitudes to the super-deceivers. However, 666 is the number of man. It is the number of incompleteness. It will soon end." Why? I have *set my king upon my holy hill of Zion* [or Jerusalem] (Psalm 2:6). God adds, "Though horrendous judgments are about to fall, look up! Your redemption draws nigh. My son, the Lamb, is about to come forth and take His proper position on earth as King of kings and Lord of lords. He shall soon arrive at Jerusalem."

The Prophet Zechariah also stated this same truth:

His feet shall stand in that day upon the mount of Olives, which is before Jerusalem on the east, and the mount of Olives shall cleave in the midst thereof toward the east and toward the west, and there shall be a very great valley; and half of the mountain shall remove toward the north, and half of it toward the south (Zechariah 14:4). Additional verses depict the establishment of Christ's earthly kingdom: *Beautiful for situation, the joy of the whole earth, is mount Zion...the city of the great King* (Psalm 48:2). *In Salem also is his tabernacle, and his dwelling place in Zion* [or Jerusalem] (Psalm 76:2). *Thou shalt arise, and have mercy upon Zion* [or Jerusalem] (Psalm 102:13). Psalm 110:2 pictures His reign and states: *The Lord shall send the rod of thy strength out of Zion: rule thou in the midst of thine enemies.* Again, *The Lord shall reign for ever, even thy God, O Zion, unto all generations. Praise ye the Lord* (Psalm 146:10). As He reigns, the people are pleased and cry, *Let Israel rejoice in him that made him: let the children of Zion be joyful in their King* (Psalm 149:2).

Isaiah the prophet predicted this time of peace. He said, *Out of Zion shall go forth the law, and the word of the Lord from Jerusalem. And he shall judge among the nations, and shall rebuke many people: and they shall beat their swords into plowshares, and their spears into pruninghooks: nation shall not lift up sword against nation, neither shall they learn war any more* (Isaiah 2:3,4).

Jesus Christ is coming soon to sit upon David's throne. How do I know this momentous event is about to occur? Because Jerusalem, where He will reign—captured by the Jews in 1967—became the eternal, undivided capital of Israel on July 31, 1980. And this is only the beginning. Soon Jerusalem will become the capital of the entire world—upon the arrival of the King of kings and Lord of lords, the Lord Jesus Christ. The way has been prepared in our day. Let's triumphantly shout the news, "The King is coming! Amen! The King is coming!" First, however, He must return for the Church (all Christians) so that we can return with Him (chapter 19, verse 14). Thus, the Rapture cannot be delayed much longer. Since we return with Him, and it is visibly manifest that we must return together soon, then the fact is clear that our remaining time upon earth is extremely limited.

At this point in our text, that time has come! How glorious is the hour of the Lord's return to Jerusalem—the capital of the world—with His people. Part of His entourage is composed of the 144,000 Jews mentioned in chapter 7. They have the Lamb's Father's name written (or inscribed) in their foreheads. This is a result of the sealing mentioned in chapter 7, verses 3 and 4.

Verse 2: *And I heard a voice from heaven, as the voice of many waters, and as the voice of a great thunder: and I heard the voice of harpers harping with their harps.*

What a majestic sound fills the heavens and the earth as the heavenly chorus, with the voice of many waters (an unusual amount of octaves), crescendos into thunder-like proportions. The multitudinous choir

is accompanied by harps—a symbol of joy. This joy
has to do with Christ's redemption.

Verse 3: *And they sung as it were a new song
before the throne, and before the four beasts, and the
elders: and no man could learn that song but the
hundred and forty and four thousand, which were
redeemed from the earth.*

The new song of these redeemed Jews is undoubtedly similar to the song of the saints presented
in chapter 5, verse 9: *And they* [sang] *a new song,
saying, Thou art worthy to take the book, and to open
the seals thereof: for thou wast slain, and hast redeemed us to God by thy blood out of every kindred,
and tongue, and people, and nation.* Still, the song of
the 144,000 differs somewhat in that it is exclusively
their own. The point is that the redeemed in every
dispensation have something about which they can
sing—the joy of the Lord. The purity, holiness, and
sanctification of this group are described in the next
verse.

Verse 4: *These are they which were not defiled
with women; for they are virgins. These are they
which follow the Lamb whithersoever he goeth. These
were redeemed from among men, being the firstfruits
unto God and to the Lamb.*

Some commentators, particularly priests in the
Middle Ages, stated that this honor was reserved for
them because they had refrained from sexual inter-
course. Such an explanation, however, is impossible
in the light of the sanctity of marriage, for *marriage is
honourable in all, and the bed undefiled* (Hebrews
13:4). That is why, *whoso findeth a wife findeth a*

good thing, and obtaineth favour of the Lord (Proverbs 18:22). The meaning, then, has to do with the undefiled walk of the redeemed Jews as stated in the next part of the verse: *These are they which follow the Lamb whithersoever he goeth.* They are free from spiritual fornication as described in James 4:4 which states: *Ye adulterers and adulteresses, know ye not that the friendship of the world is enmity with God? whosoever therefore will be a friend of the world is the enemy of God.*

Idolatry, the ultimate form of spiritual adultery, is the sin of the hour during the Tribulation period, as we have already observed in chapters 9 and 13. Yet, even during such a time as this, there are multitudes who remain true to the Lord. I dogmatically believe that the "undefiled" of verse 4 are those who have kept themselves unspotted from the world. This truth is also pictured in 2 Corinthians 11:2 concerning the Church, the bride of Christ: God says, *I am jealous over you with godly jealousy: for I have espoused you to one husband, that I may present you as a chaste virgin to Christ.* Both Christ and His Father want pure sweethearts.

The Jewish virgins in our text are most likely those referenced in Matthew 25:1-13 (the parable of the wise and foolish virgins). In all dispensations, God wants His people to be separate from the world, the flesh, and the devil. *Be ye not unequally yoked together with unbelievers: for what fellowship hath righteousness with unrighteousness? and what communion hath light with darkness? And what concord hath Christ with Belial? or what part hath he that believeth with an infidel? And what agreement hath the temple of God with idols? for ye are the temple of the living God; as God hath said, I will dwell in them, and walk in them; and I will be their God, and they shall be my people. Wherefore come out from among them, and be ye separate, saith the Lord, and touch not the unclean thing; and I will receive you, And will be a Father unto you, and ye shall be my sons and daughters, saith the Lord Almighty* (2 Corinthians 6:14-18).

These untainted Jews who walked the pathway of holiness are the firstfruits of the Tribulation period. The harvest is to follow as millions more turn to Messiah. *And so all Israel shall be saved: as it is written, There shall come out of Sion the Deliverer, and shall turn away ungodliness from Jacob: For this is my covenant unto them, when I shall take away their sins* (Romans 11:26,27).

Another attribute of the 144,000 Jews is mentioned in the next verse.

Verse 5: *And in their mouth was found no guile: for they are without fault before the throne of God.*

God hates the sin of lying. In fact, the Bible lists lying as one of the sins that will keep a man out of heaven (see Revelation 22:15). The Tribulation hour, under the Antichrist, produces a world inundated with deceit. The Antichrist works *lying wonders* (2 Thessalonians 2:9), and multitudes *believe a lie* (2 Thessalonians 2:11). Even during this age of fraud, however, the redeemed Jews do not follow Satan, who *is a liar, and the father of* [lies] (John 8:44). Oh, that there were more believers who never used deceit, who never passed rumors (usually exaggerated lies), and who refused to listen to the lies that Satan, *the accuser of* [the] *brethren*, hatches! God wants holy people in every dispensation of time. Let's be like Jesus *who did no sin, neither was guile found in his mouth* (1 Peter 2:22).

Verse 6: *And I saw another angel fly in the midst of heaven, having the everlasting gospel to preach unto them that dwell on the earth, and to every nation, and kindred, and tongue, and people.*

This verse introduces us to the first of the angels who proclaim a special message to the world. What is this everlasting gospel the angel preaches? The word *gospel* simply means "good news." It is also called *glad tidings* (Luke 1:19), *good tidings* (Luke 2:10), and *good tidings* once again (1 Thessalonians 3:6). This good news always includes the message of the blood in every dispensation. *To* [Christ] *give all the prophets witness, that through his name whosoever believeth in him shall receive remission of sins* (Acts 10:43), and remission of sins is through the blood, for *without shedding of blood is no remission* (Hebrews 9:22).

In addition to proclaiming the everlasting gospel, the angel announces that all those who have rejected the message of Jesus for the mark of the Antichrist (666) are about to be bombarded with a series of judgments from God himself.

Verse 7: [The angel said] *with a loud voice, Fear God, and give glory to him; for the hour of his judgment is come: and worship him that made heav-*

en, and earth, and the sea, and the fountains of waters.

The angel's message is God's final call to a Christ-rejecting world, and the message is "turn or burn; repent or die. This is mankind's last opportunity to receive Jesus Christ as Messiah, as Lord, yea, as the true God."

Verse 8: *And there followed another angel, saying, Babylon is fallen, is fallen, that great city, because she made all nations drink of the wine of the wrath of her fornication.*

Here we learn of the impending judgment to be unleashed upon religious and political Babylon in chapters 17 and 18. We will deal with the fulfillment of these predictions, plus the fact that all nations are made to drink of the wine of the wrath of her fornication, when we reach those sections. For the present, suffice it to say that the abominable portrait before us typifies a one-world church united to a one-world political system using every type of corruption imaginable to promote herself into prominence at the end time. Beware! The present ecumenical effort, attempting to unite all religions under a so-called "banner of brotherhood," regardless of one's belief about Christ, is the forerunner of a monstrous fornicator who makes all nations drink of the wine of her wrath.

Verse 9: *And the third angel followed them, saying with a loud voice, If any man worship the beast and his image, and receive his mark in his forehead, or in his hand,*

Verse 10: *The same shall drink of the wine of the wrath of God, which is poured out without mix-*

197

ture into the cup of his indignation; and he shall be tormented with fire and brimstone in the presence of the holy angels, and in the presence of the Lamb:

Verse 11: And the smoke of their torment ascendeth up for ever and ever: and they have no rest day nor night, who worship the beast and his image, and whosoever receiveth the mark of his name.

This third angel announces the doom of those who are worshipping the Antichrist and his image, and who have received the mark "666" in their foreheads or hands. For the weak-kneed sisters of Christendom who claim that "the God of love could never punish sinners," verses 9 through 11 are probably the Bible's most graphic picture of judgment. Although the text before us is self-explanatory, I feel it prudent to practically state the same truths twice, in order that mockers may see that there is a judgment of hellfire taught in this book, as well as throughout the Bible. Those individuals who have received the mark of the beast taste of the *wine of the wrath of God, which is poured out without mixture* [without dilution or weakening of his wrath as it is stirred up] *into the cup of his indignation.* The judgment is so horrendous as it is administered in the presence of Christ and his angels that *the smoke of* [the Antichrist's partners and pawns] *ascendeth up for ever and ever: and they have no rest day nor night, who worship the beast and his image, and whosoever receiveth the mark of his name.*

Contrary to the teaching of certain cultists, this judgment is also endless. The words *everlasting* for the lost and *eternal* for the saved are identical in the Greek, both places—heaven and hell—last for the ages of ages—eternally, everlastingly. Thus, Matthew 25:46 states: [The lost] *shall go away into everlasting punishment: but the righteous into life eternal.* I repeat, both are of equal duration.

Some may raise an objection that this punishment cannot be eternal because of the words "day and night." Nonsense! The apocalypse, or Book of Revelation, constantly uses this terminology in place of "unceasingly." For example, in chapter 4, verse 8, the four living creatures before the throne of God *rest not day and night, saying, Holy, holy, holy, Lord God Almighty, which was, and is, and is to come.* Isaiah declared this truth in chapter 66, verse 24, *For their worm shall not die, neither shall their fire be quenched.* Jesus himself had this text in mind when He said in Mark 9:43, *And if thy hand offend thee, cut it off: it is better for thee to enter into life maimed, than having two hands to go into hell, into the fire that never shall be quenched.*

The most terrible experience of time and eternity is to be lost. My wife, Rexella, sings a song that creates a soul-winner's heart within those who hear it. The chorus states:

Think what it means to be lost forever,
  No one to guide you across that cold river.
Darkness, crying, none to deliver,
  Think what it means to be lost.

Thank God, this awesome portrait does not have to be the future of any human being, for Romans 10:13 victoriously announces that *whosoever shall call upon the name of the Lord shall be saved.* Don't delay making life's most important decision.

Now, the subject of fire also causes us to recall that time during the Tribulation hour when one-third of the earth's population is reduced by fire, smoke, and brimstone (chapter 9, verse 18). Possessing a foreknowledge of all these events, and knowing that earthly sorrows can last only as long as one has life, the Holy Spirit, through John, gives an assuring promise about the future.

Verse 12: *Here is the patience of the saints: here are they that keep the commandments of God, and the faith of Jesus.*

Verse 13: *And I heard a voice from heaven saying unto me, Write, Blessed are the dead which die in the Lord from henceforth: Yea, saith the Spirit, that they may rest from their labours; and their works do follow them.*

This will be especially true during the Tribulation hour when the toils of life are so great. Remember, this is the worst time of heartache in history. Jesus said, *For then shall be great tribulation, such as was not since the beginning of the world to this time, no, nor ever shall be* (Matthew 24:21). Now, at last, it is over for some. They have died and happiness is theirs. They rest from the heartbreaks of life, exchanging them for rewards as their good works and deeds follow them.

Verse 14: *And I looked, and behold a white cloud, and upon the cloud one sat like unto the Son of man, having on his head a golden crown, and in his hand a sharp sickle.*

A white cloud—the Shekinah or "glory of God" cloud—is usually associated with Christ. This is the same cloud that went before the Children of Israel as they wandered through the wilderness (Exodus 13:21,22). It was also present at the giving of the Law (Exodus 19:9). This glorious cloud illuminated the transfiguration scene (Matthew 17:5) and *received [Christ] out of their sight* at His ascension (Acts 1:9). At the Rapture, all church-age saints, living and dead, will *be caught up together...in the clouds* (1 Thessalonians 4:17). Finally, when the Lord Jesus Christ returns to planet earth, *he cometh with clouds* (Revelation 1:7). Thus, in verse 14 of this chapter the Son of Man is seen situated upon the cloud as He comes to thrust in His sharp sickle of judgment.

Verse 15: *And another angel came out of the temple, crying with a loud voice to him that sat on the cloud, Thrust in thy sickle, and reap: for the time is come for thee to reap; for the harvest of the earth is ripe.*

Verse 16: *And he that sat on the cloud thrust in his sickle on the earth; and the earth was reaped.*

One cannot get away with sin forever: *Be sure your sin will find you out* (Numbers 32:23). Sin will catch up with you, and when it does, *they that plow iniquity, and sow wickedness, reap the same* (Job 4:8). The time of reaping has come, and the sickle, sharp and steady, does its judgmental work. Verses 17-20 describe this hour as the greatest bloodbath in history.

Verse 17: *And another angel came out of the temple which is in heaven, he also having a sharp sickle.*

Verse 18: *And another angel came out from*

the altar, which had power over fire; and cried with a loud cry to him that had the sharp sickle, saying, Thrust in thy sharp sickle, and gather the clusters of the vine of the earth; for her grapes are fully ripe.

Verse 19: *And the angel thrust in his sickle into the earth, and gathered the vine of the earth, and cast it into the great winepress of the wrath of God.*

Verse 20: *And the winepress was trodden without the city, and blood came out of the winepress, even unto the horse bridles, by the space of a thousand and six hundred furlongs.*

This final scene of Revelation 14 describes the work of two angels. The one with a sharp sickle comes from the temple in heaven, while the other with power over fire emerges from the altar. The one in command is the angel from the altar. He immediately orders that the vine be cut off and cast into the great winepress of the wrath of God. Since true children of God are branches of the vine (see John 15:5), the members of the one-world church of the Antichrist and false prophet are called members of Satan's vine. The time of their pruning or destruction has arrived at last, and they are cut off and cast into the great winepress of God's indignation.

Oh, what a purging of branches takes place during this hour! The conflict begins in the Valley of Jehoshaphat and becomes centered in the Valley of Jezreel, which is on the plain of Esdraelon near the hill of Megiddo (chapter 16, verse 16). *I will also gather all nations, and will bring them down into the valley of Jehoshaphat, and will plead with them there for my people and for my heritage Israel, whom they have scattered among the nations, and parted my land. Beat your plowshares into swords, and your pruninghooks into spears: let the weak say, I am strong. Assemble yourselves, and come, all ye heathen, and gather yourselves together round about: thither cause thy mighty ones to come down, O Lord. Let the heathen be wakened, and come up to the valley of Jehoshaphat: for there will I sit to judge all the heathen round about. Put ye in the sickle, for the harvest is ripe: come, get you down: for the press is full, the vats overflow; for their wickedness is great. Multitudes, multitudes in the valley of decision: for the day of the Lord is near in the valley of decision* (Joel 3:2,10-14). Eventually the battle encompasses the entire nation of Israel and is, of course, global in involvement as the armies of the world meet in the Middle East for the final holocaust of history—the Battle of Armageddon (see Zechariah 14:2).

The result is a 200-mile-long area soaked with blood, (one thousand six hundred furlongs, in American mathematics, is a distance of 200 miles.) Interestingly, the nation of Israel is 200 miles long, from north to south. According to Ezekiel 39:8-16, seven months will be required to bury the dead and the armaments of war will be burned for seven years afterward! The tense Middle East situation certainly signals the return of Christ.

In light of the unprecedented devastation just described, a few additional thoughts are appropriate at this time. First of all, when the Soviet Union, under the names Gog, Magog, Mechech, Tubal, and Rosh, invades Israel, the largest armies in the history of the world will converge on the Middle East. Ezekiel states that they will come up like a cloud (see Ezekiel 38:16). John tells us that *the number of the army of the horsemen* [is] *two hundred thousand thousand—* or two hundred million (chapter 9, verse 16). No wonder the conflict is so incredible.

Secondly, the weapons are the deadliest ever used in the history of mankind. *A fire goeth before him* (Psalm 97:3). *For, behold, the Lord will come with fire* (Isaiah 66:15). *The flaming flame shall not be quenched* (Ezekiel 20:47). *A fire devoureth before them* (Joel 2:3). Who? The northern army from Russia that is driven back to Siberia. Hear God's statement: *But I will remove far off from you the northern army, and will drive him into a land barren and desolate, with his face toward the east sea, and his hinder part toward the utmost sea, and his stink shall come up, and his ill savour shall come up, because he hath done great things* (Joel 2:20).

The retreat is effectual in Joel 2:30, for the prophet states: *And I* [saw] *wonders in the heavens and in the earth, blood, and fire, and pillars* [or literally columns] *of smoke*. These are the exact characteristics of a nuclear blast! *The whole land shall be devoured by the fire of his jealousy* (Zephaniah 1:18). *For, behold, the day cometh, that shall burn as an oven* (Malachi 4:1). Now we understand why the nation of Israel will be drenched with blood. No wonder Jeremiah 30:7 says, *Alas! for that day is great, so that none is like it*. Daniel 12:1 adds, *There shall be a time of trouble, such as never was*. This time is so horrendous that there will never have been anything like it in the past nor shall there be anything like it again in the future. Jesus agreed. He said in Matthew 24:21, *For then shall be great tribulation, such as was not since the beginning of the world to this time, no, nor ever shall be.* Revelation 9:18 adds, *By these three was the third part of men killed, by the fire, and by the smoke, and by the brimstone, which issued out of their mouths.*

Finally Russia is going to be smashed in the Middle East. Proof: *Therefore, thou son of man, prophesy against Gog, and say, Thus saith the Lord God; Behold, I am against thee, O Gog, the chief prince of Meshech and Tubal: And I will turn thee back, and leave but the sixth part of thee* (Ezekiel 39:1,2). Later, the Battle of Armageddon will be fought and will assuredly become history's most terrifying holocaust. However, the good news is that, as a Christian, you will not be present—and if you are not yet a believer, you do not have to be present. So I plead with you to receive Christ without delay.

15

Chapter 15 is a preparatory portion of Scripture. Its eight verses serve as an introduction to the seven vial or bowl judgments described in chapter 16.

Let's investigate.

Verse 1: *And I saw another sign in heaven, great and marvellous, seven angels having the seven last plagues; for in them is filled up the wrath of God.*

The sign John now views in heaven is awe-inspiring. Seven angels—possibly the seven angels or messengers of the seven churches mentioned in chapters 2 and 3—are about to pour out the final seven plagues upon earth. This is the completion of God's judgment when His wrath is unleashed against rebellious mankind.

Verse 2: *And I saw as it were a sea of glass mingled with fire: and them that had gotten the victory over the beast, and over his image, and over his mark, and over the number of his name, stand on the sea of glass, having the harps of God.*

As explained in chapter 4, verse 6, the *sea of glass* speaks of tranquillity. It is calm and stable, and typifies: (1) the Church at rest, or (2) God's living Word. Solomon's Temple contained a sea of glass, depicting the Word of God, as a means of sanctification. Notice that the sea of glass in our text is mixed with fire. This is a beautiful picture of believers standing firmly for Christ under the test of fire, having their feet planted on the Word of God. The Apostle Peter speaks of this matter when he says, *That the trial of your faith, being much more precious than of gold that perisheth, though it be tried with fire, might be found unto praise and honour and glory at the appearing of Jesus Christ* (1 Peter 1:7). Thus, there is no doubt whatsoever that the Tribulation saints enjoy victory over the beast, his image, his mark and the number of his name (666) by the Word of God and prayer. They died for the name of Jesus and are conquerors because of death. Had they remained alive by accepting the beast and his number, they would have been losers. Instead, they are victors, because to die in Christ is gain (see Philippians 1:21). This is why they stand upon the sea of glass—a picture of the Word of God—and are also serenaded and soothed by heaven's harpists.

Verse 3: *And they sing the song of Moses the servant of God, and the song of the Lamb, saying, Great and marvellous are thy works, Lord God Almighty; just and true are thy ways, thou King of saints.*

Verse 4: *Who shall not fear thee, O Lord, and glorify thy name? for thou only art holy: for all nations shall come and worship before thee; for thy judgments are made manifest.*

This group, saved out of the Tribulation, sings the song of Moses. The meaning? Back to Exodus,

208

chapter 14. Moses and his people were being hotly pursued by Pharaoh and his armies. Finally the Israelites arrived at the Red Sea. There God parted the waters so that His people could cross over on dry land. As Pharaoh's military geniuses followed, the waters closed in upon them, and they died. The Israelites, realizing the protection of God on their behalf in sparing them from the Egyptian ruler—a type of the Antichrist—began to sing a song of worship, praise, and adoration to Jehovah: *The horse and his rider hath he thrown into the sea* (Exodus 15:1). Now, centuries later, redeemed Jews who through death left earth's Tribulation miseries behind, sing the song of Moses and the Lamb. This does not mean they use the same lyrics as the people of Moses' day, but rather that they—as Jews—identify with Moses, the great Jewish leader. They belong to Moses, nationally and to the Lord Jesus Christ, spiritually, for their song is also about the Lamb. The words are *Great and marvellous are thy works, Lord God Almighty; just and true are thy ways, thou King of saints.*

Verse 4 reflects the attributes of the King of the nations during the Millennium. Then He is revered because the world fears and glorifies His name. Also, in homage and respect to His holiness and His mighty acts of judgment and subjugation, all nations come to worship in His presence. This is in harmony with Isaiah 2:2 and 3: *And it shall come to pass in the last days, that the mountain of the Lord's house shall be established in the top of the mountains, and shall be exalted above the hills; and all nations shall flow unto it. And many people shall go and say, Come ye, and let us go up to the mountain of the Lord, to the house of the God of Jacob; and he will teach us of his ways, and we will walk in his paths: for out of Zion shall go forth the law, and the word of the Lord from Jerusalem.*

Zechariah agrees in chapter 14, verses 16 and 17: *And it shall come to pass, that every one that is left of all the nations which came against Jerusalem shall even go up from year to year to worship the King, the Lord of hosts, and to keep the feast of tabernacles. And it shall be, that whoso will not come up of all the families of the earth unto Jerusalem to worship the King, the Lord of hosts, even upon them shall be no rain.*

Verse 5: *And after that I looked, and, behold, the temple of the tabernacle of the testimony in heaven was opened:*

The Ark of the Testimony was kept in the Temple or the Tabernacle or the Holy of Holies. Under Moses, it was concealed from the eyes of the people. Its mysteries were beyond them. That day is now finally over. The way of the Holiest is open to all, including the Tribulation saints. Now they may view His workings, because they have access to His abiding place.

Verse 6: *And the seven angels came out of the temple, having the seven plagues, clothed in pure and white linen, and having their breasts girded with golden girdles.*

The sight of the seven angels coming out of the Temple is breathtaking and frightening. In the earthly Tabernacle and Temple, men were not allowed entrance. Even the high priest could go in but once each year, and then only after rigid ceremonial standards had been observed. The angels, however, have been admitted because they are created beings of holiness to administer the upcoming bowl judgments. The pure and white linen and golden girdles worn by these angels are the same items of clothing worn by Old Testament priests. In other words, angel-priests are about to judge the world from the place where God's Law rests—the Holy of Holies. This judgment is necessary because mankind has desecrated God's laws globally. The fact that there are seven angels— the number of perfection and completeness—proves that no stone will be left unturned as they execute their seven judgments upon planet earth. Hence, as they leave the Temple, they are given their bowls or vials of judgment.

Verse 7: *And one of the four beasts gave unto the seven angels seven golden vials full of the wrath of God, who liveth for ever and ever.*

Verse 8: *And the temple was filled with smoke from the glory of God, and from his power; and no man was able to enter into the temple, till the seven plagues of the seven angels were fulfilled.*

In concluding this chapter, verse 8 conclusively proves that the Temple area is sealed to angels and men during the final forty-two months of the Tribulation hour. God's throne, which symbolizes mercy and love, is shut to the public until the period of judgment ends. This, of course, is during the outpouring of the seven bowls of unprecedented judgment. When God's judgment has been completed, men may then again approach the Mercy Seat. Until that time, however, all is hazy and dark because of the smoke which fills the Temple.

16

The information presented in the following twenty-one verses should cause all men to examine their relationship with the Almighty God. The events we are about to observe are both awesome and terrifying. In fact, the only consolation for the believer is that he will not be present when the forthcoming scenario actually takes place. By the time our study is concluded, we will understand and appreciate more than ever before the words of the Apostle Paul in Titus 2:13: *Looking for that blessed hope, and the glorious appearing of the great God and our Saviour Jesus Christ.* The final seven judgments of the Tribulation hour are about to begin.

Verse 1: *And I heard a great voice out of the temple saying to the seven angels, Go your ways, and pour out the vials of the wrath of God upon the earth.*

The voice of Almighty God issues forth from the smoke-filled Temple, directing the angels to carry out their duties. Remember, God himself is sending forth these judgments. His holiness has been offended. Mankind has worshiped a man—the Antichrist, the devil in human skin—even bowing to his image, *the abomination of desolation* (Matthew 24:15). The true and eternal God is justly angry. He cannot allow this iniquity to go unjudged.

In Isaiah 42:8 Jehovah says, *I am the Lord: that is my name: and my glory will I not give to another, neither my praise to graven images.* Again, in Exodus 20:4-6: *Thou shalt not make unto thee any graven image, or any likeness of any thing that is in heaven above, or that is in the earth beneath, or that is in the water under the earth: Thou shalt not bow down thyself to them, nor serve them: for I the Lord thy God am a jealous God, visiting the iniquity of the fathers upon the children unto the third and fourth generation of them that hate me; And showing mercy unto thousands of them that love me, and keep my commandments.* Because mankind, *en masse*, has grossly violated this commandment during the Tribulation period, the promised judgment must begin.

First bowl judgment

Verse 2: *The first* [angel] *went, and poured out his vial upon the earth; and there fell a noisome and grievous sore upon the men which had the mark of the beast, and upon them which worshipped his image.*

What a scene, as the first bowl is poured out and men become covered with ulcerated sores! They had the mark of the beast (666), and now they have the mark of God—ulcers. These festering infections probably obscure the beast's number.

Can this verse be taken literally? The plague is similar to one of past history: *And the Lord said unto Moses and unto Aaron, Take to you handfuls of ashes of the furnace, and let Moses sprinkle it toward the heaven in the sight of Pharaoh. And it shall become small dust in all the land of Egypt, and shall be a boil breaking forth with blains* [ulcerated sores] *upon man, and upon beast, throughout all the land of Egypt. And they took ashes of the furnace, and stood before Pharaoh; and Moses sprinkled it up toward heaven; and it became a boil breaking forth with blains upon man, and upon beast. And the magicians could not stand before Moses because of the boils; for the boil was upon the magicians, and upon all the Egyptians* (Exodus 9:8-11). What a terrible price men pay for not believing God!

Second bowl judgment

Verse 3: *And the second angel poured out his vial upon the sea; and it became as the blood of a dead man: and every living soul died in the sea.*

Again history records a time when the waters turned to blood: *Thus saith the Lord, In this thou shalt know that I am the Lord: behold, I will smite with the rod that is in mine hand upon the waters which are in the river, and they shall be turned to blood. And the fish that is in the river shall die, and the river shall stink; and the Egyptians shall loathe to drink of the water of the river. And the Lord spake unto Moses, Say unto Aaron, Take thy rod, and stretch out thine hand upon the waters of Egypt, upon their streams, upon their rivers, and upon their ponds, and upon all their pools of water, that they may become blood; and that there may be blood throughout all the land of Egypt, both in vessels of wood, and in vessels of stone. And Moses and Aaron did so, as the Lord*

215

commanded; and he lifted up the rod, and smote the waters that were in the river, in the sight of Pharaoh, and in the sight of his servants; and all the waters that were in the river were turned to blood. And the fish that was in the river died; and the river stank, and the Egyptians could not drink of the water of the river; and there was blood throughout all the land of Egypt (Exodus 7:17-21). If God did it once, He can certainly do it again. He is the omnipotent, all-powerful God. His promises never fail.

Pausing momentarily to review our studies, we recall that the second seal (chapter 6:3,4) brought great bloodshed upon earth and the second trumpet blast (chapter 8:8) caused a third part of the sea to become blood. In the verse presently under study, every sea creature perishes when the water is turned to blood. The result is an unbearable stench throughout the entire world as these organisms decease and decay. Think of it! That which always symbolized life—*the life of the flesh is in the blood* (Leviticus 17:11)—and symbolized salvation—*the blood of Jesus Christ* [God's] *Son cleanseth us from all sin* (1 John 1:7)—now becomes a symbol of condemnation and death. Wait! There is more. The third vial extends the destruction to all bodies of water internationally.

Third bowl judgment

Verse 4: *And the third angel poured out his vial upon the rivers and fountains of waters; and they became blood.*

Verse 5: *And I heard the angel of the waters say,*

Thou art righteous, O Lord, which art, and wast, and shalt be, because thou hast judged thus.

Verse 6: *For they have shed the blood of saints and prophets, and thou hast given them blood to drink; for they are worthy.*

Verse 7: *And I heard another out of the altar say, Even so, Lord God Almighty, true and righteous are thy judgments.*

By this time, one may have been tempted to believe that God is not just. To the contrary, God is always equitable, fair, and righteous in His dealings with men. Genesis 18:25 declares, *Shall not the Judge of all the earth do right?* No man has all the facts in his possession. Thus, he must wait until he meets God face to face. Then and only then will he be able to make unbiased decisions.

Notice that angelic beings have different responsibilities upon earth. In our text, we see the angel of (or over) the waters justifying God's actions by saying, *Thou art righteous, O Lord* [the eternal one] *...because* [of thy judgments]. In effect, the angel is saying, "The wicked beast worshipers who shed the blood of so many of Your saints and prophets may not satisfy their insatiable desire for blood by drinking it to their heart's content. They deserve what has happened to them. You have answered the prayers of Your saints under the altar" (chapter 6). As this message of vindication to the Almighty is concluded, a voice from the altar replies, "Even so," or "Amen." Justice prevails. God's judgments are true and righteous.

Fourth bowl judgment

Verse 8: *And the fourth angel poured out his vial upon the sun; and power was given unto him to scorch men with fire.*

Verse 9: *And men were scorched with great heat, and blasphemed the name of God, which hath power over these plagues: and they repented not to give him glory.*

The inhabitants of planet earth now experience the greatest heat wave in history. Many of us remember what happened in the south during the summer of 1980. Crops were parched and great numbers of people died as temperatures consistently soared over 100 degrees. Now we see what happens when the sun is out of control. Isaiah predicted this period of time in chapter 24, verses 4-6: *The earth mourneth and fadeth away, the world languisheth and fadeth away, the haughty people of the earth do languish. The earth also is defiled under the inhabitants thereof; because they have transgressed the laws, changed the ordinance, broken the everlasting covenant. Therefore hath the curse devoured the earth, and they that dwell therein are desolate: therefore the inhabitants of the earth are burned, and few men left.*

The earth becomes so drastically hot during this judgment that God has to alleviate the suffering by shortening the daylight hours. Jesus said in Matthew 24:22, *And except those days should be shortened, there should no flesh be saved: but for the elect's sake those days shall be shortened.* What did He mean? Many scholars have proposed the idea of the Tribulation period being abbreviated, but this is an impossibility because God's predestined program for the Tribulation totals seven years—or eighty-four months, or exactly 2,520 days. Since the scheduled timetable is already prophesied, not one day can be cut from the program. Verse 2 of chapter 11 mentions 1,260 days as one half of this period and no one can change God's plan. Therefore, we must find another explanation.

Is there a solution? Definitely! God shortens the daylight hours and lengthens the night seasons to keep millions alive. He accomplishes this by darkening the sun, as predicted by His Son, the Lord Jesus Christ: *Immediately after the tribulation of those days shall the sun be darkened* (Matthew 24:29). This statement harmonizes with Revelation 6:12: *And I beheld when he had opened the sixth seal, and, lo, there was a great earthquake; and the sun became black as sackcloth of hair.* God's method of shortening the daylight hours hinders the sun's death purge of earth's inhabitants by reducing the amount of ultraviolet rays bombarding the planet. This act of mercy is for His people, the saved Tribulation saints, for He adds in Matthew 24:22, *But for the elect's sake those days shall be shortened.*

Once again we need to remember that the Church, the elect bride of Christ composed of all those who were born again prior to the Rapture (chapter 4, verse 1), is at home in glory during this time. The earthly group of Tribulation saints presently being discussed constitutes the election of Romans 11:28. They are also referred to as Jacobites, or Israelites, in Romans 11:26. These are Jews. They are not members of the bride of Christ, but rather members of the wife of Jehovah.

Mankind's reaction to the scorching with fire takes the form of further rebellion. Instead of repenting and appealing to God who has power to stay the plague (verse 9), the people aim a barrage of four-letter blasphemies at the Almighty. The human heart is exceedingly wicked and callous (see Jeremiah 17:9). Even in the face of such agonizing judgment, repentance, restitution, and reconciliation are the farthest things from men's minds. Truly, they are hardened sinners.

Fifth bowl judgment

Verse 10: *And the fifth angel poured out his vial upon the seat of the beast; and his kingdom was full of darkness; and they gnawed their tongues for pain,*

Verse 11: *And blasphemed the God of heaven because of their pains and their sores, and repented not of their deeds.*

Whereas the fourth judgment produced unusual brightness through the scorching rays of the sun, the fifth bowl unleashes darkness upon the very throne of the Antichrist and throughout his empire. This could certainly be related to the shortening of the days and lengthening of the nights, as already described. Whatever the darkness is, we take it to be literal as was the Egyptian plague described in Exodus 10:21-23: *And the Lord said unto Moses, Stretch out thine hand toward heaven, that there may be darkness over the land of Egypt, even darkness which may be felt. And Moses stretched forth his hand toward heaven; and there was a thick darkness in all the land of Egypt three days: They saw not one another, neither rose any from his place for three days: but all the children of Israel had light in their dwellings.*

What a thrilling moment for the saints on earth! They see the satanically-controlled or devil-incarnated leader humiliated internationally as the power of God is unleashed upon his seat of government. This scene is equated with the "the day of the Lord." *The day of the Lord is darkness, and not light* (Amos 5:18). *Let all the inhabitants of the land tremble: for the day of the Lord cometh, for it is nigh at hand; A day of darkness and of gloominess, a day of clouds and of thick darkness, as the morning spread upon the mountains: a great people and a strong; there hath not been ever the like* [militarily], *neither shall be any more after it, even to the years of many generations* (Joel 2:1,2).

Who is the military colossus that produces such darkness and gloominess in the last days? Russia! *But I will remove far off from you the northern army, and will drive him into a land barren and desolate, with his face toward the east sea, and his hinder part toward the utmost sea, and his stink shall come up, and his ill savour shall come up, because he hath done great* [frightful] *things* (Joel 2:20). The only nation in the world north of Israel with a barren area and two oceans surrounding it is the Soviet Union. This is the same nation that comes against Israel from the north in Ezekiel 38:15 and is known by the names Magog, Meshech, Tubal, and Rosh. How near it all appears!

221

In our text, the Day of the Lord has arrived. The wicked gnaw their tongues for pain, but continue blaspheming the God of heaven. Apparently, no amount of punishment for sin can change some people. They repented not. Don't let it happen to you!

Sixth bowl judgment

Verse 12: *And the sixth angel poured out his vial upon the great river Euphrates; and the water thereof was dried up, that the way of the kings of the east might be prepared.*

Verse 13: *And I saw three unclean spirits like frogs come out of the mouth of the dragon, and out of the mouth of the beast, and out of the mouth of the false prophet.*

Verse 14: *For they are the spirits of devils, working miracles, which go forth unto the kings of the earth and of the whole world, to gather them to the battle of that great day of God Almighty.*

Verse 15: *Behold, I come as a thief. Blessed is he that watcheth, and keepeth his garments, lest he walk naked, and they see his shame.*

Verse 16: *And he gathered them together into a place called in the Hebrew tongue Armageddon.*

The sixth trumpet judgment should be recalled in the light of the sixth tipped bowl. There is a striking similarity. Chapter 9, verses 13-18, depicts the sixth angel voicing his commands. As he does, four angels are loosed from the great river Euphrates—the area of present-day Iran, Iraq, and Syria. Wow! A total of two hundred million troops (9:16) appear in the Middle East from the Orient. This has to be the largest assemblage of military men in the annals of history!

In the text before us (16:12), we witness a miraculous drying up of the Euphrates River in order that the kings of the east might cross over unhindered. The word *kings* pictures the leaders of troops. They cross the Euphrates in order to participate in the greatest Mid-East confrontation ever—the Battle of Armageddon! Actually, the conflict is a fight against the Lord and His hosts and will be discussed in detail when we arrive at its explanation point—chapter 19, verses 11-16. Upon their arrival in the Holy Land, these oriental kings or rulers join with the leaders of other nations for the war of wars as predicted in Psalm 2:2-4: *The kings of the earth set themselves, and the rulers take counsel together, against the Lord, and against his anointed, saying, Let us break their bands asunder, and cast away their cords from us. He that sitteth in the heavens shall laugh: the Lord shall have them in derision.*

How near is Armageddon? Bear in mind that both chapters 9 and 16 mention the Euphrates River as a focal point in this war. Keep your eyes on the Mid-East—especially Iran, Iraq, and Syria—in the days ahead. The Euphrates was jointly theirs when these nations were called Persia. Thus, Iran, Iraq, and Syria are a prominent identification point for the end-time war.

Between the sixth and seventh seal and trumpet judgments, we encountered parenthetical utterances. Now we find another parenthesis between the sixth and seventh bowl judgments. This we shall consider from verses 13-16, already quoted.

Verse 13 reveals three unclean spirits like frogs coming out of the mouths of (1) the dragon (Satan), (2) the beast (Antichrist), and (3) the false prophet (head of the world church). What we see, then, is an unholy trinity controlled by the power of evil spirits in an age of occultism, as explained in chapter 9, verses 20 and 21. The symbolism of frogs (for the text says "like frogs") speaks of uncleanness. The plague of frogs in Egypt produced an obnoxious stench that filled the land with indescribable odors and filth (see Exodus 8:14). Thus, the picture is clear. The counterfeit trinity—the devil, the Antichrist, and the false prophet—produce supernatural miracles through the power of the devil and his demonic spirits, thus convincing the kings of the earth that these men are gods. Because of it, the kings willingly follow them to the Middle East for the great day of God Almighty, which is Armageddon. The entire situation reeks in God's nostrils.

Verse 15 is a pause or lull before the storm. God says He will come as a thief. This again proves that the Church is not present, for that day shall not overtake believers as a thief (see 1 Thessalonians 5:4). The words of verse 15, then, constitute a final admonition to the Tribulation saints, telling them to watch for His coming and to continue walking in pathways of holiness. The terms *watcheth* and *garments* refer to slothfulness and carelessness, spiritually speaking. Let's prove this. In Christ's day, a one-piece garment was removed at bedtime. It was worn only during waking hours. Here the Lord tells the final group or gleaning of Tribulation saints to watch, for in so doing they will be awake and clothed. The command is to be prepared. Preparation voids their being found naked and ashamed.

The same is true for believers today. When Jesus comes, multitudes will stand at the Judgment Seat naked (without rewards) and ashamed, because they were not watching. Heed the warning of 1 John 2:28: *And now, little children, abide in him; that, when he shall appear, we may have confidence, and not be ashamed before him at his coming.*

Verse 16 names the location of the great day of God Almighty: Armageddon or "the mount of Megiddo"—the place where numerous battles have occurred throughout history. Armageddon will also be the scene of the final battle when the winepress of the wrath of God is released upon the nations.

Seventh bowl judgment

Verse 17: *And the seventh angel poured out his vial into the air; and there came a great voice out of the temple of heaven, from the throne, saying, It is done.*

Verse 18: *And there were voices, and thunders, and lightnings; and there was a great earthquake, such as was not since men were upon the earth, so mighty an earthquake, and so great.*

Verse 19: *And the great city was divided into three parts, and the cities of the nations fell: and great Babylon came in remembrance before God, to* *give unto her the cup of the wine of the fierceness of his wrath.*

Verse 20: *And every island fled away, and the mountains were not found.*

Verse 21: *And there fell upon men a great hail out of heaven, every stone about the weight of a talent: and men blasphemed God because of the plague of the hail; for the plague thereof was exceeding great.*

Satan is *the prince of the power of the air* (Ephesians 2:2). This is why *we wrestle...against* [evil spirits] *in high places* (Ephesians 6:12). The seventh angel, in pouring out his bowl *into the air*, destroys the last traces of Satan's abiding place. Armageddon, as will be explained in chapter 19, also destroys every nook and cranny where Satan has had a resting place. As this occurs, a voice out of the temple of heaven victoriously shouts, "It is done!" The twenty-one judgments are completed.

Interestingly, when Christ bore the judgment for our sins, He cried, *It is finished.* Now, as unregenerate mankind pays the price for their sin of not repenting and allowing Christ to bear their load, a voice from heaven again cries, *It is finished.* There will be no further judgments. Judgment number twenty-one is the finale.

The seventh outpoured bowl produces thunders, lightnings, and the most devastating earthquake ever to occur upon earth. The Prophet Haggai undoubtedly predicted this when he stated: *For thus saith the Lord of hosts...I will shake the heavens, and the earth, and the sea, and the dry land; And I will shake all nations, and the desire of all nations* [Christ] *shall come* (Haggai 2:6,7).

One should be certain to note that the final bowl judgment does not bring about the end of the world. Instead, the Lord Jesus Christ returns at this time, establishes His earthly kingdom, and rules for one thousand years (chapter 20, verse 4). Still this is the end of civilization as we have known it. The destruction divides the great city (Jerusalem) into three parts and causes every major city in all nations to fall. In addition, every island flees away and mountains become dislocated, even to the point of disappearing into the oceans. The worst judgment is reserved for Babylon, which receives the cup of the wine of the fierceness of His wrath. A detailed study of Babylon's demise will be conducted in chapter 18.

The climax is the raining down from heaven of hailstones weighing from 86 to 120 pounds. The Greek talent weighed 86 pounds, the Troy talent 96 pounds, and the Jewish talent 120 pounds. Whatever measurement is used, this hailstorm will do more than dent cars and demolish homes. It will literally pulverize everything in sight.

In spite of this plague, the inhabitants of earth continue calling God dirty names. Men never learn. Finally they must die and suffer eternal banishment from God in a fiery hell. Even then they weep and gnash their teeth (see Matthew 8:12). Although weeping denotes sorrow, the gnashing of teeth depicts cursing. No wonder God's Word says that *the smoke of their torment ascendeth up for ever and ever* (Revelation 14:11).

May none of this ever be a part of your experience. Make certain you have gotten in on the first "It is finished" cry of Jesus Christ upon the cross of Calvary. Do not keep hesitating only to finally hear the "It is done" wail of judgment number twenty-one. Christ died for you, shed His blood for the remission of your sins, and He longs to save you.

17

Chapters 17 and 18 form another parenthesis. They are expositions of two verses previously discussed. Chapter 17 explains Revelation 14:8 and chapter 18 expounds Revelation 16:19. In Revelation 14:8 we read, *And there followed another angel, saying, Babylon is fallen, is fallen, that great city, because she made all nations drink of the wine of the wrath of her fornication.*

Likewise, in chapter 16, just concluded, we learned that *great Babylon came in remembrance before God, to give unto her the cup of the wine of the fierceness of his wrath* (verse 19). As we have already discussed, the Babylon of chapter 14 is a religious system, whereas the Babylon of chapter 16 is political. The chapter before us, then, is the story of the rise and fall of the ecumenical world church, while chapter 18 describes the destruction of a political system. Let's begin our investigation of chapter 17 and discuss its prophetic implications, historically.

Verse 1: *And there came one of the seven angels which had the seven vials, and talked with me, saying unto me, Come hither; I will shew unto thee the judgment of the great whore that sitteth upon many waters:*

Here we see one of the seven angels who administered one of the seven judgments speaking to the disciple, John, inviting him to view the judgment of the great harlot who *sitteth upon many waters*. This phrase, *many waters*, speaks of religious control over humanity, internationally. Proof? Verse 15: *The waters which thou sawest, where the whore sitteth, are peoples, and multitudes, and nations, and tongues.*

Verse 2: *With whom the kings of the earth have committed fornication, and the inhabitants of the earth have been made drunk with the wine of her fornication.*

Here we discover that this worldwide religious system holds both earth's leaders and people within its grasp. The fornication committed is between these worldly leaders and the church. Remember that fornication, spiritually speaking, has to do with idolatry, including all its evil connotations and associations.

Spiritual fornication also has to do with Christianity embracing the world—leaping out of Christ's arms into those of another lover. God's Word instructs true Christians to be separated from the world (see Romans 12:2), specifically cautioning them not to fall in love with the world or anything that it contains (see 1 John 2:15). Those who disregard these commands are spiritual adulterers or fornicators. That's why James 4:4 declares, *Ye adulterers and adulteresses, know ye not that the friendship of the world is enmity with God? whosoever therefore will be a friend of the world is the enemy of God.* Harlotry and whoredom, then, speak of idolatry and worldliness.

During the Tribulation hour, a vast international religious system (the great whore of verse 1) creates impure alignments with kings, rulers, and presidents in an unprecedented way. Her control is so over-whelming that humanity becomes mentally stupefied or hypnotically drugged as they are made drunk with the intoxicating brew of these religious/political alliances.

Verse 3: *So he carried me away in the spirit into the wilderness: and I saw a woman sit upon a scarlet coloured beast, full of names of blasphemy, having seven heads and ten horns.*

At this point John, guided by the Holy Spirit, observes the *woman* (or world church) sitting *upon a scarlet coloured beast, full of names of blasphemy, having seven heads and ten horns.* We first saw this beast in chapter 13, verse 1: *I stood upon the sand of the sea, and saw a beast rise up out of the sea, having seven heads and ten horns.* We immediately recognize him to be the Antichrist, who came to power through a confederation of western nations pictured by the ten horns and ten toes discussed previously.

The only difference between the present text and verse 1 of chapter 13 is that the beast is now described as being scarlet coloured. Most commentators believe this reflects his bloody assault upon the world as he rises to power. He begins his reign with a fake peace pact (see Daniel 9:27) which he later breaks! As a result, millions are slaughtered during his rule. Now he bears the blood-red color of an executioner.

Verse 4: *And the woman was arrayed in purple and scarlet colour, and decked with gold and pre-*

cious stones and pearls, having a golden cup in her hand full of abominations and filthiness of her fornication:

As this world church on earth is described, please keep in mind that the true Church—the bride of Christ—is in heaven (chapter 4, verse 1). Her members were raptured from all nations and from many denominations. In fact, their song was recorded in chapter 5, verse 9: *Thou wast slain, and hast redeemed us to God by thy blood out of every kindred, and tongue, and people, and nation.* The lyrics clearly prove that they trusted in the precious blood of Jesus for salvation. There is no other way (see 1 Peter 1:18,19). Cain rejected the blood and tried to appease God with a vegetable offering (see Genesis 4:3), but God said, *It is the blood that maketh an atonement for the soul* (Leviticus 17:11). One cannot get to heaven by following *the commandments of men* (Matthew 15:9), observing tradition (see Mark 7:9), or as a result of works (see Titus 3:5). Thus, those who believed and obeyed God's teachings concerning the blood of the Lamb are in heaven when the false church, the great whore that sitteth upon many waters, holds sway over the earth.

This false religious system of the Tribulation hour is a complete union of the church and the world. Its members are the leftovers from all denominations. They were either doctrinally or morally wrong. One is as bad as the other. The doctrinally wrong are described in 2 Peter 2:1 and 3: *But there were false prophets also among the people, even as there shall be false teachers among you, who privily shall bring in damnable heresies, even denying the Lord that bought them, and bring upon themselves swift destruction...whose judgment now of a long time lingereth not, and their damnation slumbereth not.*

The morally wrong are pictured in Jude, verses 8-21. Now we understand why theology and morality are so important! When God says, *All have sinned* (Romans 3:23), He means all. When He declares, *The wages of sin is death* (Romans 6:23), He means punishment. When He declares, *The blood of Jesus Christ his Son cleanseth us from all sin* (1 John 1:7), He means just that! There are no two ways about it! God says what He means—and means what He says. If one rejects God's Word, he will end up among this Tribulation crowd of self-indoctrinated religionists in a world church destined for destruction.

Secondly, if one says he is a Christian but continues to live in sin, the result will be the same—even though his doctrinal theories may coincide with the true teachings of the Word. Yes, disobedience to revealed truth, as well as incorrect doctrine, keeps one from the presence of God for all eternity. This is why Titus 1:16 states: *They profess that they know God* [lip service]; *but in works* [daily living] *they deny* [God], *being abominable, and disobedient, and unto every good work reprobate* [counterfeit]. Therefore, the members of both groups remain on earth when Jesus calls His genuine children home in the twinkling of an eye. Then these leftovers from all denominations become members of the only religious body still in existence—the world church under the false prophet.

Looking at verse 4 once again, we notice that the woman or mother of the united world church is clothed in materials of *purple and scarlet-colour*. This signifies rulership, for imperial Rome bedecked its leaders in such fashionable elegance. Strange, is it not, that ecclesiastical rulers have always desired temporal authority? They have sought to control the world as well as their parishioners.

Constantine, who became Emperor of Rome in 312 A.D. and eventually head of the church, is a perfect example of this power struggle which has continued to the present hour. Shades of Nicolaitanism! Remember the church of Ephesus in chapter 2. Question: Is such a goal scriptural? No! Jesus taught His disciples to pray, *Thy kingdom come* (Matthew 6:10). When that great event takes place in chapter 19, verse 16, then and only then, is a theocracy—the government of God—established upon earth. This position of leadership is reserved for the Lord Jesus Christ, and no mortal has any business taking His place. The throne belongs exclusively to the King of kings and Lord of lords.

The colors and jewels of verse 4 picture a church composed of prelates or leaders elegantly dressed in purple and scarlet (the colors of the emperors from the time of Constantine). They are also decked with gold and precious stones and pearls (a picture of wealth) and use idols in worship (pictured by the golden cup in the woman's hand). The cup is full of (1) abominations and (2) filthiness.

Verse 5: *And upon her forehead was a name written, MYSTERY, BABYLON THE GREAT, THE*

MOTHER OF HARLOTS AND ABOMINATIONS OF THE EARTH.

Here we discover that the mother church has daughters. Her offspring are groups who either rejected the true teachings of the founder of Christendom or who had a counterfeit experience with the Son of God. They went through the motions but were never truly converted. Among them are cultists, apostates, and unconverted professors of religion—including Baptists, Catholics, Lutherans, Pentecostals, Presbyterians, and those who were members of a host of denominations. They never really knew the Lord (see Matthew 7:21-23). The fruit of daily living was spoiled. Now they are all united in one homogenized ecumenical monstrosity—the counterfeit church under the leadership of the false prophet. However, the true believers from many denominations are already on the glory side and were evacuated at the Rapture (see Revelation 4:1).

Friend, at the Judgment Day, no church—not even your church—will be the final standard of truth. Neither will tradition hold sway at the judgment bar of God. The only and absolute authority of truth, faith, and religious practice is God's Holy Word (see 2 Timothy 3:16)! This is why the Lord Jesus himself said in Mark 7:7 and 13, *Howbeit in vain do they worship me, teaching for doctrines the commandments of men. Making the word of God of none effect through your tradition, which ye have delivered.*

Verse 6: *And I saw the woman drunken with the blood of the saints, and with the blood of the martyrs* *of Jesus: and when I saw her, I wondered with great admiration.*

As John watches all the cunning antics of persecution this woman used and uses, *he* [wonders] *with great admiration.* This does not mean he admires the one who has so mercilessly destroyed so many. Instead, the original Greek is that John "wonders with a great wonder." He is mystified.

Verse 7: *And the angel said unto me, Wherefore didst thou marvel? I will tell thee the mystery of the woman, and of the beast that carrieth her, which hath the seven heads and ten horns.*

The explanation begins in the next verse.

Verse 8: *The beast that thou sawest was, and is not; and shall ascend out of the bottomless pit, and go into perdition: and they that dwell on the earth shall wonder, whose names were not written in the book of life from the foundation of the world, when they behold the beast that was, and is not, and yet is.*

The angel continues unfolding the mystery of the beast in verses 8 through 17. Then, in verse 18, the identity of the woman is revealed. Concerning the beast, the angel declares, *The beast that thou sawest was* [past tense], *and is not* [present tense]; *and shall ascend* [future tense] *out of the bottomless pit.* This is the same beast found in verse 3 and also in chapter 13, verse 1. The reason the beast *was, and is not and shall ascend out of the bottomless pit, and go into perdition* is that, as mentioned during our study of chapter 13, verse 3, he is more than likely assassinated during the Tribulation hour—and thus, *is not.* Then Satan, the great imitator, resurrects him and enters the body of this human for the final forty-two months of the Tribulation. This explanation fulfills the statement, *and yet is* (verse 8). While he is deceased, the beast is in the place of departed evil spirits—the bottomless pit. At the time of his resurrection, he ascends out of this pit, only to eventually go back into perdition at the conclusion of his reign when Christ comes (at the Battle of Armageddon) and casts him into the *lake of fire* (chapter 19, verse 20). Verse 8 also tells us that those persons whose names [are] *not written in the book of life,* are emotionally stirred as they see the beast *that was* [alive], *and is not* [because of his assassination] *and yet is* [because of his resurrection] ruling again.

Verse 9: *And here is the mind which hath wisdom. The seven heads are seven mountains, on which the woman sitteth.*

This is a tremendous text. It locates, geographically, the final world power block and headquarters for the world church as well. Historically speaking, Rome is the only city situated on seven hills. The names of her seven peaks are (1) Aventine, (2) Caelian, (3) Capitoline, (4) Esquiline, (5) Palatine, (6) Quirinal, and (7) Viminal. There is no disputing the fact. The world church, sitting on these seven hills, heading up scores of denominations, rides to power on the back of the ten-horned western federation of nations.

Verse 10: *And there are seven kings: five are fallen, and one is, and the other is not yet come; and when he cometh, he must continue a short space.*

As John receives this vision of the seven kings,

237

five have already fallen. They were (1) Julius Caesar, (2) Tiberius, (3) Caligula, (4) Claudius, and (5) Nero. Number 6—Domitian—is, at the time John receives this revelation, alive and on the throne. Number 7 is yet to come. He, of course, is the Antichrist whose reign will last briefly, or *a short space.*

Verse 11: *And the beast that was, and is not, even he is the eighth, and is of the seven, and goeth into perdition.*

This verse is a thought-twister, but easily understood when one considers it carefully. Who is king number eight if there are only seven kings in the first place? Number eight is number seven resurrected! *And the beast that was* [before his assassination], *and is not* [because of his untimely death], *even he is* [because of his resurrection] *the eighth.* He is *of the seven* because Satan, who incarnated his body while dead, also motivated the other seven. As further proof that number eight is the resurrected Antichrist (number seven), we are again told that he will eventually go into perdition. This statement is also made concerning number seven in verse 8 as well as in our text—verse 11. King number seven and king number eight are one and the same.

Verse 12: *And the ten horns which thou sawest are ten kings, which have received no kingdom as yet; but receive power as kings one hour with the beast.*

The ten horns have not become quite familiar to us. They may soon control the world. Communism, as we have learned, is not the final power block of history. Rather, this ten-toed western alliance is. The

238

power of these nations, however, will be for one hour, or for but a brief moment of time.

Verse 13: *These have one mind, and shall give their power and strength unto the beast.*

The final ten-nation western federation—after the Antichrist ousts three of the original members and replaces them—becomes so unified that everything they possess, economically and militarily, is placed under the control of this world leader (see Daniel 7:8,24).

Verse 14: *These shall make war with the Lamb, and the Lamb shall overcome them: for he is Lord of lords, and King of kings: and they that are with him are called, and chosen, and faithful.*

This verse is fulfilled in chapter 19, verses 11 through 16, when the world's armies gather together against the Lord and His anointed as pictured in Psalm 2:2: *The kings of the earth set themselves, and the rulers take counsel together, against the Lord, and against his anointed.* The Lamb (Christ) is the *Lord of lords, and King of kings.* The called, chosen, and faithful who accompany Him are the armies of heaven (chapter 19, verse 14) composed of the believers (the true Church) who were raptured out of the world in chapter 4, verse 1, and who then waited in heaven seven years to return with the Bridegroom.

Verse 15: *And he saith unto me, The waters which thou sawest, where the whore sitteth, are peoples, and multitudes, and nations, and tongues.*

As explained in our discussion of verse 1, the woman sitting upon many waters is the world church who exercises religious control over mankind internationally.

Verse 16: *And the ten horns which thou sawest upon the beast, these shall hate the whore, and shall make her desolate and naked, and shall eat her flesh, and burn her with fire.*

The Antichrist eventually betrays his religious followers. They bowed and scraped to his image, but now he no longer wants to share the limelight and glory with them. Thus, the individual leaders of the countries in the ten-nation confederacy turn against the world church. They hate her, strip her of all possessions (the gold, precious stones, and pearls of verse 4), and destroy her by burning her remains to the ground. Who places such a plan of action in the hearts of these rulers? None other than God Almighty!

Verse 17: *For God hath put in their hearts to fulfil his will, and to agree, and give their kingdom unto the beast, until the words of God shall be fulfilled.*

Imagine, God does it all! This portion of Scripture emphasizes the futility of politics. Despite the methods and manipulations of man, God's plan always comes to pass. He sets up and knocks down world rulers at will (see Psalm 75:7). They are but pawns in the game of life (see Proverbs 21:1). God's will prevails regardless of what humans attempt to do. Christian, get souls saved! This is your God-given goal. Let the world spend time on temporal issues. The cause of Christ is eternal!

Verse 18: *And the woman which thou sawest is*

that great city, which reigneth over the kings of the earth.

This great end-time city is located within the Common Market nations and proves that the political and religious power brokers exist together simultaneously. Since the world church forms at the time when ten western nations unite—and both the European Economic Community and World Council of Churches began unity proceedings in 1948—Christ's coming must be near. How long, O Lord, ere we shout that glad song, "Christ returneth, hallelujah!" Yes, "Hallelujah!" Amen!

18

In the next twenty-four verses, we shall witness the destruction of political Babylon. This Babylon is different from the one just discussed. Chapter 17 concerned religious Babylon, whereas chapter 18 pictures political, or commercial, Babylon. Religious Babylon was called "mystery Babylon," but commercial Babylon is referred to as "Babylon the great." Religious Babylon was presented as a woman or a mother, while commercial Babylon is portrayed as a city—a *great city*, a *mighty city*, and eventually a burning city. Religious Babylon was situated on seven hills, whereas political Babylon is visible from the sea (see verses 17, 18, and 21). Religious Babylon was destroyed by the kings of the earth (17:16), but political Babylon will be destroyed by horrendous judgments from the hand of God. When religious Babylon was destroyed, the kings rejoiced. When political Babylon is demolished, however, the kings and merchants of the earth *lament* [and weep] *for her* (18:9,15). Let's study political Babylon.

Verse 1: *And after these things I saw another angel come down from heaven, having great power; and the earth was lightened with his glory.*

John says, *after these things*. After what things? After the fulfillment of religious Babylon's destruction. John's statement is further proof that the two Babylons are entirely different and distinctive of one another. Only after the events of chapter 17 does John see God's judgment upon political Babylon in the verses that follow.

The angel bringing the warning of impending judgment is powerful and glorious. His appearance lightens the entire globe. Quite possibly, this is a christophany or appearance of Christ, as He is *the light of the world* (John 8:12).

Verse 2: *And he cried mightily with a strong voice, saying, Babylon the great is fallen, is fallen, and is become the habitation of devils, and the hold of every foul spirit, and a cage of every unclean and hateful bird.*

God's judgment of commercial Babylon has begun. The angel's cry is, *Babylon the great is fallen, is fallen*. Why? She has *become the habitation of devils, and the hold of every* [evil] *spirit imaginable*. She is a cage containing every vicious, filthy, and hateful bird in existence.

A walk through New York City, Detroit, Chicago, Los Angeles, Hollywood, or San Francisco would be helpful at this point. America's major cities—and minor ones as well—are loaded with lust-ridden sinners seeking sex thrills through prostitutes, R- and X-rated movies, and pornographic bookstores. Our beloved America could possibly fit the description of political Babylon as a *cage* [containing] *every unclean and hateful bird* controlled by foul spirits and demons who inhabit the land and its people. God help us to have an old-fashioned, Holy Spirit-empowered revival in "the land of the free and the home of the brave." Otherwise, God's judgment may soon fall.

Verse 3: *For all nations have drunk of the wine of the wrath of her fornication, and the kings of the earth have committed fornication with her, and the merchants of the earth are waxed rich through the abundance of her delicacies.*

Just like religious Babylon, this political system has turned to idolatry and fornication. As we saw in chapter 17, these terms refer to the worship of strange gods and a love of this world's material goods. Seeking prestige and power, commercial or political Babylon has promoted and joined ungodly world alliances. The text states that the nations of earth have partaken *of the wine of the wrath of her fornication, and the kings of the earth have committed* [spiritual] *fornication with her* for gain. Hence, the merchants of the earth have become exceedingly wealthy by "wheeling and dealing" with this nation who is super-abundantly loaded with *delicacies*.

Verse 4: *And I heard another voice from heaven, saying, Come out of her, my people, that ye be not partakers of her sins, and that ye receive not of her plagues.*

Verse 5: *For her sins have reached unto heaven, and God hath remembered her iniquities.*

The believers of the Tribulation hour—those who trusted in the shed blood of the Lamb and refused the mark of the beast—are told to *come out of her* [and

245

partake not] *of her* [evil deeds]. They are to live holy lives in the midst of *a cage* [full of] *unclean and hateful bird*[s] whose sins have *reached unto heaven* and caused an abominable stench in the nostrils of the Almighty. They are to be careful of materialism and to refrain from illegal gain through the love of the delicacies of this world.

Verse 6: *Reward her even as she rewarded you, and double unto her double according to her works: in the cup which she hath filled fill to her double.*

Verse 7: *How much she hath glorified herself, and lived deliciously, so much torment and sorrow give her: for she saith in her heart, I sit a queen, and am no widow, and shall see no sorrow.*

Here we see God's law of sowing and reaping coming into effect: *They that plow iniquity, and sow wickedness, reap the same* (Job 4:8). Humanity cannot get away with sin forever. God hates sin. It is inconsistent with His holiness. Except for God's mercy, most of us would have been dead and in hell long ago. His grace, however, passes all human understanding. *The Lord is...longsuffering to us-ward, not willing that any should perish, but that all should come to repentance* (2 Peter 3:9). Still God cannot tolerate sin forever, and the reaping of political Babylon's iniquity must finally take place.

What a terrible experience as Babylon receives a double portion of judgment. Literally, the verse should say, "The double is to be doubled." This was the punishment under the law of Moses (see Exodus 22:4,7). Now God says, "Double the judgment upon Babylon according to her works. Reward her even as she rewarded you." Babylon has glorified herself and lived deliciously. Her wealthy became wealthier and her poor became poorer. As a nation, she did not care about the poor, for she said, "I am a queen. I shall see no sorrow. I do not want to look at the needs of the impoverished."

There is a possibility that James 5:1-6 predicted the judgment administered in Revelation 18:1,7: *Go to now, ye rich men, weep and howl for your miseries that shall come upon you. Your riches are corrupted, and your garments are motheaten. Your gold and silver is cankered; and the rust of them shall be a witness against you, and shall eat your flesh as it were fire. Ye have heaped treasure together for the last days. Behold, the hire of the labourers who have reaped down your fields, which is of you kept back by fraud, crieth: and the cries of them which have reaped* [the poor] *are entered into the ears of the Lord of sabaoth. Ye have lived in pleasure on the earth, and been wanton; ye have nourished your hearts, as in a day of slaughter. Ye have condemned and killed the just; and he doth not resist you.*

The end of the age will not see communism enthroned. Instead, capitalism will be the ruling power as ten western nations bleed the world's inhabitants of their possessions. Now, don't misunderstand. I hate the atheistic, godless monstrosity called "communism." It will be destroyed, as will Russia, in the Middle East (see Ezekiel 39:1,2). However, "double trouble" is also coming for those exploiters of the masses—the rich who starve the poor—according to

247

the verses just investigated. Their judgment takes place as Babylon is burned.

Verse 8: *Therefore shall her plagues come in one day, death, and mourning, and famine; and she shall be utterly burned with fire: for strong is the Lord God who judgeth her.*

Verse 9: *And the kings of the earth, who have committed fornication and lived deliciously with her, shall bewail her, and lament for her, when they shall see the smoke of her burning,*

Verse 10: *Standing afar off for the fear of her torment, saying, Alas, alas that great city Babylon, that mighty city! for in one hour is thy judgment come.*

When the news of Babylon's destruction is received, earth's kings, monarchs, potentates, and presidents immediately begin to weep. Their source of wealth has been disintegrated. They are joined by members of the Chamber of Commerce.

Verse 11: *And the merchants of the earth shall weep and mourn over her; for no man buyeth their merchandise any more.*

Let's view the commodities. Not a single item is really necessary. In fact, the entire display may be classified as "luxurious worldly baubles used to impress high society." Imagine, even the mark of the beast won't hinder wealth in the western world! Just look at the expensive dainties listed in the following portion of Scripture.

Verse 12: *The merchandise of gold, and silver, and precious stones, and of pearls* [for investment portfolios], *and fine linen, and purple, and silk, and*

248

scarlet [for fashionable dress], *and all thyine wood, and all manner vessels of ivory, and all manner vessels of most precious wood, and of brass, and iron, and marble* [for high-class furniture],

Verse 13: *And cinnamon, and odours, and ointments, and frankincense* [for sensuousness. Also, a stockpile of] *wine, and oil, and fine flour, and wheat, and beasts, and sheep, and horses* [for the satisfying of flesh], *and chariots* [for the getaway], *and slaves* [for labour to increase wealth], *and* [finally the] *souls of men* [for lust and other demeaning practices].

But judgment must come. The treasures of the Tribulation enterprises do not last. Neither will they last for you, if this is all you want out of life. Why?

Verse 14: *And the fruits that thy soul lusted after are departed from thee, and all things which were dainty and goodly are departed from thee, and thou shalt find them no more at all.*

They will be destroyed in one hour (verses 10 and 17).

Verse 15: *The merchants of these things, which were made rich by her, shall stand afar off for the fear of her torment, weeping and wailing,*

Verse 16: *And saying, Alas, alas, that great city, that was clothed in fine linen, and purple, and scarlet, and decked with gold, and precious stones, and pearls!*

Verse 17: *For in one hour so great riches is come to nought. And every shipmaster, and all the company in ships, and sailors, and as many as trade by sea, stood afar off,*

Verse 18: *And cried when they saw the smoke of*

her burning, saying, What city is like unto this great city!

Verse 19: *And they cast dust on their heads, and cried, weeping and wailing, saying, Alas, alas, that great city, wherein were made rich all that had ships in the sea by reason of her costliness! for in one hour is she made desolate.*

No comment is needed at this point, for the preceding texts are self-explanatory. As the world weeps over the destruction of political Babylon, all heaven breaks forth in praise.

Verse 20: *Rejoice over her, thou heaven, and ye holy apostles and prophets; for God hath avenged you on her.*

To this point there has only been one other command to rejoice recorded in the Book of Revelation. All has been solemn and sad. At the overthrow of Babylon, however, the cherubim, seraphim, and other angelic orders are told to praise the Lord. The holy apostles and prophets—representatives of all Old and New Testament saints—are instructed to join them. Why? The chief enemy of the people has been destroyed.

The world persecuted the prophets, apostles, and saints of God during every age. Oftentimes great suffering was inflicted upon them: [Some] *were tortured, not accepting deliverance; that they might obtain a better resurrection: And others had trial of cruel mockings and scourgings, yea, moreover of bonds and imprisonment: They were stoned, they were sawn asunder, were tempted, were slain with the sword: they wandered about in sheepskins and goatskins; being destitute, afflicted, tormented; (Of whom the world was not worthy:) they wandered in deserts, and in mountains, and in dens and caves of the earth* (Hebrews 11:35-38). Now such oppression is finished forever! *Babylon...is fallen, is fallen.* Praise the Lord! The world can no longer touch God's people *for God hath avenged you on her*—or from the Greek, which is stronger: "God hath judged your judgment on her."

Verse 21: *And a mighty angel took up a stone like a great millstone, and cast it into the sea, saying, Thus with violence shall that great city Babylon be thrown down, and shall be found no more at all.*

Some Bible scholars identify this stone as Christ. Acts 4:11 states: [Christ] *is the stone which was set at nought of you builders, which is become the head of the corner.*

The stone strikes at the end time when ten toes or ten western nations are aligned. Daniel 2:34 states: *Thou sawest till that a stone was cut out without hands, which smote the image upon his feet* [composed of ten toes] *that were of iron and clay, and brake them to pieces.*

This explanation is repeated in Daniel 2:44 and 45: *And in the days of these kings shall the God of heaven set up a kingdom, which shall never be destroyed: and the kingdom shall not be left to other people, but it shall break in pieces and consume all these kingdoms, and it shall stand for ever. Forasmuch as thou sawest that the stone was cut out of the mountain without hands, and that it brake in pieces the iron, the brass, the clay, the silver, and the gold;*

251

the great God hath made known to the king what shall come to pass hereafter: and the dream is certain, and the interpretation thereof sure.

The Lord Jesus Christ may well be the stone that pulverizes Babylon. So thorough is the stone's destruction that Babylon is finished forever.

Verse 22: *And the voice of harpers, and musicians, and of pipers, and trumpeters, shall be heard no more at all in thee; and no craftsman, of whatsoever craft he be, shall be found any more in thee; and the sound of a millstone shall be heard no more at all in thee;*

Entertainment ceases in this "laugh-a-minute" commercial empire. All music and hilarity is forever silenced. The craftsmen—including tool and die makers, auto mechanics, and machinists—are put out of business as all production is halted in Babylon, once the international center of commerce.

Verse 23: *And the light of a candle shall shine no more at all in thee; and the voice of the bridegroom and of the bride shall be heard no more at all in thee: for thy merchants were the great men of the earth; for by thy sorceries were all nations deceived.*

Lights are extinguished, possibly through energy deficiencies. Marriages cease, and heartbreak inundates the land. No longer is there time for mirth, joy, love, and romance.

Verse 24: *And in her was found the blood of prophets, and of saints, and of all that were slain upon the earth.*

The closing verses of this chapter reveal three reasons for God's judgment of Babylon: (1) her love of wealth and riches—[her] *merchants were the great men of earth*; (2) her abusive usage of drugs—*for by* [her] *sorceries were all nations deceived.* (The word *sorceries* in this text again comes from the Greek word *pharmakeia*, translated *pharmacy* in English. The term connotes "getting high on" or "getting kicks out of" drugs.); and (3) her hatred, abuse, and persecution of the people of God—for *in her was found the blood of prophets, and of saints, and of all that were slain upon the earth.*

Who is Babylon? Certain scholars think that the term refers to the ancient city of Babylon on the banks of the Euphrates River in present-day Iraq. Interestingly, the city is currently being rebuilt. Others, including such prophecy scholars as Dr. S. Franklin Logsden, believe Babylon to be the United States of America—a leader of the western world aligned with the Antichrist's ten-toed kingdom.

Some great scholars believe that America and *Babylon the great* are one and the same because of the information presented in the prophecies of Isaiah and Jeremiah, plus the words of John the seer in Revelation, chapter 18.

Consider the following momentarily. Isaiah 18:1,2 depicts a latter-day nation that amazingly resembles modern America. This nation (1) has the insignia of wings—similar to our national emblem, the bald eagle; (2) is a land that is beyond the sea from Israel; (3) is scattered and peeled—meaning it is widely spread out or has great land areas; (4) is meted out—or staked out—by acres and miles; and (5) is a land whose rivers are spoiled—or polluted.

Likewise, in chapters 50 and 51 of the book bearing his name, Jeremiah presents conclusive evidence that a latter-day Babylon—far different from and superior to ancient Babylon—will spring into existence. As one studies Jeremiah's remarks, he is amazed to see that modern America seems to be the fulfillment of these predictions because: (1) she is a nation of *mingled people* (Jeremiah 50:37); (2) she is a nation whose *mother shall be sorely confounded* and who coexists with the "mother" at the hour of her decline (50:12); (3) she *dwellest upon many waters* (51:13); (4) her wealth plagues the nations of the earth to the point of insane jealousy (51:7); (5) her space exploits are so utterly fantastic that she tries to *mount up to heaven* (51:53); and (6) she exists when Israel is back in her land. (Order my videocassette entitled "America in Prophecy" for a detailed study of this subject.)

19

Chapter 19 is exhilarating because it begins with a heavenly host singing an *Alleluia* chorus, and this is a Hebrew word meaning "praise Jehovah" or "praise the Lord." Chapter 19 contains the only mention of the term in the New Testament, and we will find it four different times in the following six verses.

Verse 1: *And after these things I heard a great voice of much people in heaven, saying, Alleluia; Salvation, and glory, and honour, and power, unto the Lord our God:*

John says, *after these things.* After what things? After the destruction of religious and political Babylon. Then what? Then he hears the tremendous sound of a multitude conducting a praise and testimony meeting in heaven. Probably led by the martyred saints of the Tribulation hour (chapter 7, verse 9), this group eventually includes all the redeemed in glory. They are rejoicing because (1) evil has run its course; (2) the Tribulation hour is concluding; (3) Christ is preparing to return with His saints; (4) the armies of the world are about to be demolished; (5) swords will then be remade into plowshares and spears into pruninghooks (see Isaiah 2:4); and (6) Christ will soon establish His millennial kingdom upon the earth. Such "good news" would make anyone shout, "Amen! Praise the Lord!"

The reason this praise is directed to One whose attributes are: (1) *salvation*, (2) *glory*, (3) *honour*, and (4) *power* is revealed in the next verse.

Verse 2: *For true and righteous are his judgments: for he hath judged the great whore, which did corrupt the earth with her fornication, and hath avenged the blood of his servants at her hand.*

Verse 3: *And again they said, Alleluia. And her smoke rose up for ever and ever.*

The refrain is repeated as God's people acknowledge the fact that Babylon's doom is eternal. Never again will religious or political alliances bring men into bondage. Never again will man be duped, deluded, and destroyed through pompous ceremonialism. No, Babylon's smoke ascends up for the ages of ages—forever and forever!

Verse 4: *And the four and twenty elders and the four beasts fell down and worshipped God that sat on the throne, saying, Amen; Alleluia.*

At this point the twenty-four elders (those we observed casting their trophies or crowns at Jesus' feet following the Rapture and Judgment Seat of Christ in chapter 4) join the praise session. The world system that so harassed and persecuted them has finally been judged. The four beasts (identified as cherubim and seraphim in chapter 4) also lend their voices in glorifying God. They are rejoicing over the fact that they did not follow Lucifer, the head angel, as so many of their group did when he rebelled against the Almighty (see Isaiah 14:12-14). Now they are eternally secure, whereas the fallen angels are everlastingly damned.

Verse 5: *And a voice came out of the throne, saying, Praise our God, all ye his servants, and ye that fear him, both small and great.*

This voice is undoubtedly an angel encouraging the heavenly host to continue the praise session. He is the celestial cheerleader at one of heaven's most momentous and climactic hours.

Verse 6: *And I heard as it were the voice of a great multitude, and as the voice of many waters, and as the voice of mighty thunderings, saying, Alleluia: for the Lord God omnipotent reigneth.*

This is the final chorus as all heaven joins together in song. The multitudinous voices resound so loudly that the roar is likened to the sound of *many waters* and *mighty thunderings*. Why not? The prayer of the ages, *Thy kingdom come*, uttered by millions upon millions through the centuries, is about to be answered. Thus, the exclamation: [Praise Jehovah!] *for the Lord God Omnipotent* [soon] *reigneth.*

Verse 7: *Let us be glad and rejoice, and give honour to him: for the marriage of the Lamb is come, and his wife hath made herself ready.*

Verse 8: *And to her was granted that she should be arrayed in fine linen, clean and white: for the fine linen is the righteousness of saints.*

At the hour of Christ's return to earth with His bride (the Church), His honeymoon is launched for 1,000 years. These verses are further proof that the Rapture is a pre-Tribulational event. The marriage of the Lamb takes place in heaven, not on earth. The Bride prepares herself at the Judgment Seat of Christ (which also takes place in heaven) before the wedding. These are time-consuming events. Then she returns with her lover—the Lord Jesus Christ—from heaven.

The Saviour is the Bridegroom because He is *the Lamb of God,* [who] *taketh away the sin of the world* (John 1:29). The marriage partners at this glorious event include the Lamb (Christ) and His bride (the Church). Question: Where have they been during the Tribulation hour depicted in chapters 6 through 18? The answer: Heaven! You see, the Church was raptured in Revelation 4:1 and has not been mentioned again until this point—the time of preparation for the wedding.

During the seven years that earth dwellers suffered judgment from heaven, the Bride was being investigated in heaven, for 2 Corinthians 5:10 states: *We must all appear before the judgment seat of Christ; that every one may receive the things done in his body, according to that he hath done, whether it be good or bad.* Second Corinthians 11:2 continues: *For I am jealous over you with godly jealousy: for I have espoused you to one husband, that I may present you as a chaste* [pure] *virgin to Christ.* For many who were unfaithful to Christ during the engagement period (their years of service upon earth), this will be a time of humiliation (see 1 John 2:28).

Since we are then betrothed or engaged to Christ from the time of our conversion until the moment of the Rapture, God commands that we live consistently holy lives (see 1 Peter 1:16). Then, immediately after we are called home in the "twinkling of an eye," the pre-marital examination concerning our faithfulness as His sweetheart begins. Today's signs definitely indicate that the hour is near. Our next appointment has been scheduled. How heartbreaking the report should the Bridegroom say, "I have discovered a problem." Child of God—don't be among the losers—live victoriously!

In preparation for the marriage ceremony itself, every believer will be attired in the wedding garment he made upon earth. The material will be composed of the good works remaining after the Judgment Seat has occurred. Someone may ask, "Doesn't the Bible teach that believers are clothed in the righteousness of Christ?" Definitely (see 2 Corinthians 5:21). This is how one becomes a Christian in the first place. However, the word *righteousness* in the original Greek of verse 8 is not singular—(righteousness based upon Christ's work) but plural—(righteousnesses based upon the believer's life and deeds upon earth). At the *judgment seat of Christ* (2 Corinthians 5:10), every work—good or bad—will be investigated. Then those works will be placed in the fires of testing (see 1 Corinthians 3:13). At that time *if any man's work abide which he hath built thereupon, he shall receive a reward. If any man's work shall be burned, he shall suffer loss* [of rewards]*: but he himself shall be saved; yet so as by fire* [by the skin of his teeth] (1 Corinthians 3:14,15).

The two texts just referenced describe the preparation of the bride of Christ (all Christians) for the wedding (the marriage of the Lamb). Clearly, the wedding gown is composed of the believers' righteousnesses (good works) performed on earth in honor of the lover of her soul. When this great moment arrives—undoubtedly soon, yes, perhaps today—what will you have? What will your wedding garment picture? Oh, I plead with you to live for Christ. Give Him your very best and all that you have. If you do, your rewards will be great, your joy complete, and your heavenly entrance abundant (see 2 Peter 1:11).

Verse 9: *And he saith unto me, Write, Blessed are they which are called unto the marriage supper of the Lamb. And he saith unto me, These are the true sayings of God.*

This verse discloses the fact that the marriage of the Lamb will include a reception with many guests invited. Please note that the Bride and the Bridegroom are never guests. They are the ones for whom the ceremony is performed. Who, then, are those in attendance at the Marriage Supper? The guests include all believers up to Pentecost as well as the Tribulation saints. John—the disciple Jesus loved (see John 19:26) and the one who wrote the Book of Revelation—said, *He that hath the bride is the bridegroom: but the friend of the bridegroom, which standeth and heareth him, rejoiceth greatly because of the bridegroom's voice: this my joy therefore is fulfilled* (John 3:29). No wonder our text states: *Blessed* [or happy] *are they which are called unto the marriage supper of the Lamb.*

The bride is composed of all believers who become members of the body of Christ from the Day of

260

Pentecost until the Rapture. Now we find that the guests are those who trusted in the Lord either prior to Pentecost or following the Rapture. Since the marriage takes place in heaven, and the Old Testament and Tribulation believers are part of the earthly group, their only hope of participating in this event of the ages is that the wedding reception and Marriage Supper take place on earth. This is exactly what happens.

The fact that the marriage takes place in heaven and the supper occurs on earth is beautifully portrayed by the parable of the ten virgins: *Then shall the kingdom of heaven be likened unto ten virgins, which took their lamps, and went forth to meet the bridegroom. And five of them were wise, and five were foolish. They that were foolish took their lamps, and took no oil with them: But the wise took oil in their vessels with their lamps. While the bridegroom tarried, they all slumbered and slept. And at midnight there was a cry made, Behold, the bridegroom cometh; go ye out to meet him. Then all those virgins arose, and trimmed their lamps. And the foolish said unto the wise, Give us of your oil; for our lamps are gone out. But the wise answered, saying, Not so; lest there be not enough for us and you: but go ye rather to them that sell, and buy for yourselves. And while they went to buy, the bridegroom came; and they that were ready went in with him to the marriage: and the door was shut. Afterward came also the other virgins, saying, Lord, Lord, open to us. But he answered and said, Verily I say unto you, I know you not. Watch therefore, for ye know neither the day nor the hour wherein the Son of man cometh* (Matthew 25:1-13).

Notice that verse 6 of the above text states: *Behold, the bridegroom cometh; go ye out to meet him.* The reason the emphasis is on the Bridegroom instead of the Bride is because the Lord Jesus is all in all. Even John says, *Let us be glad and rejoice, and give honour to him: for the marriage of the Lamb is come* (Revelation 19:7). Believers—members of the Bride—ought always to remember that the glory is His. He redeemed us. We would be nothing were it not for Jesus. These texts, then, explain the marriage, the supper, the guests, and the location.

Verse 10: *And I fell at his feet to worship him. And he said unto me, See thou do it not: I am thy fellowservant, and of thy brethren that have the testimony of Jesus: worship God: for the testimony of Jesus is the spirit of prophecy.*

If there were any portion of the Book of Revelation John would like to omit, this would be the verse. He has just done a foolish thing. He allowed himself to become so enamored with the angel delivering the message that he began worshipping a created being. Such recording of human weaknesses proves that God wrote the Bible, for man would have omitted his mistakes. God, however, records them in order to show the world that *all have sinned, and come short of the glory of God* (Romans 3:23).

As John bows his knee to this created being, the angel cries, "Don't do it. Angels are but *ministering spirits, sent forth to minister for them who shall be*

262

heirs of salvation (Hebrews 1:14). Get up! I am only a servant of God, as you are."

John has just learned an important lesson. Have you? Beware of any religion that honors or reveres angels—including the angel Moroni of Mormonism. Such practice is wrong: *Let no man beguile you of your reward in...worshipping of angels* (Colossians 2:18). Even the angel's command in our text is, "worship God." Thus, it is obvious that we are not to worship men, women, angels, or idols (see Exodus 20:4,5). Worship God!

Verse 11: *And I saw heaven opened, and behold a white horse; and he that sat upon him was called Faithful and True, and in righteousness he doth judge and make war.*

Verse 12: *His eyes were as a flame of fire, and on his head were many crowns; and he had a name written, that no man knew, but he himself.*

Verse 13: *And he was clothed with a vesture dipped in blood: and his name is called The Word of God.*

Verse 14: *And the armies which were in heaven followed him upon white horses, clothed in fine linen, white and clean.*

Verse 15: *And out of his mouth goeth a sharp sword, that with it he should smite the nations: and he shall rule them with a rod of iron: and he treadeth the winepress of the fierceness and wrath of Almighty God.*

Verse 16: *And he hath on his vesture and on his thigh a name written, KING OF KINGS, AND LORD OF LORDS.*

These verses graphically portray the coming of Christ to earth. This event is called "The Revelation" among theologians because this is the moment the Lord reveals himself to the inhabitants of earth. The same scene was observed in chapter 11, verse 15, as well. Remember, chapters 12 through 19 simply repeat the materials presented in chapters 6 through 11.

For centuries, the world has scoffingly cried, *Where is the promise of his coming?* (2 Peter 3:4). Now the mocking abruptly ceases. Why? Breathtaking signs accompany the One who sits on this white horse—as He comes to judge and make war on the world: *Immediately after the tribulation of those days shall the sun be darkened, and the moon shall not give her light, and the stars shall fall from heaven, and the powers of the heavens shall be shaken: And then shall appear the sign of the Son of man in heaven: and then shall all the tribes of the earth mourn, and they shall see the Son of man coming in the clouds of heaven with power and great glory. And he shall send his angels with a great sound of a trumpet, and they shall gather together his elect* [saved Jews and Tribulation saints] *from the four winds, from one end of heaven to the other* (Matthew 24:29-32).

The scene before us is a literal event because John sees heaven opened. This is thrilling. Heaven's door is opened but twice in the Book of Revelation—once in chapter 4, verse 1, and now in chapter 19, verse 11. Chapter 4 pictures the Rapture; chapter 19 pictures the Revelation. The door was opened in chapter 4 to receive the saved; now the door is opened again in order that the saints may return with the rider on the white horse—the King of kings and the Lord of lords. Don't let anyone tell you that there is but one appearing at Christ's return. Two opened doors tell the truth, the whole truth, and nothing but the truth.

The Rider in verse 12 has *eyes...as a flame of fire,* which are piercing and purging. He can immediately see through the sham and hypocrisy of men. These are the same eyes we viewed in chapter 1, verse 14. As King, Christ has on His head the crowns of royalty. He also has a special name that will only be exposed at the hour of His return. Until then He alone knows this name and its meaning.

In verse 13, we see that the Lord wears *a vesture dipped in blood*—a picture of the judgment He is bringing to earth. None can doubt that this Judge is anyone but the Lord Jesus Christ, for His name is called the Word of God. John often called Him by this name. In fact, he was the only New Testament writer to use this title. John 1:1 states: *In the beginning was the Word, and the Word was with God, and the Word was God.* Verse 14 adds, *And the Word was made flesh.* He again calls Christ *the Word of life* in 1 John 1:1.

At this moment John sees the *Word of God* coming in judgment. He also observes a great host called *the armies* [of] *heaven* following Him upon white horses. Notice that they come from heaven; they are not already present on earth. They are the saints who were raptured in chapter 4, verse 1—the Bride who *made herself ready and* [wore] *fine linen, clean and white* in verse 8 of this present study. Tens of thousands—yea, millions upon millions in number—avoided the Tribulation hour and are now returning with the King for the conflict at Armageddon. They are privileged to stand with Him as He comes *to execute judgment upon all, and to convince all that are ungodly among them of all their ungodly deeds which they have ungodly committed, and of all their hard speeches which ungodly sinners have spoken against him* (Jude 15). The time of reaping has arrived.

As Christ returns to subjugate the earth dwellers, He does so with a sword in His mouth (see verse 15). This sword is nothing less than the Word of God.

His Word always smites men in their consciences and lives. This is exactly what happened to the officers of the chief priests and Pharisees when they came to the Garden of Gethsemane, seeking Jesus, *As soon then as he had said unto them, I am he, they went backward, and fell to the ground* (John 18:6). Oh, *the word of God is quick, and powerful, and sharper than any twoedged sword* (Hebrews 4:12).

We note in verse 15 that Christ and His Word alone smash the nations at Armageddon. The armies of heaven only observe as He treads the winepress of the fierceness and wrath of Almighty God. This moment brings the fulfillment of Daniel 2:34, which predicts that *a stone...cut out without hands* pulverizes the image—the ten-nation confederacy. Then the stone instantly expands and fills the entire earth with a new kingdom, never to be destroyed. Its leader is the King of kings and Lord of lords. No one can miss

Him, for His vesture and thigh coverings bear His title—King of kings and Lord of lords. The King has come! Oh, hallelujah! The King has come!

Verse 17: *And I saw an angel standing in the sun; and he cried with a loud voice, saying to all the fowls that fly in the midst of heaven, Come and gather yourselves together unto the supper of the great God;*

Verse 18: *That ye may eat the flesh of kings, and the flesh of captains, and the flesh of mighty men, and the flesh of horses, and of them that sit on them, and the flesh of all men, both free and bond, both small and great.*

The devastating scene described in these verses is the result of the Battle of Armageddon (chapter 16, verse 16) fought in the valleys of Megiddo and Jehoshaphat, not Russia's invasion of Israel (see Ezekiel 38 and 39). Russia made her move in the middle of the Tribulation hour. Why? The Antichrist came to power, made a false peace pact with the nations, and then broke it in the midst of the seven years (see Daniel 9:27). At that point Russia invaded the Holy Land, for she went *up to the land of unwalled villages;* [saying] *I will go to them that are at rest, that dwell safely* (Ezekiel 38:11).

Prior to the appearance of the Antichrist in chapter 13, the nation of Israel is not at rest or dwelling safely. This situation changes when he comes to power, takes control, and initiates his peace plan. Then Israel and all the world proclaim, "Peace, peace," but it does not last, *For when they shall say, Peace and safety; then sudden destruction* [comes] *upon them* (1 Thessalonians 5:3). Russia quickly takes

267

advantage of the opportunity and moves against Israel, for she is at rest, dwelling safely. Moscow's act of
aggression, however, proves to be her "Waterloo,"
for she is destroyed by the hand of God (see Ezekiel
39:1-3).

Conversely, the battle described in this present
chapter occurs as God destroys the Antichrist and his
ten-horned empire. The following passages vividly
portray the terrible, catastrophic judgment which occurs in preparation for, and fulfillment of, Armageddon:

*For, behold, in those days, and in that time, when
I shall bring again the captivity of Judah and Jerusalem, I will also gather all nations, and will bring them
down into the valley of Jehoshaphat, and will plead
with them there for my people and for my heritage
Israel, whom they have scattered among the nations,
and parted my land. Assemble yourselves, and come,
all ye heathen, and gather yourselves together round
about: thither cause thy mighty ones to come down,
O Lord. Let the heathen be wakened, and come up to
the valley of Jehoshaphat: for there will I sit to judge
all the heathen round about. Put ye in the sickle, for
the harvest is ripe: come, get you down: for the press
is full, the vats overflow; for their wickedness is
great. Multitudes, multitudes in the valley of decision: for the day of the Lord is near in the valley of
decision. The sun and the moon shall be darkened,
and the stars shall withdraw their shining. The Lord
also shall roar out of Zion, and utter his voice from
Jerusalem; and the heavens and the earth shall shake:
but the Lord will be the hope of his people, and the*

268

strength of the children of Israel. So shall ye know that I am the Lord your God dwelling in Zion, my holy mountain: then shall Jerusalem be holy, and there shall no strangers pass through her any more (Joel 3:1,2,11-17).

Verses 14-20 of chapter 14, and verses 17-21 of chapter 16, already studied, also have to do with the Battle of Armageddon. Thus, we see that before the Marriage Supper of the Lamb becomes a reality, the supper of the great God occurs. This event begins as an angel summons all the fowls (or vultures) of heaven to gather together for a feast, *For wheresoever the carcase is, there will the eagles be gathered together* (Matthew 24:28). At this gathering they eat the flesh of deceased kings, captains, mighty men, horses, their riders, and all men from every rank and position of life. What a horrible nightmare as men suffer the consequences of their rebellion against God.

Finally the one who made life so miserable upon earth, who gave men a number (666), who would not let them buy or sell without the number of his name, and who had millions of believers beheaded because they refused his number, is judged by God himself!

Verse 19: *And I saw the beast, and the kings of the earth, and their armies, gathered together to make war against him that sat on the horse, and against his army.*

Verse 20: *And the beast was taken, and with him the false prophet that wrought miracles before him, with which he deceived them that had received the mark of the beast, and them that worshipped his* *image. These both were cast alive into a lake of fire burning with brimstone.*

What a conclusion! Two world leaders—one political, the other religious; one posing as God, the other promoting him—now discover that their charade is over. They are cast alive into the lake of fire burning with brimstone—the final abode of all God-haters and Christ-rejecters for time and eternity. A thousand years later, when Satan joins them (chapter 20, verse 10), they are still suffering torment day and night. Oh, who is foolish enough to preach immediate disintegration or annihilation in the light of such plain texts?

Verse 21: *And the remnant were slain with the sword of him that sat upon the horse, which sword proceeded out of his mouth: and all the fowls were filled with their flesh.*

The battle has ended. None is spared!

20

Chapter 20 introduces us to the most beautiful, peaceful, and rewarding age this world will ever know—the Millennium, or the one-thousand-year reign of the Lord Jesus Christ as *KING OF KINGS; AND LORD OF LORDS. He will sit on the throne of David in Jerusalem, and the government shall be upon his shoulder: and his name shall be called Wonderful, Counsellor, the mighty God, The everlasting Father, The Prince of Peace. Of the increase of his government and peace there shall be no end* (Isaiah 9:6,7).

Before beginning our study of this chapter, may I take a moment to refute the reasoning of critics who deny this doctrinal truth? Those who oppose the teaching of a literal one-thousand-year reign of Christ upon earth are in direct opposition to the Word of God! Their claim that the doctrine is dangerously built on a single chapter of the Bible proves that they are not good students of God's Holy Word, for many passages both teach and reflect this truth. Let's investigate.

First of all, if Israel has no future, dozens of Old Testament prophecies immediately go down the drain.

For example, Genesis 49 and Deuteronomy 33, with all of their benedictions upon the people of Israel, must be scrapped if there is no place upon earth where they find fulfillment. To spiritualize or allegorize the literal truths concerning Israel's future is to be willfully blinded. I have spent thousands of hours in God's Book and could never honestly or intellectually arrive at such a conclusion.

Secondly, there must be a Millennium, or scores of verses become hollow platitudes of meaningless predictions. Consider the following texts—they could never depict heaven because they occur on earth. If so, there must be a time and place for their fulfillment, because none of them has yet occurred.

The wolf also shall dwell with the lamb (as nature is tamed) (Isaiah 11:6).

But they shall sit every man under his vine and under his fig tree; and none shall make them afraid (Micah 4:4).

Behold, a king shall reign in righteousness (Isaiah 32:1).

And in the days of these kings shall the God of heaven set up a kingdom, which shall never be destroyed...and it shall stand for ever (Daniel 2:44).

The Lord...shall suddenly come to his temple (Malachi 3:1).

Ezekiel describes this Temple, built and located upon the earth (see chapters 40 through 48). Israel will be the head—not the tail—of the nations in that day (see Zechariah 8:23).

And they shall build houses, and inhabit them;

and they shall plant vineyards, and eat the fruit of them (Isaiah 65:21).

The Lord Jesus Christ referred to the period of time during which these events take place as the regeneration. *And Jesus said unto them, Verily I say unto you, That ye which have followed me, in the regeneration when the Son of man shall sit in the throne of his glory, ye also shall sit upon twelve thrones, judging the twelve tribes of Israel* (Matthew 19:28). Likewise, Peter declared, *And* [God] *shall send Jesus Christ, which before was preached unto you: Whom the heaven must receive until the times of restitution of all things, which God hath spoken by the mouth of all his holy prophets since the world began* (Acts 3:20,21).

The word *restitution* means "a reconstitute" and is similar to the regeneration of Matthew 19:28. In addition, Paul stated in Ephesians 1:21 that there is an age *which is to come.* This same age is called *the dispensation of the fulness of times* (Ephesians 1:10). Again these terms refer to the rule of Christ and His people over the earth—not angels, as the spiritualizers would have us believe. Angels ruling the earth is an impossibility, *for unto the angels hath he not put in subjection the world to come* (Hebrews 2:5). Instead, *the most High ruleth in the kingdom of men* (Daniel 4:17). The title, *the most High* [God], *or the most High* is Christ's millennial title throughout the Psalms, the Book of Daniel, and the Book of Hosea. The *most High* [God] will also bear the title *King of Israel* in that day (John 1:49). All upon earth will obey Him for [He] *shalt break them with a rod of iron*

273

(Psalm 2:9). The result: *Thy people shall be willing in the day of thy power* (Psalm 110:3). Earth's inhabitants will love the Lord Jesus so much during the kingdom age that *daily shall he be praised* (Psalm 72:15). Yes, *His name shall endure forever* (Psalm 72:17).

The center of all this kingdom activity is Jerusalem, not heaven's golden shores. Proof? *Yet have I set my king upon my holy hill of Zion* (Psalm 2:6). *Out of Zion shall go forth the law, and the word of the Lord from Jerusalem* (Isaiah 2:3). [They] *shall worship the Lord in the holy mount at Jerusalem* (Isaiah 27:13). *And the Redeemer shall come to Zion* (Isaiah 59:20). *The Lord also shall roar out of Zion, and utter his voice from Jerusalem* (Joel 3:16). *Thus saith the Lord...I will dwell in the midst of Jerusalem* (Zechariah 8:3). *Yea, many people and strong nations shall come to seek the Lord of hosts in Jerusalem* (Zechariah 8:22).

The preceding evidence is proof enough! Only the spiritually blind can deny the fact of a literal Millennium. Only the willfully ignorant can claim that the teaching is based on just one chapter of the Bible. Our brief review has but touched the hem of the garment concerning millennial truth. Believe God, not men. Now, since *mille* means "thousand" and *annum* means "years," let's begin our study of chapter 20 which presents the *mille annum*, Millennium, or the one-thousand-year reign of Christ on the earth.

Verse 1: *And I saw an angel come down from*

heaven, having the key of the bottomless pit and a great chain in his hand.

Verse 2: *And he laid hold on the dragon, that old serpent, which is the Devil, and Satan, and bound him a thousand years,*

Verse 3: *And cast him into the bottomless pit, and shut him up, and set a seal upon him, that he should deceive the nations no more, till the thousand years should be fulfilled: and after that he must be loosed a little season.*

What a victorious sight John now sees—an angel coming from heaven with a key and a chain in his hand for the purpose of opening the bottomless pit and binding Satan for one thousand years. Some scholars believe the angel to be Christ himself because he has the keys of hell and death (chapter 1, verse 18). This is a distinct possibility. However, one who possesses keys often loans them to another when help is needed. Thus, the angel might be Michael, the archangel. The important observation here is that Christ's ownership of the keys—which open the pit of the abyss for Satan—is by virtue of His completed work upon Calvary's cross. Remember His statement in verse 18 of chapter 1: *I am he that liveth, and was dead;* [Calvary]*; and, behold, I am alive for evermore* [the Resurrection]*, Amen; and have the keys of hell and of death.*

The chain carried by the angel is used to bind the villain of the ages—called *the dragon, that old serpent...the Devil, and Satan*—for 1,000 years. What horrid titles the evil one bears! *Dragon*, in Hebrew, pictures a hideous monster. The term *old serpent* portrays the slithering snake who brought ruination upon the entire human race through his deceitful work in the Garden of Eden (see Genesis 3:1-6). *Satan* means "slander," for he is *the accuser of* [the] *brethren* as we learned in chapter 12, verse 10, and he is also the father of slanderers and gossips (see John 8:44). *Devil* means "adversary" or "foe," and surely Satan has been a foe of Christ and His followers until this present moment in our text. Now, at last, he is cast into the *bottomless pit,* shut up and sealed for a Millennium (verse 3).

The *bottomless pit* is not the *lake of fire* into which the beast and false prophet were cast in chapter 19, verse 20. Rather, it is a temporary prison where Satan is incarcerated for ten centuries in order that peace, prosperity, happiness, and holiness may exist on earth during Christ's millennial reign. At the end of this time, he is *loosed* [for] *a little season,* leads one final revolt against God, and is subsequently cast into the eternal *lake of fire...where the beast and the false prophet are* (chapter 20, verse 10).

Verse 4: *And I saw thrones, and they sat upon them, and judgment was given unto them: and I saw the souls of them that were beheaded for the witness of Jesus, and for the word of God, and which had not worshipped the beast, neither his image, neither had received his mark upon their foreheads, or in their hands; and they lived and reigned with Christ a thousand years.*

John now observes thrones occupied for judgment. Who sits upon them? Members of the first resurrection—which includes the Old Testament saints, Church Age saints, and Tribulation saints. The resurrection of the Old Testament believers is described in Daniel 12:1 and 2, and the resurrection of New Testament saints in 1 Thessalonians 4:16-18 and 1 Corinthians 15:15-54. As we have seen, the resurrection of the martyred Tribulation saints undoubtedly occurs at the *glorious appearing of Christ* (Titus 2:13) when He returns to earth. Chapter 6, verses 9 through 11, presented this view. At that point these martyrs awaited their resurrection but were told to wait *yet for a little season, until their fellowservants also and their brethren, that should be killed as they were, should be fulfilled.*

Thus, we see that the thrones are occupied by resurrected believers from Adam onward, inclusive of the last Tribulation martyrs. Each has been a participant in the first resurrection. These saints are entitled to sit upon thrones because they are members of the *royal priesthood* (1 Peter 2:9). Christ has made them *kings and priests* (chapter 5, verse 10).

Verse 5: *But the rest of the dead lived not again until the thousand years were finished. This is the first resurrection.*

The closing sentence of this verse, *This is the first resurrection,* should have been the conclusion of verse 4. The transition from verse 4 to verse 5 would then be: *And they lived and reigned with Christ a thousand years.* [This is the first resurrection.] *But the rest of the dead lived not again until the thousand years were finished.* This clarifies the issue. The dead of verse 5—raised a thousand years later—

could not be part of the first resurrection (those of verse 4)—because...

Verse 6: *Blessed and holy is he that hath part in the first resurrection: on such the second death hath no power, but they shall be priests of God and of Christ, and shall reign with him a thousand years.*

Since the remaining dead come forth one thousand years later, we immediately understand that they cannot be part of the first resurrection. Those who take part in the first resurrection reign with Christ during the Millennium, while the members of this group remain in their graves. They, in turn, are raised for the Great White Throne Judgment after the 1,000 years.

Verse 7: *And when the thousand years are expired, Satan shall be loosed out of his prison,*

Verse 8: *And shall go out to deceive the nations which are in the four quarters of the earth, Gog and Magog, to gather them together to battle: the number of whom is as the sand of the sea.*

Verse 9: *And they went up on the breadth of the earth, and compassed the camp of the saints about, and the beloved city: and fire came down from God out of heaven, and devoured them.*

This portion of Scripture has caused many people great concern. They ask, "Why should Satan be loosed for a short season? What purpose could God have in unchaining this monster after one thousand years of blessed peace?" The answer is, "The free will of man."

All persons who enter the Millennium are redeemed people (Isaiah 60:21 and Joel 2:28). However, one must remember that procreation still takes place during this era of time because those who survived the Tribulation hour enter the Millennium with human bodies. The believers upon the thrones possess resurrected bodies and do not bear children, but the others do. Consequently, the children born during this one-thousand-year period are born with the old Adamic, or sin, nature which has been an inherent part of man ever since the fall of Adam and Eve. Many of them, of course, accept Christ as their personal Saviour, but many do not! In addition, since Satan is bound, there is little to tempt them. They simply do not face the problems and trials which have confronted mankind in past ages. Satan's release, then, is to determine whether or not Christ is real to these children of the Millennium, or whether they have been submissive simply because He ruled *with a rod of iron* (chapter 19, verse 15).

The truth is revealed as millions follow the devil. Yes, even after living with the Lord Jesus Christ for ten centuries, much of mankind rebels. Verses 8 and 9 inform us that Satan deceives the nations internationally (pictured by the four corners of the earth), and gathers them together for one last battle. The army is gigantic in number...*as the sand of the sea*. Once again the camp of God's people—the beloved city of Jerusalem—is surrounded, just as the armies of the Tribulation hour gathered against Jerusalem to battle (see Zechariah 14:1). Then, in an instant, God destroys them all with a devouring fire from heaven.

To whom do the names Gog and Magog refer? In Ezekiel 38 and 39, they identify Russia. Not so in verse 8. Instead, they most likely indicate the memory of past brutality—much like the names *Pearl Harbor, Hiroshima, and Iraq* do today. As Gog and Magog (Russia) invades Israel and comes against Jerusalem during the Tribulation hour, such an indelible impression is left upon all the world that now—one thousand years later—the details are still vivid. Thus, this past war, fought in the same area, is brought to mind as Satan once again attempts to destroy Israel.

Verse 10: *And the devil that deceived them was cast into the lake of fire and brimstone, where the beast and the false prophet are, and shall be tormented day and night for ever and ever.*

This is the end for the deceiver of the ages. He is cast into the place *prepared for the devil and his angels* (Matthew 25:41). Many centuries were required for this slanderous culprit to reach his final destination. Now that he has arrived, he will experience nothing but continual torment—day and night—for ever and ever. Amen!

We need to digress for a moment at this point, because many persons—Christians included—harbor a misconception about hell. Whenever they see or hear the term, they picture a place where a little red-suited gremlin stokes the fires and torments his victims with a pitchfork. Satan is neither the stoker nor does he torment his followers—and, as we have observed, he does not enter hell until after the Millennium. As we have already learned, Satan is the *god of this world* [system] (2 Corinthians 4:4), *the prince of the power of the air* (Ephesians 2:2), and the ruler of heavens one and two—the aerial and stellar heavens. He retains this position until he is cast out of heaven (see chapter 12, verses 7-9). He then reigns on earth for the final forty-two months of the Tribulation period. Upon Christ's return to earth, Satan is bound in the *bottomless pit*, and then, following the Millennium, is released for a short season. Finally, he is cast into hell, or *the lake of fire and brimstone*, where he is tormented for all eternity. An understanding of these truths is essential to both victorious living and correct interpretation of the Book of Revelation.

We now come to the most awesome portion of Scripture in the entire Bible—the judgment of the wicked.

Verse 11: *And I saw a great white throne, and him that sat on it, from whose face the earth and the heaven fled away; and there was found no place for them.*

Verse 12: *And I saw the dead, small and great, stand before God; and the books were opened: and another book was opened, which is the book of life: and the dead were judged out of those things which were written in the books, according to their works.*

Verse 13: *And the sea gave up the dead which were in it; and death and hell delivered up the dead which were in them: and they were judged every man according to their works.*

Verse 14: *And death and hell were cast into the lake of fire. This is the second death.*

Verse 15: *And whosoever was not found written in the book of life was cast into the lake of fire.*

Again John says, *I saw.* The term is found thirty-seven times in this book. What a privilege was his! This time he views the gloomiest hour of history—the judgment of the wicked—as well as Christ sitting upon a *white throne*. White is the symbol of purity, justice, and holiness in Scripture. *Though your sins be as scarlet, they shall be white as snow* (Isaiah 1:18). *His wife hath made herself ready. And to her was granted that she should be arrayed in fine linen, clean and white* (chapter 19, verses 7 and 8).

Since "white" stands for all that is honorable and right, what does it symbolize? Integrity—for Christ, Who is *the truth* (John 14:6), is himself the Judge. Notice that the term is *Great White Throne*. This pictures a great judgment that is about to fall on those who have rejected the "so great salvation" question (see Hebrews 2:3).

How does one know that the tender, loving Jesus is the One who sits upon the throne as Judge? The answer is found in John 5:22: *For the Father judgeth no man, but hath committed all judgment unto the Son*. Again, the Father *hath given him authority to execute judgment also, because he is the Son of man* (John 5:27). The One raised from the dead—the Lord Jesus Christ—is the Judge, according to Acts 17:31: [For] *he hath appointed a day, in the which he will judge the world in righteousness by that man whom he hath ordained; whereof he hath given assurance unto all men, in that he hath raised him from the dead*. That moment is now before us!

What a solemn scene as unregenerate mankind comes face to face with God for the investigation of all their evil deeds. Every transgressor is present:

presidents and paupers, high society snobs and skid row derelicts. Yes, this group includes every Christ-rejecter of the ages, small and great, rich and poor, free and bond. *Marvel not at this: for the hour is coming, in the which all that are in the graves shall hear his voice, and shall come forth; they that have done good, unto the resurrection of life* [the first resurrection]*; and they that have done evil, unto the resurrection of damnation* [the resurrection for judgment] (John 5:28,29). Make no mistake about it, *there shall be a resurrection of the dead, both of the just and unjust* (Acts 24:15).

As the unsaved stand before a holy God, the books are opened. Yes, He has record of every wicked deed sinners have ever committed. Nothing remains hidden. Adultery, abortion, drunkenness, drug addiction, harlotry, hatred, lawlessness, murder, rebellion, sexual promiscuity, wife-swapping, and every other abominable practice is then exposed in detail.

How is all this possible? God is both omniscient (all knowing) and omnipotent (all-powerful). The psalmist said in chapter 139, verses 1 and 2, *O Lord, thou hast searched me, and known me. Thou knowest my downsitting and mine uprising.* God knows everything about every member of the human race. God adds, *I know the things that come into your mind, every one of them* (Ezekiel 11:5). I know when you have eyes *full of adultery, and that cannot cease from sin* (2 Peter 2:14). I know when your tongue is about to curse, *For there is not a word in my tongue, but, lo, O Lord, thou knowest it altogether* (Psalm 139:4). *I*

283

the Lord search the heart (Jeremiah 17:10). This statement is extremely important, *For out of the heart proceed evil thoughts, murders, adulteries, fornications, thefts, false witness, blasphemies* (Matthew 15:19).

God's books will be totally accurate because He sees every move humans make: *The eyes of the Lord run to and fro throughout the whole earth* (2 Chronicles 16:9). *All things are naked and opened unto the eyes of him with whom we have to do* (Hebrews 4:13). That aborted fetus flushed into oblivion, that sex act in a parked car or motel room, that crooked deal for illegal gain—everything is indelibly inscribed in the journal of the Almighty bookkeeper. One cannot hide from God, whoever He may be! Furthermore, no mistakes will be made, for the dead will be judged *out of those things which were written in the books, according to their works.* We also see that every unbeliever will be present, for the bodies come forth from land and sea and the souls come from Hades (or hell). Then, body, soul, and spirit are reunited to stand before God.

Many have never realized that there is a time when the wicked are released from hell. This is not a new doctrine or man-made theory. (Order my full-length audio cassette, "Hell Without Hell," for a thorough study of this subject.) However, for the moment, let's examine a few facts regarding this teaching.

The New Testament contains two Greek words—*Hades* and *Gehenna*—both of which are translated *hell* in our English Bible. The Lord Jesus Christ used both words repeatedly. Why two words? Are there two places? Yes! A simple illustration will help us understand.

Everyone knows the difference between a local jail and a penitentiary. When an individual is arrested for a crime, he is not placed in the penitentiary until he has had a trial. Instead, he is locked up in the local jail (city or county), where he awaits his trail. Then, upon being found guilty, he is transferred to the penitentiary, where he serves his sentence. The next statement is of extreme importance. Get it! When Jesus used the word *Hades*, He referred to the local jail—the place where the sinner is bound until the judgment morning. Then, on Judgment Day, the sinner comes out of the local jail (*Hades*), stands before the Judge (the Lord Jesus himself), is found guilty, and is subsequently transferred to the final penitentiary of souls (*Gehenna*). The lake of fire is usually synonymous with *Gehenna*.

The eleven instances where Christ mentioned *Hades* are as follows: Matthew 11:23; 16:18; Luke 10:15; 16:22,23; Acts 2:27; 2:31; 1 Corinthians 15:55; Revelation 1:18; 6:8; 20:13; and Revelation 20:14.

Gehenna is mentioned twelve times by the Saviour: Matthew 5:22; 5:29; 5:30; 10:28; 18:9; 23:15; 23:33; Mark 9:43; 9:45; 9:47; Luke 12:5; and James 3:6.

After studying the twenty-three texts, one observes that verses 13 and 14 of our present study now make perfect sense: *Death* [the grave] *and hell* [Hades] *delivered up the dead which were in them.* The plural pronoun "them" indicates two places: *the grave* and *Hades*—one for the body and the other for the soul. Next *they were judged every man according to* his *works* (that's the trial). Then *death and* [Hades—Greek] *were cast into the lake of fire* [*Gehenna*—the final penitentiary].

Why are they transferred? *Gehenna* differs from *Hades* in that *Gehenna* is a place where there are degrees of suffering. After one has been examined and judged as to how much light he had (how often he heard the message of salvation and rejected it), he is assigned to this place called *Gehenna,* where there are degrees of suffering according to one's light and works. Thus, the final hell will differ for all, depending on one's evil deeds and the number of times he rejected Christ's offer of love.

Now we understand Romans 2:5 a little better: *But after thy hardness and impenitent heart treasurest up* [storest up, savest up] *unto thyself wrath against the day of wrath.* This is why *it shall be more tolerable* [more bearable, more endurable] *for the land of Sodom in the day of judgment, than for* [Capernaum] (Matthew 11:24). What was Capernaum's sin? Capernaum had greater light since Christ visited the city and preached to her citizens. This is also why the Pharisees *receive the greater damnation* (Matthew 23:14).

Clearly, sinners are raised from *death* and *Hades*, judged by Christ at the Great White Throne, and then transferred to *Gehenna.* The "good news," however, is that none of this happens to those who are trusting in the merits of the shed blood of Jesus. When one trusts Christ, his name is written in the *book of life.* The judgment just discussed is only for those whose names are not found inscribed in the book (see verse 15). If one is saved, he need never be concerned about hell as his eternal destiny, for *he that believeth on* [Christ] *is not condemned* (John 3:18). He is also *passed from death unto life* (John 5:24). Thus, *there is therefore now no condemnation to them which are in Christ Jesus* (Romans 8:1). Amen.

The great judgment is only for those who participate in the final resurrection which occurs after the 1,000-year or millennial reign of Christ upon earth. Those who were raised prior to the Millennium are eternally secure, for *blessed and holy is he that hath part in the first resurrection: on such the second death hath no power* (verse 6).

21

The final two chapters of the Book of Revelation present the glorious future which awaits every believer of all dispensations and ages. The eternal state of both the saved and lost is described in the first eight verses of this chapter. In addition, verses 9 through 27 present a glowing description of the New Jerusalem. The view is absolutely breathtaking. Let's begin our study.

Verse 1: *And I saw a new heaven and a new earth: for the first heaven and the first earth were passed away; and there was no more sea.*

The passing away of the first heaven and earth occurred at the conclusion of the Great White Throne Judgment. This was part of the renovation of the world which Jesus predicted in Matthew 24:35 when He said, *Heaven and earth shall pass away.* The time and method are described in 2 Peter 3:7,10-13. Listen carefully to these solemn words: *The heavens and the earth, which are now, by the same word are kept in store, reserved unto fire against the day of judgment and perdition of ungodly men. But the day of the Lord will come as a thief in the night; in the which the heavens shall pass away with a great noise, and the elements shall melt with fervent heat, the earth also and the works that are therein shall be burned up. Seeing then that all these things shall be dissolved, what manner of persons ought ye to be in all holy conversation and godliness, Looking for and hasting unto the coming of the day of God, wherein the heavens being on fire shall be dissolved, and the elements shall melt with fervent heat? Nevertheless we, according to his promise, look for new heavens and a new earth, wherein dwelleth righteousness.*

In the new world, the sea is eliminated, possibly because of its connotation with wickedness: *The wicked are like the troubled sea, when it cannot rest, whose waters cast up mire and dirt* (Isaiah 57:20). Another reason may be that oceanic vegetation is no longer necessary.

Verse 2: *And I John saw the holy city, New Jerusalem, coming down from God out of heaven, prepared as a bride adorned for her husband.*

Two Jerusalems are mentioned in Scripture (see Galatians 4:25,26 and Hebrews 12:22). One is earthly and the home of the believers during the millennial period. The other is heavenly—the New Jerusalem, or celestial city, which hovers over the earth eternally following the post-millennial creation of the new heaven and earth. The New Jerusalem is undoubtedly the one Christ has been preparing for 2,000 years, for the Saviour said in John 14:2, *I go to prepare a place for you.* This magnificent masterpiece descending toward earth reminds one of the elegant beauty of a bride on her wedding day.

Verse 3: *And I heard a great voice out of heaven*

saying, Behold, the tabernacle of God is with men, and he will dwell with them, and they shall be his people, and God himself shall be with them, and be their God.

To this point in time, God's Tabernacle has been located in heaven. Now we discover a change of address. The Almighty descends to earth with His heavenly entourage, settling in the New Jerusalem to begin global operations from this satellite city. The redeemed—in their glorified bodies—live in the New Jerusalem. Those with bodies of flesh—those who were born and saved during the millennial hour— enter the eternal state with their natural bodies. They live on earth, in and under the light of the Holy City (see chapter 21, verse 24). The true beauty of the entire scene is that God dwells in the midst of His people, for a voice cries, *Behold, the tabernacle of God is with men, and he will dwell with them, and they shall be his people, and God himself shall be with them, and be their God.*

Another exciting fact is that believers, with their glorified bodies, will be able to travel as fast as the speed of light, yea, as fast as their thoughts. Thus, they will traverse back and forth to earth from their city in space—the New Jerusalem—in a moment of time. Presently the world's scientists predict that men will be living in space cities before the year 2,000. They don't know the half of it! Amen!

Verse 4: *And God shall wipe away all tears from their eyes; and there shall be no more death, neither sorrow, nor crying, neither shall there be any more pain: for the former things are passed away.*

This verse should be a favorite among God's people. Think of it! Pain, sorrow, crying, and death are forever eliminated in this land of eternal life. No wonder the redeemed are able to triumphantly shout, *O death, where is thy sting? O grave, where is thy victory?* (1 Corinthians 15:55). Never again will a funeral procession take place, for death, *the last enemy,* will have been destroyed (see 1 Corinthians 15:26). In addition, everything associated with death is also eliminated for time and eternity. Glory! No more disease, heart attacks, automobile accidents, wars or rumors of wars. "It is finished" is truly the national anthem of eternity.

Although these truths are wonderful in themselves, the greatest fact is that the Lord's people *see His face* (see chapter 22, verse 4). In addition, sin has ceased to exist because Satan is eternally incarcerated in Gehenna, *the lake of fire* (see chapter 20, verse 10). A new day in a new heaven suspended above a new earth has arrived because...

Verse 5: *He that sat upon the throne said, Behold, I make all things new. And he said unto me, Write: for these words are true and faithful.*

Verse 6: *And he said unto me, It is done. I am Alpha and Omega, the beginning and the end. I will give unto him that is athirst of the fountain of the water of life freely.*

God speaks to John, saying, *It is done.* As Christ completed His redemptive work for sinners on the cross, He cried, *It is finished.* Now God, who has made all things new, again announces, *It is finished,* or done. His will has been accomplished in Jesus

Christ—namely, that the earth should be free from the curse of sin and that its inhabitants should be conformed to His very likeness. This has happened. *It is done.* God adds, *I am* [the] *Alpha and Omega, the beginning and the end.* Alpha and Omega are the first and the last letters of the Greek alphabet. Hence, the explanation, the beginning and the end. But what does it mean? In Christ, all creation began without sin (see Colossians 1:15-19). Now, in Christ, it has ended without sin.

In this glorious city—New Jerusalem—the spiritual thirst of God's people is also satisfied forever. While on earth, Jesus said to the woman of Samaria, *Whosoever drinketh of this water* [in the well] *shall thirst again: But whosoever drinketh of the water that I shall give him shall never thirst; but the water that I shall give him shall be in him a well of water springing up into everlasting life* (John 4:13,14). That time has come, and God states: "I will give unto him that is athirst of the fountain of the water of life freely." It is yours to possess throughout the ages. Enjoy yourselves!

However, make no mistake about it. The eternal prize of being in the presence of God in the New Jerusalem, where there is no more death, sorrow, crying, pain, or thirst, is only for those who trust in the merits of the shed blood of Christ.

Verse 7: *He that overcometh shall inherit all things; and I will be his God, and he shall be my son.*

Who is the overcomer? The one who believes that Jesus is the Son of God (see 1 John 5:4). Oh, be sure of your salvation, because the next verse mentions a motley group of sinners that misses the eternal paradise upon earth.

Verse 8: *But the fearful, and unbelieving, and the abominable, and murderers, and whoremongers, and sorcerers, and idolaters, and all liars, shall have their part in the lake which burneth with fire and brimstone: which is the second death.*

This text plainly states that those who were condemned at the judgment of chapter 20, verses 11-15, have been cast into the *lake of fire,* or Gehenna. They were not given a reprieve, a commuted sentence, or a second chance, as some sentimentalists teach. Revelation 21 is the eternal state.

No more changes are possible. Those who stood before God's Great White Throne did not make it. Who were they?

1. *The fearful*—those who rejected Christ to escape the ridicule of men.

2. *The unbelieving*—those who rejected the doctrine of Christ's deity and shed blood as the only means of obtaining eternal life. Jesus said, *Ye shall die in your sins...if ye believe not that I am he* [or that I am God] (John 8:24). In John 5:40, the Saviour again said, *Ye will not come to me, that ye might have life.*

3. *The abominable*—those who engaged in wicked practices. They spoke the language of christendom but never lived it: *They profess that they know God; but in works they deny him, being abominable, and disobedient, and unto every good work reprobate* (Titus 1:16).

4. *The murderers*—including those who carried

294

hatred within their hearts and minds for others. If you don't believe it, listen to the following: *Whosoever hateth his brother is a murderer: and ye know that no murderer hath eternal life abiding in him* (1 John 3:15).

5. *The whoremongers*—those who engaged in fornication (premarital sex), adultery (extra marital flings), or perverted sex.

6. *The sorcerers*—those who practiced drug usage for "kicks" and "highs."

7. *The idolaters*—those who worshiped or revered anyone or anything other than the living and true God, or who used idols in worship. Remember God's warning, *Little children, keep yourselves from idols* (1 John 5:21).

8. *All liars*—those who deceived others, distorted the truth, and destroyed mankind by lies.

Verse 9: *And there came unto me one of the seven angels which had the seven vials full of the seven last plagues, and talked with me, saying, Come hither, I will shew thee the bride, the Lamb's wife.*

Here one member of the angelic host which administered the final seven judgments now speaks to John, saying, "Come here. I want to show you the Bride, the Lamb's wife, the one who *made herself ready* [in] *fine linen, clean and white* (chapter 19, verses 7 and 8) and who returns with Him for the 1,000-year honeymoon (chapter 19, verses 11 through 16)." At this point the Bride is envisioned in her final resting place.

Verse 10: *And he carried me away in the spirit to a great and high mountain, and shewed me that*

295

great city, the holy Jerusalem, descending out of heaven from God.

The Bride is pictured as the city of the New Jerusalem because a city is composed of people. Buildings, streets, and light are but aids to the residents. For example, one refers to a city as "clean" or "wicked." Why? Because of its people. Now, as John views God's heavenly creation, he is impressed by (1) the brilliance of the city (verses 9-14), (2) the size of the city (verses 15-17), and (3) the beauty of the city (verses 18-21). He describes the city as...

Verse 11: *Having the glory of God and her light was like unto a stone most precious, even like a jasper stone, clear as crystal;*

Verse 12: *And had a wall great and high, and had twelve gates, and at the gates twelve angels, and names written thereon, which are the names of the twelve tribes of the children of Israel:*

Verse 13: *On the east three gates; on the north three gates; on the south three gates; and on the west three gates.*

Verse 14: *And the wall of the city had twelve foundations, and in them the names of the twelve apostles of the Lamb.*

In Bible times walls were erected for protection. However, since war is forever finished, one may question the presence of this wall in the New Jerusalem. The answer? It serves as a reminder that the God of love protected His people while on earth. This wall is an eternal memorial to the fact that our lives have been hidden *with Christ in God* (Colossians 3:3).

The city also has twelve gates, each inscribed with one of the names of the twelve tribes of the Children of Israel.

The gates are staffed with angels who welcome those possessing the right and privilege of entering the city (chapter 22, verse 14). The twelve angels standing at these entrances are possibly those who worked jointly with each tribe during the earthly sojourn of the people of Israel. We also note that, just as the gates are inscribed with the names of the twelve tribes, the foundations of the wall itself contain the names of Christ's twelve apostles. Next let's consider the size of the city.

Verse 15: *And he that talked with me had a golden reed to measure the city, and the gates thereof, and the wall thereof.*

Verse 16: *And the city lieth foursquare, and the length is as large as the breadth: and he measured the city with the reed, twelve thousand furlongs. The length and the breadth and the height of it are equal.*

Verse 17: *And he measured the wall thereof, an hundred and forty and four cubits, according to the measure of a man, that is, of the angel.*

The angel measures the city with a golden reed or measuring rod. Since the streets are composed of gold and the city is pure gold as well (verse 18), a gold yardstick is appropriate. (It's a good thing that thieves are excluded—1 Corinthians 6:10—otherwise heaven's freeways would disappear!)

Verse 16 informs us that the New Jerusalem is tetragonal, or foursquare in shape. The city is a perfect cube because its width, length, and height are equal. In fact, the angel discovers its dimensions to be 12,000 furlongs wide, long, and high. Most scholars believe this to be a distance of 1,500 miles. Dr. A. C. Gaebelein says, "Twelve thousand furlongs constitutes fifteen hundred miles." Seiss states: "The golden city is 1,500 miles square; for 12,000 stadia make 1,500 miles."

Placed over the United States of America, the heavenly city would extend from the northernmost point of Maine to the southernmost point of Florida and from the eastern seaboard to Colorado. In fact, the major cities of the world are mere villages in comparison with the New Jerusalem.

Because it also extends 1,500 miles upward into space, it could literally contain every person who has ever been born, plus additional billions as well.

The wall extends around the city and is approximately 216 feet in height, for a cubit is the distance from the elbow to the end of the middle finger (approximately eighteen inches).

Now let's look into the magnificent beauty of God's Holy City.

Verse 18: *And the building of the wall of it was of jasper: and the city was pure gold, like unto clear glass.*

Verse 19: *And the foundations of the wall of the city were garnished with all manner of precious stones. The first foundation was jasper; the second, sapphire; the third, a chalcedony; the fourth, an emerald;*

Verse 20: *The fifth, sardonyx; the sixth, sardius; the seventh, chrysolite; the eighth, beryl; the ninth, a* *topaz; the tenth, a chrysoprasus; the eleventh, a ja-cinth; the twelfth, an amethyst.*

Verse 21: *And the twelve gates were twelve pearls: every several gate was of one pearl: and the street of the city was pure gold, as it were transparent glass.*

Wow! Notice first that the wall of jasper represents Christ, in His radiant glory, surrounding His saints. Next the pure gold city typifies the righteousness of God's holy nature, and then the precious colorful stones—startlingly brilliant—picture the Lord's attributes as well as various aspects of His redemptive work.

Imagine the scene when the light of the city—the Lord Jesus Christ (verse 23)—shines through the brilliancy of these stones! When John's vision becomes a reality—then and only then—we will begin to understand the term *the glory of God!*

The beautiful city also pictures the saints of all ages joined together in love, for the names of the twelve tribes of Israel are coupled with the names of the apostles. This means that all of God's people from all dispensations have finally been joined together in one truly ecumenical brotherhood. No longer will we be Baptists, Lutherans, Methodists, Nazarenes, or Presbyterians. Instead, we will be united brethren! What a glorious day when we lay aside eternally the tags that so often divide us.

Verse 22: *And I saw no temple therein: for the Lord God Almighty and the Lamb are the temple of it.*

On earth, God always had a dwelling place—a temple or tabernacle—where men could come to worship and commune with Him. Such a place is no longer needed, for the tabernacle of God is now with men. He has chosen to dwell with them (chapter 21, verse 3).

Verse 23: *And the city had no need of the sun, neither of the moon, to shine in it: for the glory of God did lighten it, and the Lamb is the light thereof.*

While on earth, Jesus said, *I am the light of the world* (John 8:12). Now, in the eternal city, Christ, in all His radiant splendor and glory, shines forth so magnificently that darkness becomes an impossibility. No wonder there shall be no night there!

Verse 24: *And the nations of them which are saved shall walk in the light of it: and the kings of the earth do bring their glory and honour into it.*

Verse 25: *And the gates of it shall not be shut at all by day: for there shall be no night there.*

Verse 26: *And they shall bring the glory and honour of the nations into it.*

These verses undoubtedly picture the multitudes who came through the Millennium as born-again, regenerated believers. They did not follow Satan in the final rebellion upon his release from the bottomless pit. Therefore, they entered the eternal state in bodies of flesh. Their rulers, kings, and presidents—also born again and still living in earthly bodies—now bring their glory and honour into the New Jerusalem as well. They come to praise Him who is all in all. As they arrive, there is no fear of assassination, recrimination, terrorism, or robbery. Such events are no longer possible. God is present. Satan is destroyed. Temptation is forever past. Thus, the gates of the city are never locked. Security is needless in the land of eternal day where there is no night. At this point, however, the warning flag is again lifted.

Verse 27: *And there shall in no wise enter into it any thing that defileth, neither whatsoever worketh abomination, or maketh a lie: but they which are written in the Lamb's book of life.*

22

This closing chapter of the Book of Revelation continues our thrilling "sightseeing tour" of the New Jerusalem, and reaffirms the fact that only those who possess the righteousness of Christ are granted admittance and residence.

Verse 1: *And he showed me a pure river of water of life, clear as crystal, proceeding out of the throne of God and of the Lamb.*

Verse 2: *In the midst of the street of it, and on either side of the river, was there the tree of life, which bare twelve manner of fruits, and yielded her fruit every month: and the leaves of the tree were for the healing of the nations.*

The first two verses of chapter 22 establish the fact that, in our new glorified bodies, we, as inhabitants of the Holy City, will continue to enjoy the habit of eating. Why not? When we see Jesus, *we shall be like him* (1 John 3:2). Since He ate in His glorified body (see Luke 24:43), why wouldn't we? Our text also describes the best drink we will ever enjoy—pure, refreshing water direct from the throne of God. Think of it! Distilled or chemically treated water is no longer necessary, for pollution has become non-existent!

Not only do we have crystal clear water to drink, but we also enjoy delicious health-producing fruit. In fact, the *tree of life* bears twelve manner of fruits and produces them monthly.

This is interesting.

When Adam and Eve sinned by partaking of the *tree of knowledge of good and evil* (Genesis 2:17), God drove them out of the Garden of Eden. He then stationed an angel before its entrance in order to keep them from eating the fruit of the *tree of life*, lest they eat and live eternally in their sinful state.

Now a new day has arrived. The saints are in the very presence of God, and may eat of *the tree of life* to their heart's content. Undoubtedly this tree plays a part in promoting one's endless existence, for even the leaves contain healing or health for the nations living under, or in the light of, the city. The word *health* is the proper translation, not *healing*. Since there is no sorrow, sickness, or pain, healing is unnecessary because eternal health is for all. In the heavenly city, doctors and nurses are permanently retired. Hallelujah!

Verse 3: *And there shall be no more curse: but the throne of God and of the Lamb shall be in it; and his servants shall serve him:*

The curse, which originated in the Garden of Eden and was partially removed during the Millennium, is now obliterated forever.

Verse 4: *And they shall see his face; and his name shall be in their foreheads.*

Think of it! We will observe the beauty of our Saviour's countenance daily as we live in His presence forever and ever.

When we look at the One who is altogether lovely and He, in turn, looks at us, He will observe His name indelibly inscribed upon our foreheads. This is our seal of eternal ownership! Oh, how wonderful to belong to Jesus!

Verse 5: *And there shall be no night there; and they need no candle, neither light of the sun; for the Lord God giveth them light: and they shall reign for ever and ever.*

Because Christ, in all His glory, illuminates the city and its inhabitants—those who walk in the light of the city—no other type of natural or artificial lighting is required. Even the sun which warmed the former earth for so many centuries is no longer necessary. The warmth of the love of God shines upon His people for the ages of ages in this land of eternal day.

Verse 6: *And he said unto me, These sayings are faithful and true: and the Lord God of the holy prophets sent his angel to shew unto his servants the things which must shortly be done.*

At this point the angel tells John the reason God has allowed him to experience this vision of the revelation. He says, "The God of the holy prophets who is truth and cannot lie, sent me to tell you that the things you have heard and seen must come to pass speedily."

Verse 7: *Behold, I come quickly: blessed is he that keepeth the sayings of the prophecy of this book.*

In verse 6, our Lord told John that the things

written in this Book of Revelation must shortly be done or "come to pass speedily." Then He adds in verse 7, *Behold, I come quickly* [or speedily]. The term *speedily* is not used in relationship to hours, days, months, or even years. Rather, it speaks of a series of events happening in rapid succession once they begin. In other words, when these things begin to come to pass (see Luke 21:28), the signs and events will fall into place so speedily—one after another—that a state of preparedness should be maintained. Hence, the admonition: *Blessed* [or happy] *is he that keepeth the sayings of the prophecy of this book.* Such an individual will be ready for the Lord's return.

Verse 8: *And I John saw these things, and heard them. And when I had heard and seen, I fell down to worship before the feet of the angel which shewed me these things.*

Verse 9: *Then saith he unto me, See thou do it not: for I am thy fellowservant, and of thy brethren the prophets, and of them which keep the sayings of this book: worship God.*

Poor mortals never learn! John had already made the mistake of bowing before an angel and being rebuked in chapter 19, verse 10. Now he does it again! Fortunately, we have a God of love. He is willing to forgive the same mistake *seventy times seven* (Matthew 18:22). Only by His grace, love, compassion, and forgiveness are any of us able to continue. Thank you, Lord Jesus!

Verse 10: *And he saith unto me, Seal not the sayings of the prophecy of this book: for the time is at hand.*

Following God's revelation to Daniel, the prophet was told to *seal the book* [until] *the time of the end* (Daniel 12:4).

John, however, is forbidden to seal the Book of Revelation because *the time is at hand,* or has come. In the Greek, the word *time* is *kairos,* and means "opportune moment" or "correct season." Thus, the angel is saying, "The time for the revealing of prophetic truth has come. People are to be made aware of the future. They must learn the history of the churches and the plan of the ages. Then, as they live in these periods of time, they will understand God's program. They will also realize that, once the events begin, they will speedily come to pass. Knowing this, they will prepare. Therefore, do not seal the prophecy of the sayings of this book."

Our study of the Book of Revelation has revealed that the Rapture, the Tribulation, and the Great White Throne Judgment will soon come to pass. As a result, some will realize that little time is left and will ask Christ to save them. Others will continue to harden their hearts. The decision is every individual's to make. One's acceptance or rejection of God's truth and the Lord Jesus Christ as one's personal Saviour will determine where one spends eternity and what one will be forever. Hence, the next statement...

Verse 11: *He that is unjust, let him be unjust still: and he which is filthy, let him be filthy still: and he that is righteous, let him be righteous still: and he that is holy, let him be holy still.*

Choose this day what you shall be eternally!

Verse 12: *And, behold, I come quickly; and my*

307

reward is with me, to give every man according as his work shall be.

God's prophetic time clock is ticking, and every event will certainly and speedily come to pass.

Verse 13: *I am Alpha and Omega, the beginning and the end, the first and the last.*

God is saying, "When I come, I will finish the work of redemption which I began, for I am the Alpha and Omega, *the author and finisher of* [the] *faith* (Hebrews 12:2)." If you receive the gospel invitation, you will be happy for...

Verse 14: *Blessed are they that do his commandments, that they may have right to the tree of life, and may enter in through the gates into the city.*

According to Dr. C. I. Scofield, a better rendering of verse 14 is, "Blessed are they that wash their robes that they may have right to the tree of life." If one is seeking rights to the tree of life by commandment-keeping, he is planning to arrive in the eternal state by his works. This, of course, is impossible as we have learned through Titus 3:5, Romans 4:5, and numerous other texts.

Dr. A. C. Gaebelein, Dr. H. A. Ironside, Dr. J. A. Seiss, and practically all noted Bible scholars also translate the verse, "Blessed are they that wash their robes (in the blood of the Lamb) that they may have right to the tree of life, and may enter in through the gates into the city." Those who reject the message of the blood and salvation by grace through faith in the completed work of Christ (see Ephesians 2:8,9) are reminded:

Verse 15: *For without are dogs, and sorcerers,*

and whoremongers, and murderers, and idolaters, and whosoever loveth and maketh a lie.

This is the crowd pictured in Revelation 21:8. The *dogs* are identical to the *abominable* of chapter 21. The abominable never lived it (see Titus 1:16), and the dogs went back to their dirt—their old sinful habits (see 2 Peter 2:22). Both verses speak of individuals who lack the "new birth" experience—the one and only way a person can become a new creation in Christ Jesus (see 2 Corinthians 5:17). There is absolutely no doubt about the destiny of those who reject God's message and the truths revealed in the Book of Revelation, for...

Verse 16: *I Jesus have sent mine angel to testify unto you these things in the churches. I am the root and the offspring of David, and the bright and morning star.*

The message of the revelation is true because Christ inaugurated and guarantees it. Who would dare question Him? In this verse, the Lord also calls himself the root and offspring of David. As the root, He is David's Lord—the preexistent God (see Psalm 110:1). As his offspring, He is David's son, the incarnate Christ (see Matthew 22:41-46).

This is a beautiful picture of the God-man, the Lord Jesus Christ. Jesus is also *the bright and morning star*. In fact, Peter calls Him *the day star* (2 Peter 1:19).

Now listen intently, for this is deeply moving. God so loves sinners that His compassionate heart must extend the gospel call one last time before the book closes. Oh, that modern-day ministers were as evangelistic as the Heavenly Father! Hear Him:

Verse 17: *And the Spirit and the bride say, Come. And let him that heareth say, Come. And let him that is athirst come. And whosoever will, let him take the water of life freely.*

In this text, God compassionately declares, "Believe in Me; come to Me. Invite Me into your heart and life. You have everything to gain and nothing to lose. Everyone and everything is pulling for you: (1) the Holy Spirit is, (2) the bride of Christ is, (3) everyone who hears and believes is, (4) the glorious city in which the Bride dwells is saying, 'Don't you want me for your eternal home?' Finally (5) your own spiritual thirst is crying out, 'I want to be satisfied.'" Why not come and drink? The water of life is free. It is without cost or obligation for everyone, and *whosoever will* may come!

If you have rejected this invitation, if you have considered the message of the Book of Revelation unimportant, or if you are among those who believe that the Book of Revelation is not part of the canon of Scripture—that it is but a collection of riddles, simply a symbolic hoax perpetrating a myth—beware! For God himself warns one and all...

Verse 18: *For I testify unto every man that heareth the words of the prophecy of this book, If any man shall add unto these things, God shall add unto him the plagues that are written in this book:*

Verse 19: *And if any man shall take away from the words of the book of this prophecy, God shall take away his part out of the book of life, and out of the* *holy city, and from the things which are written in this book.*

What a strong judgmental warning! What a serious admonition from the Almighty to take the Book of Revelation seriously! God means what He says and says what He means. One is not to meddle with or handle lightly the truths which mean so much to the God of heaven and earth, for...

Verse 20: *He which testifieth these things saith, Surely I come quickly. Amen. Even so, come, Lord Jesus.*

God's last promise as the Book of Revelation closes is, *Surely, I come quickly.* When one sees the beginning of these events and the rapid succession of signs following speedily, Jesus will come quickly— or suddenly. The response of His people is: *Amen.* This expression literally means, *so be it* (Jeremiah 11:5). And then they immediately add, *"Even so, come, Lord Jesus."*

The final message to the Church is that our Lord will return. Until this glorious event takes place and He calls us to himself *in the twinkling of an eye,* my prayer for every born-again child of God reflects the benediction of this blessed book:

Verse 21: *The grace of our Lord Jesus Christ be with you all. Amen.*

BIBLIOGRAPHY

Chafer, Lewis Sperry, *Systematic Theology*

Church, Jerry R., *Prophecy in the News*

Computer Digest

de Liguori, Alphonse, "The Glories of Mary,"
     Europe magazine

French, Nancy, *Computer World* magazine

Gaebelein, A.C., *The Revelation*

Gaverluk, Emil, *Caleb Communications U.S.A.*

Gibbons, Edward, *The History of the Rise and Fall of the
     Roman Empire*

Hilsop, Alexander, *The Two Babylons*

Hoar, William P., *Review of the News*

Ironside, H.A., *Lectures of the Book of Revelation*

Larkin, Clarence, *Dispensational Truth*

Logsdon, S. Franklin, *Is the U.S.A. in Prophecy?*

McAulfee, Kathleen, *Omni* magazine

Mendlovitz, Saul, *Review of the News*

Peterson, Paul, *Sinister World Computerization*

Scofield, C.I., *Scofield Reference Bible*

Scott, Paul, *Washington News Intelligence Syndicate*

Seiss, J.A., *The Apocalypse: Lectures on the Book of
     Revelation*

Spaak, Henry, *Society for Worldwide Interbank
     Financial Telecommunications*

Stoner, Peter, *Science Speaks*

Ulmer, Kevin, *Omni* magazine

Unger, Merrill F., *Unger's Bible Dictionary*

Vaticano Illustrato II

Wolfson, Seymour, *The Detroit News*

For a complete list of recordings, books, and other re-
source materials by Dr. Jack Van Impe, write for our
lastest catalog:

JACK VAN IMPE MINISTRIES
P.O. Box 7004 • Troy, Michigan 48007
In Canada: Box 1717, Postal Station A
Windsor, Ontario N9A 6Y1

Other Books by Jack Van Impe

AIDS Is for ~~Life~~ Death
Documented factual information about this deadly modern-day plague. Hundreds of authoritative medical and news reports listed alphabetically by subject for instant reference.

The Walking Bible
The "inside" story of Dr. Jack Van Impe. Forty years of the triumphs and tragedies of a remarkable man of God. New updated version includes new chapters and photographs.

Sin's Explosion
Though sin permeates and inundates the land, God specializes in bringing sinners to himself when sin is rampant. Includes scores of stirring quotes from great revival leaders. This book is a must for every library.

11:59...and Counting!
What does the future hold for you and your loved ones? The questions that plague humanity are answered in this detailed account of mankind's march toward the Tribulation, Armageddon, and the hour of Christ's return.

Israel's Final Holocaust
Over 240,000 in print! One of the most helpful explanations of Israel's role in end-time Bible prophecies ever published. What will the final holocaust be...and how will it affect you?

ALCOHOL: The Beloved Enemy
Liquor and the Bible. Thoroughly covers the alcohol question, including historic background, current research, and statistics that may shock you. Bible help for a major

problem. Every verse on the subject of wine from Genesis to Revelation is explained.

Sabotaging the World Church
Exposes the lovelessness among the brethren, using major excerpts from Dr. Van Impe's previous book, *Heart Disease in Christ's Body*. The answer to the problem is found in the Word of God and requires every member of Christ's body to endeavor *to keep the unity of the Spirit in the bond of peace* (Ephesians 4:3).

The Spirit of Antichrist
A handbook to enlighten and prepare soldiers of the cross for the battle of the "latter days." Every page is loaded with spirtual armaments for the believer's warfare against satanic powers and beings. A Spirit-empowered volume that will help insure total victory!

The Baptism of the Holy Spirit
Dr. Van Impe's easy-to-understand study of who the Holy Spirit is, what He does, and why His baptism is for every believer. Includes what the Bible says about the personality, attributes, gifts, fruit, and power of the Holy Spirit.

God! I'm Suffering, Are You Listening?
Why do good people go through seemingly senseless suffering? Dr. Van Impe explains from a biblical perspective why even Christians suffer and the best way to make the most of misfortune.

The Happy Home: Child Rearing
Many parents are confused about how to raise their children to love and serve God. Dr. Van Impe provides sound Bible principles, as well as practical advice for raising children to be happy Christian adults.

Escape the Second Death
Five powerful salvation messages especially directed to the unsaved. A great witnessing tool. Explains the Bible way to be born again. (Excerpted from *The Spirit of Antichrist*)

Exorcism and the Spirit World
What every Christian should know about Satan, demons, and demonic activity. Reveals the dangers of association with the occult, describes Satan worship, and tells how to defeat demon forces through the delivering power of the Holy Spirit.

The True Gospel
The only "good news" is that Christ died for our sins, was buried, and rose again. There is no other good news. Dr. Van Impe also covers Christ's last seven sayings upon the cross, and the importance of His resurrection.

**Everything you always wanted
to know about Prophecy**
But didn't know who to ask! Dr. Van Impe answers questions on the Rapture, the Judgment Seat of Christ, the Tribulation, and more. Headlines and international events interpreted in the light of Christ's soon return. This booklet will challenge you to live a life of holiness and service.

The Judgment Seat of Christ
Sheds light on the misunderstood subject of God's judgment. Covers the five judgments of the Bible, including the judgment of works, and a special section on the believer's crowns to be awarded on Judgment Day.

This Is Christianity
Millions who claim to be Christians, including church members, are not because they have never been born again.

The message of this book will help you understand this vital subject and know what it means to be a follower of Christ.

The Cost of Discipleship and Revival
To be a true follower of Jesus Christ, the Bible says you must take up your cross and die to self. But just what kind of price do you have to pay? Find the answer, plus keys to revival, in the pages of this enlightening book.

What Must I Do to Be Lost?
Are you trusting in the traditions of men, your church, your good works? All the doctrines of the church will not get you into heaven. There is only one way to be saved—find out how in the pages of this book.

Religious Reprobates and Saved Sinners
A timely message by Dr. Van Impe that distinguishes "religion" from genuine salvation. If you've ever wondered how to separate the wolves from the sheep, you must read this frank, tell-it-like-it-is booklet!

YOUR FUTURE—
An A-Z Index to Prophecy
An A-Z listing of biblical terms and major prophetic teachings in the Bible. *Your Future* is an exhaustive, easy-to-use reference tool. For the first time, you can have fingertip access to finding and understanding all the prophetic scriptures that affect...Your Future!

Order from:
Jack Van Impe Ministries
P.O. Box 7004
Troy, Michigan 48007

In Canada:
Box 1717, Postal Station A
Windsor, Ontario N9A 6Y1

360-902-4745

1/4/2000 @ 10:00 AM